THE POLITICS OF NATIONAL SECURITY

THE POLITICS OF NATIONAL SECURITY

Congress and U.S. Defense Policy

A TWENTIETH CENTURY FUND BOOK

Barry M. Blechman

with the assistance of
W. Philip Ellis

New York   Oxford
OXFORD UNIVERSITY PRESS
1990

Oxford University Press

Oxford   New York   Toronto
Delhi   Bombay   Calcutta   Madras   Karachi
Petaling Jaya   Singapore   Hong Kong   Tokyo
Nairobi   Dar es Salam   Cape Town
Melbourne   Auckland

and associated companies in
Berlin   Ibadan

Copyright © 1990 by The Twentieth Century Fund

Published by Oxford University Press, Inc.,
200 Madison Avenue, New York, New York 10016

Oxford is a registered trademark of Oxford University Press

Library of Congress Cataloging-in-Publication Data
Blechman, Barry M.
The politics of national security : Congress and U.S. defense
policy : a twentieth century fund book / Barry M. Blechman.
p.   cm.
ISBN 0-19-506467-4
1. United States—National security.   2. United States—
Military policy.   3. United States. Congress.   4. United States—
Foreign relations—1981–1989.   I. Title.
UA23.B543   1990
355'.033073—dc20   89-48916   CIP

2 4 6 8 9 7 5 3 1

Printed in the United States of America
on acid-free paper

This book is dedicated to
Janne Emilie Nolan

The Twentieth Century Fund is a research foundation undertaking timely analyses of economic, political, and social issues. Not-for-profit and nonpartisan, the Fund was founded in 1919 and endowed by Edward A. Filene.

Foreword

Over the past two decades, presidents of both parties have complained that Congress has been too involved in defense policy, spending, and management. Congress and its partisans have responded by citing the constitutional power of the purse, the dangers of secrecy and centralization, and the practical political reality of a public that holds both branches accountable for the major policies of the United States. Recognizing the legitimacy of the claims of both the executive and the legislative branches means accepting an inevitable measure of conflict. This book is about how these competing views of power and responsibility are accommodated and reconciled. It should contribute to an understanding of the continuing necessity to cope with the institutional partisanship that is built into the American system of checks and balances.

The subject could not be more timely. As this foreword is being written, the countries of central and eastern Europe literally are redefining their economic and political makeup. Several may be in the midst of major shifts in territorial jurisdiction. Ethnic tensions and nationalist sentiments are rising to levels not seen in a half century. Economists are confident that some of the changes are sure to result—at least in the short run—in sharp increases in prices and unemployment. Most observers believe that the strongest military power in the region is the nation with perhaps the smallest chance of achieving significant gains in prosperity.

Out of context, this description of events sounds like cause for alarm. Yet, because the new Europe may be structured on the ideas of democratic capitalism, the upheavals have produced an unprecedented surge of optimism in the West. Even though destabilization in Europe has drawn us into war twice in this century, the United States is debating how to spend the "peace dividend" that would result from a reduction of involvement abroad. Indeed, the arguments about defense policy over the next decade are likely to be unusually intense—in part because they inevitably will take place during the sorting out period of the new European order.

Members of both the executive and legislative branches are confronted by the necessity of changing the way they see the world. Should the course of events in Europe turn dangerous, the threat to world peace could well be the greatest since World War II. Even without such mighty events, redefining U.S. strategic interests is sure to be untidy and even unsettling. A generation of policymakers has "relied" on the certainty of the Soviet threat (and of de facto spheres of influence) to guide their thinking about defense policy.

In the past, Congress often weakened its constitutional powers by permitting the executive relatively broad latitude in defense matters. After all, the period since 1945 involved the clearest external threat in the nation's peacetime history. As this perceived danger recedes, consensus about basic defense needs may prove even more elusive than it has since the Vietnam War. The role of Congress in the making of national security policy appears certain to expand. Yet political disagreements on this subject are likely to come to resemble fights over domestic issues more than they have in the past. Without a clear danger, one might ask, "So what?" Perhaps the answer is that we need to be especially clear-headed in reformulating security plans for an uncertain future.

International negotiations, as a practical matter, require a semblance of national unity. The president and Congress seldom speak with one voice, although they often work hard to define a common view of the national interest. In this sense, Barry M. Blechman's provocative analysis of how the two branches function on crucial issues has value far beyond the specifics of particular national defense disputes. In an era of increasing international interdependence, on economic and other matters, the nation's need to have the national policy process function well is growing.

Blechman, a respected Washington expert on defense, shows here why Congress has a legitimate and constructive role in the making of national security policy—and by implication on broader international questions. The Twentieth Century Fund appreciates his effort to produce this timely study, which is sure to contribute to the continuing debate over America's place in the post–cold war world.

March 1990   Richard C. Leone, Director
The Twentieth Century Fund

Preface

The White House and the Capitol building in Washington, separated by a physical distance of little more than a mile, sit on opposite sides of a gulf in attitudes and prejudices so vast as to defy most efforts to bridge them. The president and the Congress, the respective inhabitants of these two buildings, represent widely divergent perspectives on the sources, the means, and the impact of American policy options. These differences of outlook color all policy debates, but perhaps none so virulently as issues of U.S. defense and national security—fateful subjects in which presidents claim more than usual powers, just as citizens and their elected representatives are often more than usually concerned.

In a career that so far spans 26 years in Washington, I have been fortunate enough both to have served two stints in the executive branch, in the Pentagon and the State Department, and also to have worked closely with numerous members of the Congress. This association with the two, often disparate, branches has given me an appreciation of their relative strengths and weaknesses. It has made clear to me how poorly the country is served when the institutional clashes between the two branches, however predictable, overwhelm consideration of the national interest. It has also encouraged me to believe that a collaborative relationship may yet be developed—a relationship that would permit each branch to fulfill its special needs and perspectives, but also allow each to bring its unique talents, knowledge, and skills to the formulation and implementation of American defense policy.

By describing the evolution of congressional roles in U.S. defense policy in the period since the Vietnam War, I seek to demonstrate the reasons for, and the surprising endurance of, the legislature's newly assertive posture in foreign affairs, and also to describe its consequences for the national interest—both positive and negative. These new congressional roles have emerged despite the efforts of every recent president, from Lyndon Johnson to Ronald Reagan, to minimize the legislature's access and influence. Only when the Executive Branch accepts the fact of congressional influence as a permanent feature in the landscape of U.S. policymaking can the specific formulations of congressional activities be modified to ensure that the legislature plays its part as constructively as possible. George Bush still has the opportunity to cause the reforms described in this volume to come to fruition.

My understanding of the Congress is derivative. Never a member nor full-time employee, I have learned by observing, by listening, and by working informally with dozens of members and their staffs on a variety of projects. Some of the members interviewed for this project are cited in the footnotes; others chose to remain anonymous. Because of the sensitivity of their positions, none of the staff members who contributed to this book are named directly. I can only indicate my respect for the dedication, professionalism, and competence of these talented men and women by way of this book. I hope that they find it worthy.

The book is the result of a project sponsored by the Twentieth Century Fund. Of the many individuals associated with the Fund who helped along the way, I am particularly grateful to Marcia Bystryn, Beverly Goldberg, Carol Kahn, and Roger Kimball for their assistance.

I was very fortunate during the course of the project to have had a series of extraordinarily able research assistants, each of whom contributed significantly to my knowledge of the subject before passing on to more exciting pursuits. I remain deeply indebted to W. Philip Ellis, Kevin O'Prey, Marc Smyrl, and Margaret Sullivan—not only for their solid research and insightful analyses, but also for their good cheer and delightful companionship.

It would not have been possible for me to have completed this book without the help of Dr. David J. Schoetz of the Lahey Clinic in Burlington, Massachusetts. If his standards of performance, professionalism, and humanity were ever matched in Washington, the ideals of the brave men and women who founded and have fought for this Republic would lie much closer to hand.

Finally, I would like to thank Janne E. Nolan, to whom this book is dedicated. Born knowing more about politics than I will be able to learn in a lifetime, Janne was an inspiration and advisor throughout this project. Far more importantly, in the most difficult moments in Washington and Massachusetts, she did no less than to preserve my soul. I will always be grateful.

January 1990   B. M. B.
Washington, D.C.

Contents

THE POLITICS OF NATIONAL SECURITY

1

The Congress and Defense Policy Since Vietnam

Throughout the summer and fall of 1987 the nation was treated to the spectacle of the U.S. Senate striving desperately to save itself from itself. Over a six-month period, against the determined efforts of a small band of Democratic and Republican senators, the majority of the Senate employed an extraordinary series of parliamentary and rhetorical maneuvers to avoid invoking the "war powers" it had been granted in a historic struggle with the executive branch only fourteen years before.

The 93d Congress had passed the War Powers Resolution over President Richard Nixon's veto in 1973. Impatient with the difficulty of utilizing traditional means—primarily the power of the purse—to force the executive branch to end the war in Vietnam, and determined to ensure that no future commitment of U.S. armed forces in combat take place without prior approval of the legislative branch, Congress passed this unprecedented legislation. Among other things, it required that the president:

Consult with Congress before introducing United States Armed Forces into hostilities or into situations where imminent involvement in hostilities is clearly indicated by the circumstances. . . .

[In such situations] submit within 48 hours . . . a report . . . setting forth . . . the circumstances . . . the constitutional and legislative authority . . . the estimated scope and duration of the hostilities or involvement. . . .

3

Upon submission of such a report the resolution specified that a clock would be set in motion, requiring that:

> Within sixty calendar days after a report is submitted . . . the President shall terminate any use of United States Armed Forces . . . unless the Congress . . . has declared war or has enacted a specific authorization for such use of United States Armed Forces. . . .[1]

The situation in the Persian Gulf was one in which "imminent involvement in hostilities" was "clearly indicated by the circumstances." After seven years of war between Iran and Iraq, both nations had taken to mounting frequent and increasingly deadly attacks on oil tankers and other neutral shipping plying the waters of the gulf. In March the United States agreed to protect eleven Kuwaiti oil tankers by placing them under U.S. flags and providing U.S. warships to escort them. In May, well before the start of this "reflagging" operation, a U.S. frigate, the *Stark,* operating in the gulf was attacked by an Iraqi fighter aircraft. Thirty-seven American sailors were killed, another twenty-one wounded. In July, when the first U.S. convoy set sail, one of the tankers *(Bridgeton)* struck a mine that had been placed by Iranian Revolutionary Guards. In September U.S. helicopters attacked and disabled an Iranian ship that had been observed planting additional mines. In October armed U.S. helicopters attacked a group of Iranian patrol boats that had fired upon a U.S. observation helicopter, sinking one of them. Later that month, following a successful Iranian missile attack on a reflagged tanker at a Kuwaiti oil-loading facility, U.S. warships and naval commandos attacked three platforms in the gulf that were being used by Iran to monitor shipping and to coordinate attacks.[2]

As the level and scope of violence in the gulf escalated, the United States introduced more powerful forces into the region. By October the U.S. Navy's Middle East force, based in Bahrain, had been increased from three or four destroyers and a command ship to twelve major warships and several smaller vessels. Eleven more U.S. warships, including the aircraft carrier *Ranger* and the battleship *Missouri,* patrolled the northern Arabian Sea, just outside the gulf. The former carried nuclear as well as conventional ordnance for its strike aircraft, while the latter was known to be equipped with nuclear-armed Tomahawk cruise missiles. Sixteen additional U.S. warships were deployed elsewhere in the Indian Ocean.

Given the refusal of local states, including Kuwait, to provide bases for the U.S. forces and the small size of the U.S. installation at Bahrain, temporary support facilities were constructed on barges and platforms. In recognition of the risks of military operations in the gulf, the Defense Department on August 25 decided to authorize "extra danger" pay for U.S. military personnel assigned there.

By the fall of 1987, thus, the War Powers Resolution was clearly pertinent to the Persian Gulf situation. United States forces had been involved in hostilities four times in six months with no signs of diminishing risks. The situation was a classic example of a de facto, gradual assumption of a foreign defense commitment that could embroil U.S. forces in combat over a sustained period of time. As the year progressed, the United States was increasingly committed to thwarting Iran's war aims, and to preventing it from disrupting traffic through the gulf.

This was precisely the type of situation that had inspired the 1973 act. Under it the president was required to report to the Congress—prior to commitments of U.S. forces or immediately thereafter—and the Congress was required to vote its consent. If not, the troops would have to be withdrawn *automatically.* Yet in this case, neither the administration nor the Congress was prepared to invoke the law.

The question of the relevance of the War Powers Resolution was first brought up within the administration itself. According to reports, when the question of reflagging Kuwaiti tankers was first raised, White House Chief of Staff Howard H. Baker, Jr., argued that the resolution should be invoked. This was not a typical administration view, but rather reflected Baker's previous three terms as a senator from Tennessee, including four years as the Republican majority leader. The more typical executive branch perspective was expressed by an anonymous senior official as follows: "We don't think much of the War Powers Resolution to begin with and we certainly don't want to report to Congress when we don't have to. . . ."[3]

Such reluctance was not surprising; every administration since President Nixon's has labored to avoid any action that might legitimate the resolution—and most particularly its most onerous provision, paragraph 4(a)(1), which sets in motion the time limit on continued involvements in situations with actual, or imminent risk of, hostilities.

What was surprising in 1987, however, was that a majority of the Senate also seemed "not to think much of the War Powers Resolution.'' As a small group of senators made repeated efforts to force the administration to pay attention to it, a far larger number sought to have the Congress ignore it. A straight-up motion to invoke the resolution was defeated in May; in September, a filibuster prevented a vote on an amendment to the Defense Department's budget authorization that would have required implementation of War Powers. Senator Dale L. Bumpers (D.-Ark.) subsequently termed the resolution a ''eunuch,'' Senator Paul S. Trible (R.-Va.) called it a ''nullity,'' while Senator Lowell P. Weicker (R.-Conn.), chief sponsor of efforts to invoke War Powers for the gulf, called it ''de facto dead.''[4]

Later that month Senate leaders, resorting to a familiar Washington tactic to avoid action, floated the idea of establishing a commission to reconsider the War Powers Resolution. Senator Sam Nunn (D.-Ga.) may have said it best: ''I think the law's unworkable, but we have a duty to try to make it work.''[5]

In late October a pale substitute for War Powers was introduced by Senators Robert C. Byrd (D.-W.Va.), the majority leader, and John W. Warner (R.-Va.), known to be speaking for the administration. The resolution would have required the administration to report on the situation in the gulf within thirty days, after which the Congress would have another thirty days to do something (without stating what that might be)—or to do nothing at all. Pointedly, the bill would have negated the War Powers Resolution's automaticity; U.S. forces would have been withdrawn from the gulf only if the Congress had acted affirmatively, not as a result of its inaction. Even so, the Byrd–Warner proposal was initially rejected 47 to 51. It was finally passed, 54 to 44, after Byrd made clear to his colleagues that failure to act on even this limpid bill was making a mockery of the Congress's war powers all together: '' 'I think the Senate looks simply terrible,' Byrd said, pacing at his desk. 'It can't move. It's muscle-bound. . . . It can't act. I hope Senators will choose to step up to their responsibilities.' ''[6] However, since no corresponding legislation was acted upon in the House, the Byrd–Warner bill turned into a dead letter.[7]

This extraordinary performance on Capitol Hill in fact had little to do with the substantive merits or demerits of the War Powers Resolution, or even the wisdom or foolishness of the U.S. actions in the Persian Gulf. It was both more personal and more political—the Congress simply was not prepared to take responsibility either for the international consequences of compelling the withdrawal of U.S. forces from the gulf or for the domestic consequences of the combat that might follow approval of the president's action. The Congress struggled to avoid invoking War Powers because it did not want to be held accountable for either outcome; it was not prepared to choose. It wanted the administration alone to remain responsible, leaving the members of the legislature free to criticize or to applaud, depending upon the outcome of events.

This reluctance to assume responsibility for the involvement of U.S. forces in combat, inherent in most legislators' perceptions of their proper roles, was strengthened the one time the Congress had acted independently to enforce the War Powers Resolution. During the deployment of U.S. Marines in Lebanon in 1983, after a similar minuet over a period of months, the Congress had determined that the War Powers Resolution applied, but it extended the deadline for its approval of the intervention (or the automatic withdrawal of U.S. forces) from the sixty days specified to eighteen months. One month after that action, 241 U.S. Marines were killed by a terrorist's truck bomb, and the contingent was withdrawn soon thereafter. By invoking the resolution but not demanding the troops' withdrawal, Congress implicitly assumed some of the responsibility for the U.S. losses. Voters apparently understood this. The tragedy was thus effectively removed as a political issue. As one Democratic congressman said, "I voted for the Lebanon involvement against my better judgement, and then felt foolish. I was criticized severely, not for the policy, but for supporting Reagan."

Congress's ambivalence on "war powers" is consistent with its approach to a broad range of issues concerning U.S. military affairs. In the early and mid-1970s, in the aftermath of Vietnam and Watergate, the Congress shifted sharply the previous balance between the legislative and executive branches in the formulation and implementation of U.S. defense policy. Writing wholly new types of legislation, and creating new institutions and procedures to support its newly defined roles and powers, the Congress boldly established a more assertive posture than had ever before been imagined for the legislature in the conduct of foreign policy. It put special emphasis on military aspects of the nation's foreign relations.

By the end of the decade, however, few enthusiasts for the Congress's new authority could be found in Washington—even on Capitol Hill. Controversy has raged throughout the 1980s over the constitutionality, the consequences, and the wisdom of the legislature's expanded role in defense policy. Yet with few exceptions, efforts to turn back the clock have been unsuccessful. Institutional pressures and personal interests have been too strong to permit a simple reversal of the changes made in the 1970s. Just as new political realities have led the Congress to assert a greater role in defense policy, they have prevented a straightforward return to the days of executive dominance. The Congress may not necessarily want all the responsibilities of its new powers, but it is totally unprepared to yield the principles of the rights it fought so hard to secure.

The result of this ambivalence has been a continuing dispute over the proper role of Congress in various aspects of defense policy. In addition to commitments of U.S. military forces abroad, this struggle between the executive branch and the legislature has focused on the defense budget, arms control negotiations, arms sales, and covert operations. Spokesmen for the administration have maintained repeatedly that congressional interventions hamper its ability to conduct U.S. defense policy. Officials in both Democratic and Republican administrations have argued that, even when the Congress does not act to assert its new powers, the mere existence of relevant legislation introduces uncertainties that could undermine essential U.S. interests. For their part, congressional advocates argue that the 1970s legislation only reasserted congressional powers that had long, and wrongfully, been neglected. They criticize successive administrations for refusing to implement the spirit of the new legislation, for acting in bad faith, and for needlessly complicating what might have been smooth cooperation between the branches in fulfillment of their respective constitutional responsibilities.

The primary result of the continuing struggle has been inconsistency and incoherence in U.S. policy. The congressional revolution of the 1970s has come and gone, and so too the conservative Thermidor of the early 1980s, but a synthesis continues to elude the U.S. system of government. The congressional desire to play a major, visible role in defense policy remains effective, as does the executive desire to minimize congressional involvement. The two branches often compromise, but only on specific cases, not on principle. As a result, U.S. defense policy becomes uncertain and halting; those dependent upon predictability in U.S. policy—leaders of friendly governments, U.S. defense industry executives, arms control negotiators, and many others—are reluctant to enter into long-term agreements or to predicate their decisions on promises.

It is clearly in the U.S. interest to resolve this clash of wills. The new congressional role cannot be reversed, but neither can it be as far-reaching and pervasive as might have been assumed in the mid-1970s. What is necessary is a pragmatic assessment of the two branches' interests and objectives, and a mutual understanding of how they each affect U.S. policy. A new implicit agreement on their respective rights and obligations might result from such an assessment, one that takes more realistic account of the political forces that inevitably dominate both congressional and executive decision making. The value of such a review might ultimately be the formulation of more coherent and stable policies.

The Assertion of Congress's Will, 1973–1978

Defense policy has been a recurrent source of conflict between the Congress and the executive branch throughout U.S. history. Application of the constitutional system of checks and balances to the conduct of the nation's military affairs has never been easy or straightforward. The words in the Constitution may be clear enough, but their interpretation has always been controversial when it comes to the ambiguities that surround almost any aspect of the nation's defense posture. In considering the practicalities of decisions on various aspects of defense policy, moreover, the Constitution's allocation of powers is inherently contradictory, setting up conflicts between the legislative and executive branches in which the judicial branch is reluctant to intervene. Even relatively activist courts become timid when "national security" is said to be at stake.

For most of the nation's history its foreign relations were narrowly defined, its military establishment small, and its overseas involvements episodic. In this context conflicts over the Constitution's intent with respect to defense policy were of only limited consequence. With the establishment during World War II of a permanent U.S. military presence abroad, however, and with the "militarization" of U.S. foreign policy in response to Soviet initiatives and the nation's own ideologically expansionist ambitions, U.S. defense policy was transformed into a set of activities and postures with far broader ramifications.

Accordingly, the relative power of the two branches of government in setting U.S. defense policy attained far greater significance. Indeed, the march of military technology alone—creating not only weapons of mass destruction but also so-called conventional military forces with the mobility, flexibility, and firepower to be used anywhere in the world—has made the stakes of the conflict over the control of defense policy a matter of, literally, life and death.

The Congress was slow to wake to the transformation of U.S. defense policy following World War II. Throughout the 1950s and early 1960s the legislature was content to go along with presidential initiatives, ceding authority and postdating its approval of military actions from Korea through the Middle East to the Gulf of Tonkin.[8]

It was the Vietnam War, of course, that changed all this—wrenching the Congress into the harsh realities of life in the late twentieth century. In the late 1960s and early 1970s the intensifying economic and social consequences of Vietnam, and eventually its impact on the basic fabric of American life as American deaths and casualties mounted and as returning veterans and alienated students bespoke the profound divisions in American society, finally led Congress to act. It began to lose patience with successive administrations' unwillingness, or inability, to stop the nation's losses. It was primarily the younger members of Congress who stirred this rebellion—often against the wishes and power of more senior congressional leaders—just as it was the younger generation of Americans who created the political forces that made the congressional "usurpation" possible.

Other events added momentum to the congressional drive—the Watergate scandal, most importantly, but also the revelations of intelligence agencies' illegal intrusions into U.S. domestic affairs. Together these events gave the impression, only slightly exaggerating the reality, of an executive branch out of control, a combination of circumstances demanding congressional action to protect the American people from their own president.

As the Congress pushed successfully against its own leaders, as well as against the executive branch, tasting the greater freedom of action made possible in the political climate of the mid-1970s, its forays into sectors of defense policy previously reserved exclusively for the president drove deeper and wider. Actions to cut off funding for the Vietnam War and to curtail U.S. military forces in Southeast Asia were soon followed by congressional reviews of U.S. military commitments and deployments in other parts of the world. Attention was also paid, apparently for the first time in U.S. history, to less visible aspects of U.S. foreign policy entanglements: covert operations and arms sales. Congressionally enforced modifications of a planned weapons sale to Jordan in 1974, and termination of U.S. covert support to factions struggling to control the newly independent nation of Angola in 1976, marked early high points in the Congress's new defense activism.

A sudden concern about the defense budget was symptomatic of the Congress's perception of its new authority in defense matters. Defense spending was scaled back substantially in the early 1970s, going beyond the so-called Vietnam Peace Dividend to cut deeply into the Pentagon's plans to modernize and expand other types of forces. Nor did the Congress use its "power of the purse" only as a broad economic instrument. For the first time in its history, it began to play an active role in shaping the structure of U.S. military forces. Through countless amendments to various budgetary vehicles, the Congress sought to shift priorities in U.S. defense planning and to alter the disposition and characteristics of U.S. military forces. Every senator seemed to have his favorite egregious weapon system that, he claimed, should be canceled or modified in some significant way.

No corner of defense policy seemed immune to congressional scrutiny. A 1975 law, for example, required that the administration assess and report on the "arms control impact" of new weapon systems. An amendment passed in 1976 required the secretary of defense, in consultation with the secretary of state, to consider the relationship between the military force structure and foreign policy.

Beneath the superficiality of such minor congressional incursions into defense policymaking, however, more important changes were taking place in the resources and organization of the U.S. Congress and in the legislated procedures governing the formulation and implementation of various aspects of defense policy—changes that institutionalized the new interventionist attitude and guaranteed its continuance, even as political tides shifted.

The personal staffs of senators and House members, and the staffs assigned to relevant committees, expanded markedly beginning in the late 1960s: the professional staff of the Senate Armed Services Committee, for example, grew from nine to seventeen between 1969 and 1978; that of the House Armed Services Committee, from nine to twenty-six. The character of those staffs changed as well, with a premium on individuals who had the expertise to challenge the executive branch. New institutions were created to provide analytic support for congressional defense initiatives, and older institutions were expanded; the Congressional Budget Office, created in 1974, had a defense staff of twenty-five by 1978. The Office of Technology Assessment was created in 1972 and devoted a considerable portion of its work to the analysis of defense issues. Relevant sections of the Congressional Research Service of the Library of Congress and the General Accounting Office grew by fifty percent or more between 1969 and 1978. These changes are summarized in Table 1-1; all told, congressional resources devoted to the review and analysis of defense issues nearly doubled during the 1970s.

Procedural changes were even more important. The creation in 1974 of a comprehensive congressional budgetary review process made clear the trade-offs between defense and domestic programs, as well as the consequences of changes in taxes or fiscal policy for defense resources. Passage in 1974 of the so-called Nelson amendment, introduced by then-Senator Gaylord Nelson (D.-Wis.), required for the first

TABLE 1-1. Changes in Congressional Staff Devoted to Defense, 1969–1988*

Organization	1969	1978	1988
Armed Services committees			
House	9	26	40
Senate	9	17	32
Appropriations committees			
House	1	8	13
Senate	2	3	7
Budget committees			
House	0	2	3
Senate	0	3	4
Congressional Budget Office	0	25	25
Congressional Research Service	7	18	28
General Accounting Office	820	1,220	1,100

*Number of people.

Sources: Information provided by the committees and organizations cited in the table, and from Charles B. Brownson, ed., *Congressional Staff Directory* (Washington, D.C., 1969, 1978, and 1988).

time that the Congress be apprised of, and have an opportunity to review, sales of U.S. weapons to nations overseas. Creation of separate Senate and House intelligence committees in 1976 and 1977, respectively, and the adoption of the so-called Hughes–Ryan amendment (named after Senator Harold Hughes [D.-Iowa] and Congressman Leo Ryan [D.-Calif.]) requiring congressional notification of covert operations by the Central Intelligence Agency, seemed to curtail the extraordinary freedom once enjoyed by the nation's intelligence agencies. Most importantly, passage in 1973 of the War Powers Resolution seemed to guarantee that future U.S. military expeditions overseas would be possible only if the executive branch and the Congress had consulted beforehand and were in agreement that such ventures would serve the nation's interests. Furthermore, they would continue only as long as the branches continued to agree on the wisdom of the military involvement.

By the late 1970s, the Congress appeared to have totally reversed the balance in defense matters between the executive and legislative branches. It seemed to have gained the whip hand not only in the formulation of U.S. defense policy but even in its implementation. The attitude was perhaps best summarized by Senator Sam Nunn: "Congress and the people lost a lot of respect for the executive branch. . . . The trend toward more Congressional involvement is irreversible. . . ."[9] A respected political scientist, Robert Dahl, portrayed the new relationship between Congress and the executive branch in more forceful terms:

> It is . . . the responsibility of the Congress to see that so far as possible the executive branch has no discretionary power to abuse, however awkward this may make the conduct of foreign affairs. If and when a chief executive demonstrates that he and his principal aides are worthy of trust, the Congress can properly relax some of its controls—but not before.[10]

Hyperbole aside, the ascendance of Congress in the 1970s represented a true revolution in the conduct of the nation's military affairs. Thomas M. Franck and Edward Weisband, thoughtful chroniclers of this extraordinary change in the U.S. system of government, writing at the height of the congressional ascendance in 1979, put it this way:

> Revolutions are the ultimate triumph of politics over law. The Congressional revolution, paradoxically, was the defeat of politics by law. . . .

If it was the genius of the U.S. Constitution to conceive a government of laws, not men, then the revolution carried out by Congress from 1973 to 1978 has restored the Constitution's reach to embrace the conduct of foreign relations.[11]

But is it possible, indeed, for the nation's foreign affairs, particularly in their military aspects, to be run effectively by the Congress? Can the inherent inflexibility of legislation substitute adequately for the pragmatic compromises and spontaneous judgments that characterize most international interactions? Are any staff and procedural infrastructure sufficient to assist 100 senators and 435 congressmen—most of whom have no expertise (and often little interest) in military issues, and little time to devote to these subjects—to judge the merits of the complex issues of contemporary defense policy? Can a body as poorly disciplined and as "democratic" as the Congress reach binding decisions that lead to coherent and consistent policies? Would the inevitable responsiveness of the Congress to the demands of parochial political forces not inexorably overwhelm consideration of national interests? In short, was not the Congress's ascendance the triumph of politics over executive decision making, not the victory of laws over politics?

It was, of course, politics that brought on the congressional ascendance in the first place. One consequence of the Vietnam War was that defense issues had become politically salient. They had become important to the success or failure of those who would serve in the Congress and who would govern the nation. It had become potentially rewarding for politicians to be seen to be playing influential roles in the formulation of defense policy; indeed, members of Congress were expected to have thought about these issues and to be able to articulate coherent positions. And it had become potentially disabling for politicians to be seen to be on the wrong side of defense issues—"wrong" being defined by the particular constituency served.

Congressional views on defense issues thus not only became more prominent, they also reflected the diversity of American society, just as the foreign policy views of American society were themselves becoming more diverse. Congress was taking over the defense policy arena just as the dominance of the traditional, male, Caucasian, Eastern establishment perspective on foreign affairs (as on other things) was being overwhelmed. The Congress both benefited from this new diversity and helped ensure its prominence.

The Vietnam War accentuated generational as well as socioeco-
nomic class distinctions. But the underlying changes in American society primarily reflected the first coming of age of the baby-boom generation, the entry into political life of a generation of Americans
unscarred by either the Great Depression or World War II. The dynamic center of the nation's economic and social life was moving west
and south, diluting the Atlanticist tug of the Eastern elite. Affluence
was becoming increasingly widespread. Hispanics, Asians, and blacks
were beginning to play more important roles, bringing new demands
for domestic programs and new foreign policies. The changing economy, technology, and educational system were transforming the role
of women in the political process as well. Important attitudinal diver-
gencies between men and women in key aspects of defense policy
were brought to the fore as women became more important in the
selection and election of political candidates.

As the nation's economy was becoming more interdependent with
economies elsewhere in the world, the salience of developments in
foreign nations was brought home to farmers in the Middle West,
businessmen in the "new South," and consumers all over the country.
It also made them aware of the potential impact of the foreign policies
pursued by their government.

The return of casualties from Vietnam, living and dead, brought
home the cost of foreign military adventures even more pointedly. The
effect of television on American perceptions of Vietnam has been doc-
umented into cliché. The revolution in communications technology
brought worldwide events into American homes more directly than
ever before. Americans in all parts of the country increasingly turned
to their elected representatives to protect their new awareness that their
personal interests were closely affected by the United States's foreign
policies.

Senator Nancy L. Kassebaum (R.-Kans.) summarized the impact of
television on citizens' interest in foreign affairs in this way:

> It builds emotional responses. It shows the consequences of involvement
> abroad, or the effects of events abroad, in a way never experienced be-
> fore. It broadens the audience for foreign affairs and intensifies their
> responses.[12]

Technology revolutionized the cost, reliability, and availability of
travel and long-distance telephone connections and revolutionized the

practice of politics as well. Politicians gained access to more constituents than was ever thought possible. Technology changed the expectations of citizens by offering a proliferation of channels for politicians to communicate with voters. It also revolutionized the cost of running for public office.

There were two phases in this process. Television was part of the political scene in the 1950s and 1960s, but its application still reflected the old, clubby back-room relationship between politicians and the print media. Senior figures received the overwhelming share of air time, almost always in a carefully managed and favorable environment. In the late 1960s and 1970s, however, the introduction of Minicams, satellite links, and cable and ultrahigh frequency stations increased the coverage of current affairs and the demand for "news." At the same time, the celebration of investigative reporting in the wake of Watergate was also changing the tone of television news coverage. Air time was available to virtually all politicians, but there were risks if the legislator was ill prepared. The politicians who used the new medium successfully understood the premium placed on directness, brevity, criticism, and controversy.

The television revolution democratized the political process in the sense that it diminished the influence of political parties as effective arbiters of political candidacies and loosened the iron grip of ·the congressional seniority system. It changed the standards by which politicians would be judged, reducing the value of effective behind-the-scenes legislation in favor of the ability to present a pleasing visual image accompanied by an effective twenty-second "sound byte."

In order to remind constituents of their "service" to them, incumbents needed to persuade the networks—or local stations in their districts—to feature them on the evening news. A stance on a controversial public issue made this much easier. With defense issues so prominent in the wake of Vietnam, staking out positions on military subjects became a part of every political campaign. Even better was to be seen playing a role in government decisions—by chairing hearings, sponsoring legislation, proposing new policies, and consulting with (or attacking) executive branch officials. The key was to be seen as an independent and forceful advocate imposing the special perspectives and objectives of constituents on a recalcitrant executive branch.

These developments transformed the practice of politics and the perceptions of politicians as well as of the electorate. They dramatically altered the Congress's approach to domestic policy, to be sure. But with the congressional role in defense policy previously so minimal, the most dramatic impact of these events, by far, was felt in military affairs.

The Failure of the Thermidor, 1980–1986

It was the Congress's misfortune, perhaps, that its ascendance in defense policy coincided with an extremely difficult period in the United States's foreign relations. The fall of U.S. allies in Phnom Penh and Saigon in 1975 had far greater effects on American voters than most observers were willing to admit at the time. Despite the nation's overwhelming relief with the removal of U.S. troops, daily televised images of South Vietnamese scrambling frantically to escape the victorious armies of the North, climaxed by the frenzied evacuation of the U.S. mission and its dependents from the roof of the embassy in Saigon, seared the American consciousness. Although few credited the administration's claim that the government of South Vietnam would have survived had the Congress not cut military aid, this claim established a pattern of contrasts between congressional assertiveness at home and U.S. "defeats" abroad.

In 1978 the picture was repeated in Iran. As Americans watched the mobs overthrow the shah, then viewed the rabid anti-Americanism of the Ayatollah Khomeini's supporters during the humiliation of the U.S. embassy staff in Tehran, and finally saw the miserable failure of the hostage rescue mission in 1980, they wondered what was happening to the power and prestige of the United States. Although the Congress had done nothing overtly that could be said to have hastened the fall of the shah, there was again the coincidence of what was seen as a U.S. "defeat" abroad and the Congress's ascendance at home.

A new Soviet assertiveness in the Third World contributed further to these perceptions. Only one specific incident was blamed directly on congressional intervention in defense policy—the victory of the Soviet-backed Popular Movement for the Liberation of Angola (MPLA) faction in 1976. But other visible Soviet involvements and alleged "gains" in Third World nations—Ethiopia in 1977–1978, Yemen in 1978, Nicaragua beginning in 1979—again coincided with Congress's more visible role in the formulation of U.S. defense policy. Demonstrating the bipartisan character of presidential complaints, President Jimmy Carter blamed congressional restrictions on U.S. military activity abroad for a 1978 incursion by allegedly Soviet-backed rebels into Zaire's Shaba province, and had administration officials compile a list of "intolerable legislative restraints."

Underlying all this was the changing balance of military power between the great powers. Throughout this period, the Soviet Union's strategic nuclear capabilities were increasing relative to those of the United States, a development trumpeted by conservative U.S. political factions seeking to undermine both the Carter administration and its determined push for arms control agreements. Public attitudes toward defense spending swung accordingly. In 1975 only twenty percent of respondents thought that the defense budget should be increased; by 1980, fully fifty-six percent were persuaded that the United States was not spending enough on defense. It took Ronald Reagan's landslide election in 1980 for a majority of the Congress to recognize the country's growing unease with the trends in relative U.S. and Soviet military capabilities, and to swing overwhelmingly in favor of greater defense spending.[13]

The new Republican administration and its conservative allies in the media, the policy community, and even the Senate were determined to roll back congressional advances into defense policy. In the pantheon of villains as defined by the Right, the Democratic congresses of the 1970s were third only to Jimmy Carter and Fidel Castro (and clearly ahead of Leonid Brezhnev). The Republican party platform in 1980, for example, severely criticized congressional cuts in defense budgets during the 1970s and pledged to ". . . seek the repeal of ill-considered restrictions sponsored by Democrats, which have debilitated U.S. intelligence capabilities while easing the intelligence collection and subversion efforts of our adversaries."[14]

Throughout his campaign Reagan hammered on the theme that the Congress had crippled the United States's ability to defend its foreign interests. Conservative columnists and policymakers attacked congressionally imposed restrictions—real and imagined—on military operations, on the activities of intelligence agencies, on arms sales, on military deployments and assistance programs, and particularly on the size and structure of U.S. military forces themselves.

With both the presidency and the Senate in the hands of the Republicans, and a conservative mood apparently dominant in the country, the time appeared propitious for a major reversal of the 1970s shift between the branches. Senator John G. Tower (R.-Tex.), the new chairman of the Armed Services Committee, summarized the spirit of this Thermidor best:

> The 1970s were marked by a rash of Congressionally initiated foreign policy legislation that limited the President's range of options on a number of foreign policy issues. . . . Not only was much of this legislation ill conceived, if not actually unconstitutional, it has served in a number of instances to be detrimental to the national security and foreign policy interests of the United States. . . . If we are to meet the foreign policy challenges facing us in the 1980s, we must restore the traditional balance between Congress and the President. . . . To do so, much of the legislation of the past decade should be repealed or amended.[15]

In the end, though, almost nothing was accomplished. To the contrary, with only a few specific exceptions the Congress's role in defense policy expanded even further in the 1980s.

The defense budget was increased sharply with the full participation of the conservative Congress elected in 1980. However, throughout the 1980s, Congress continued to become increasingly more assertive in determining the characteristics of U.S. military forces and weapons, modifying ever more weapon programs in ever greater detail. Moreover, beginning in 1985 the Congress first leveled off and then reversed the continuing defense buildup requested by the administration. And in 1986, against the administration's fervent opposition, Congress passed a sweeping reorganization of the U.S. military establishment that reduced the power of the individual armed services in favor of joint military institutions.

The Congress's role in arms control was similarly expanded in the 1980s. Building on the Senate's treaty power, and the legislature's power of the purse, Congress at times compelled the administration to enter into certain negotiations or to modify its bargaining position. It reversed, or at least moderated, administration decisions to cease observing the 1979 Strategic Arms Limitation Treaty and to interpret the 1972 Antiballistic Missile (ABM) Treaty radically differently from the way it had been observed. And it preserved the option to negotiate still another treaty, on antisatellite weapons, which the administration would have preferred to foreclose. Members of the Congress even conceived of a new arms control idea—nuclear risk reduction centers—then persuaded the Soviet Union and the administration to take the idea seriously, and monitored progress until the idea was implemented by a formal U.S.–Soviet agreement in 1987. Far from reversing the Congress's new role in arms control, the 1980s witnessed a huge increase in that role.

Arms sales, the area of defense policy thought by many to be the least justified of the new congressional involvements, also survived administration efforts to curb congressional input. Here, too, Congress intervened successfully more often in the 1980s than in the 1970s.

By the time the Reagan administration took office in 1981, the Congress had already modified the Hughes–Ryan amendment so as to reduce reporting requirements for covert operations. In 1985 the Clark amendment, named after then-Senator Dick Clark (D.-Iowa), prohibiting U.S. support for antigovernment guerrillas in Angola, was repealed. But congressional oversight of covert operations also became stronger in the 1980s, if anything, with specific legislated restrictions modifying several operations that the administration either planned or began in Central America. As revealed during the Iran–Contra hearings in 1987, the Reagan administration found a variety of ways to circumvent some of these restrictions, but the circumventions required, and the relative smallness of the operations as a result, are more a testament to congressional power than to congressional weakness.

Finally there is the War Powers Resolution itself, from the conservative viewpoint the most dangerous of the congressional interventions. The Reagan administration made no serious effort to eliminate or even amend the legislation, contenting itself—like the three administrations before it—with the fact that Congress itself demanded only the most minimal attention be paid to the law's stated requirements.

After eight years the executive's Thermidor to the Congress's 1970s revolution in defense policy can only be judged a total failure.

The Persistence of Politics

It is extremely significant that the Congress was able to maintain, even expand, its role in defense policy against the wishes of the most popular president in modern history and in the throes of a strongly conservative tide in U.S. politics. It suggests that the changes in the U.S.

political system that led to the new congressional roles are here to stay—at least for the relevant future. It demonstrates that the institutions and procedures legislated in the aftermath of Vietnam were not idiosyncratic deviations from the mainstream of historic trends in the U.S. system of government. On the contrary, the new balance between the branches of government clearly reflects fundamental alterations in the nation's perceptions of the international system and the U.S. role in that system. The American people have extended the system of checks and balances, always prevalent in domestic policy, to the realm of foreign and defense policy. This is a new development in U.S. government, and one whose implications have yet to be fully understood.

We must now assess the consequences of this new assertive congressional role and judge, from an objective perspective, the implications for the nation's interests. Most Americans, the author included, believe that the executive in the past had been too unfettered, too far removed at times from the objectives and values of the American people. The degree of congressional involvement that existed prior to the 1970s was insufficient to ensure that popular perspectives effectively bounded executive decisions.

But has the Congress exercised its new power in a manner that ensures "popular" representation in the formulation of defense policy, but does not interfere with the day-to-day, detailed management of the nation's foreign affairs? Has the Congress considered the broad national interest along with the narrow interests of local constituents? Has the Congress implemented its new role with any degree of consistency and predictability?

The answers to these questions are often negative. Congress has tended to apply the powers seized in the 1970s with a heavy hand, sacrificing overall consistency and coherence of national policy for narrow interests and short-term objectives. This is the natural consequence of the political calculus that inevitably dominates congressional decision making. If the Congress is to play a more farsighted role in defense policy, the form and boundaries of its new functions will have to be modified and shaped in order to minimize opportunities for parochial political interests to dominate decisionmaking.

The following chapters assess Congress's recent involvements in five primary aspects of U.S. defense policy—the defense budget and military strategy, arms control, arms sales, covert operations, and commitments of U.S. forces overseas. The final chapter offers recommendations on how to reshape congressional participation in military affairs, maintaining the new balance between the two branches of government while ensuring more effective formulation and implementation of U.S. defense policy.

| 2 |

The Military Budget
and the Management
of Defense Resources

For the first fifteen to twenty years following World War II, only a few members of Congress had any serious impact on the nation's defense posture. The chairman of the House Defense Appropriations Subcommittee in particular, along with the few others charged with responsibility for defense appropriations, was able to influence the distribution of defense resources in significant ways. According to contemporary accounts, Congressman George H. Mahon, a Democrat from the 19th District in Texas, was the critical figure. He chaired the House subcommittee for nearly thirty years (1949–1978), during which time he scrubbed the budget vigorously, not only seeking to uncover inefficiencies in the management of defense resources, but also questioning the basic rationale and justification for a variety of weapon programs.

Senior figures on the legislative committees for military affairs have also been influential at various times in the nation's history, serving to vent popular concerns about inadequacies in the nation's force posture, as in the air power hearings chaired by Senator James Symington (D.-Mo.) in 1956. The legislative committees have also served as sounding boards for debate within the armed services, permitting internal critics of established defense policies to voice their dissents. General Billy Mitchell's famous testimony on the efficacy of air power, for example, credited with helping to overcome the army's resistance to building up U.S. air forces during the interwar years, was given before the House Military Affairs Committee in 1925.[1]

With these few exceptions, however, the Congress generally went along with the executive branch with respect to both the management of the Defense Department and the size and composition of defense spending. This is not to say that members of Congress always supported the president's defense policy without reservation. In the 1940s and early 1950s, for example, many members were critical of what they perceived as administration foot-dragging or incompetence with respect to the expansion of strategic air power, the deployment of air defenses, and the development of guided missiles. Nonetheless, most members refrained from seeking to overturn executive decisions because of their technical ignorance and a certain sense that it was not legitimate to challenge military judgments. Raymond Dawson, a scholar writing in the early 1960s, expressed this perspective clearly:

> The task confronting Congress in acting upon [the defense] budget is overwhelming. Its members have, *and can have,* no adequate facilities for formulating alternative programs in any systematic fashion; for this they must rely on military dissent. They must accept in the main what is submitted, grappling with thousands of items and reams of documentary exhibits. . . . . [emphasis added].[2]

Twenty-five years later, the most jarring aspect of Dawson's statement is his assumption that the Congress could not possibly acquire the analytic capabilities necessary to construct independent alternatives to the executive's defense proposals. Most members today believe that they are fully capable of challenging the executive branch on defense issues. In fact many observers, including this author, believe that for much of the 1980s the Congress did a much better job of making overall budgetary choices than did the secretary of defense.

Political factors clearly played a role in the Congress's previous reluctance to challenge the executive's defense choices. In the periods preceding and immediately following World War II there was little for politicians to gain either by supporting or by opposing a president on defense budgetary issues; the attentive audience was simply too limited. To the degree that the public voted on the basis of defense issues, moreover, the popular bias strongly favored the president's decisions, which were presumed to reflect the judgments of the nation's senior military leaders. A member of Congress had to have had a very distinguished military record of his own, had to have found persuasive evidence of high-ranking dissent within the armed forces, or else had to have been truly unconcerned about reelection to risk a challenge to the executive on the defense budget. Memories of World War II, refreshed by Korea only five years later, coupled with the prestige of the military and the popular perception of an unblemished U.S. military record, all contributed to what Sam Huntington termed the ''inviolability'' of the executive branch's defense proposals—a stark contrast to the Congress's then-contemporary willingness to challenge executive judgments in domestic and even foreign policy.[3]

A more assertive congressional role in the management of defense resources began to emerge in the 1960s. Political change came first; defense issues—the ''missile gap,'' the adequacy of U.S. conventional forces, the wisdom of the Eisenhower policy of massive retaliation—were important questions in the 1958 midterm election and were raised even more pointedly in the 1960 presidential campaign. The fact that these questions constituted campaign issues suggested a new level of public awareness and concern, an implication borne out in public opinion polls at the time.

Tangible change in the Congress's approach to defense budgetary issues began first in the legislative committees in the early 1960s, foreshadowing the broader congressional assault on defense policy that followed the Vietnam War. The armed services committees began to assume substantive budgetary roles for the first time, eventually supplanting the subcommittees on defense appropriations as the preeminent congressional authority on defense management.

Beginning in the late 1960s the Congress's rank and file—increasingly more skeptical of the Pentagon and the administration than their generally more senior colleagues on the defense committees—began to demand a more significant role for the full legislature in decisions on the nation's defense posture. Military strategy, defense management procedures, and weapon development programs all came under increasing fire. The extensive congressional debate on the Safeguard antiballistic missile system in 1968–1970 was the most prominent of these challenges, but by the early 1970s navy aircraft carriers and fighters, army tank and helicopter development programs, and air force bombers and advanced missile concepts were all subjects of detailed congressional investigations.

By the mid-1970s Congress had created new institutions and procedures to enable it to engage in more detailed and better-informed scrutiny of the defense budget, including the assessment of defense requests against different criteria. The rules of the game changed drastically. The previous clubby relationship between Defense Department officials and the few members who paid attention to defense matters was replaced by a tense atmosphere of wary partnership. More members and new committees began to play critical roles; the resources available to the Congress to analyze defense issues multiplied impressively.

This expansion of the congressional role in defense budget making continued in the 1980s. Within just a few years of Ronald Reagan's election to the presidency, the Congress had become even more critical of the executive branch's management of defense resources than it had been in the 1970s. Its dissatisfaction with the administration's defense program became more pronounced, its frustration with the combative style of Secretary of Defense Caspar W. Weinberger grew more intense, and consequently its scrutiny of defense budget requests and weapon programs became more detailed and more assertive. In the 1980s the Congress also legislated changes in Defense Department procedures in order to improve the planning and management of the nation's defense resources. This culminated in 1986 in the most far-reaching restructuring of the nation's defense establishment in almost thirty years.

The Congress came under heavy criticism for its new role in defense management. Officials of the executive branch, retired military officers, and executives of defense industries attacked it for alleged capricious interference in the defense budget, for permitting parochial interests to sidetrack national objectives, for being too shortsighted, and for imposing restrictions that make it virtually impossible to protect the nation's security efficiently. Questions were raised also about the extensive contributions to key legislators' campaign funds by political action committees tied to defense corporations. Moreover, there were questions about financial ties between defense contractors and some members of Congress serving on defense committees, and about the possibility that these financial links purchased undue influence. A study by Common Cause, the self-styled citizens' lobby, for example, found that in 1987 members of the Armed Services and Defense Appropriations committees received more than $500,000 in honoraria from the nation's weapons manufacturers.[4]

Some of these criticisms have been expressed even by congressional defense experts. Senator Sam Nunn, for example, chairman of the Armed Services Committee, has lamented the legislature's neglect of broad policy questions in favor of detailed management issues:

> I cannot remember when we have had a floor debate on our national military strategy and how well we are doing in carrying out that strategy. We have not had a serious debate about the important relationship between our national objectives, our military strategy, our capabilities, and the resources to support that strategy. . . . Instead, we are preoccupied with trivia. . . . [It] is preventing us from carrying out our basic responsibilities for broad oversight.[5]

Has the Congress gone too far in asserting its role in defense issues? Is its approach to these questions misdirected? I would say no to the first question, yes to the second.

The changes in congressional institutions and procedures that have taken place since the 1960s have enabled the Congress to play an informed and independent role in the design and management of defense resources. They have forced successive administrations to change course in important ways, bringing their policies within the broad boundaries supported by public attitudes. Just as congressional pressures forced the Carter administration to spend more for defense in the 1970s, they forced the Reagan administration to reverse its defense buildup in the 1980s. Congressional initiatives have helped shape the size and structure of the nation's armed forces, alter the administrations' spending priorities, and reorganize the Defense Department. For the most part, these initiatives have resulted in a more effective and prudent defense program, and a military force posture that reflects, to a greater extent than it might otherwise, both the nation's objective interests and the public's subjective concerns.

Still, a price has clearly been paid for the Congress's extensive involvement in defense matters. Its routine participation in annual budgetary decisions necessarily disrupts the efficient management of defense programs. Similarly, the dominance of parochial interests in congressional decision making leads not infrequently to inefficiencies, as when an overriding concern to protect constituents' economic interests makes it difficult to realize the potential savings from modernizing and rationalizing the defense infrastructure. The short-term horizon for congressional evaluations of decisions sometimes results in wasted expenditures and neglected defense needs. The Congress's responsiveness to short-term swings in the public mood sometimes results in instabilities in defense funding and consequent inefficiencies in weapon acquisition programs. Most importantly, the Congress continues to get lost in the "trees" of detailed defense programs, losing sight of the "forest" of broader issues in defense planning and military strategy.

Current congressional budgetary procedures are also extraordinarily inefficient, placing unreasonable demands on both defense officials and members of Congress. They virtually exhaust the time available for the Congress to spend on defense subjects, including oversight and debate of the broader purposes of U.S. defense policy and how well or poorly they are being accomplished.

Congress has not the resources, the incentives, nor the organization to review and evaluate each year the thousands of individual programs that make up the nation's defense posture. Nor was it intended by the Constitution that the Congress replace the president and his subordinates in these executive functions. As Stanley Heginbotham, formerly a senior official of the Congressional Research Service, has pointed out, the Congress has none of the characteristics that enable bureaucracies to function effectively: it has no definitive hierarchical structure, the functional specialization of its subunits (committees) is very limited, responsibility for effective operations is not assigned to specific individuals, the persona of its members cannot be separated from their office, and its members are rewarded or penalized on the basis of criteria that have little, if anything, to do with effective decision making. Together, these factors mean that the Congress "has extremely limited capacity to develop coherent proposals of its own and less ability to provide continuous support for operational activities." Yet these are the functions that the Congress has increasingly assumed in defense matters in recent years.[6]

That the Congress has moved into its current role is not an accident of history. It is the result of successive administrations pursuing defense policies that departed too radically from the public's beliefs of what the nation's security required and refusing to modify these policies in response to repeated expressions of congressional dissatisfaction. Significant reform of congressional overextension, then, will become possible only when an administration becomes more responsive to the realities of public and congressional moods—and more accepting of the legitimacy of congressional oversight. It is up to the executive branch to rebuild the public's and, thus, the Congress's confidence in the ability of the Defense Department to manage the nation's defense posture effectively. Only if that were accomplished would, or should, the Congress become willing to relax its now intrusive posture.

Reform proposals that might be considered would:

- Permit greater congressional attention to broader questions of U.S. military strategy and defense policy.
- Remove the replication now typical of the congressional process.
- Reduce the burden of the Congress's defense budget review on both the executive and the legislative branches.
- Make possible more stable and realistic financial planning by the Department of Defense.
- Ensure a more efficient use of whatever amounts of money are appropriated for the nation's defenses.

At the same time, they would permit the Congress to retain its ability to intervene in the specifics of those programs that, for whatever reason, require detailed attention.

Before considering these proposals specifically, it is important to understand (1) how and why the Congress extended its role in defense planning in the first place and (2) how congressional decisions on defense issues are actually taken.

Congress Takes Control of the Defense Budget

Prior to 1962, the legislative committees for military affairs played only a sporadic role; they had, in effect, abdicated their powers to authorize appropriations. Authorizations were not required annually and were phrased in such general terms and pegged at such high levels as not to interfere with decisions being taken by the Defense Department. The secretary of the air force, for example, was authorized to "procure 24,000 serviceable aircraft . . . as he may determine," without any specification of the mixture of fighters and bombers, or whether airlift or cargo aircraft should be purchased. Congressional guidance on missile development and procurement was even more vague: the secretaries of the air force and navy, separately, were authorized "to procure and construct guided missiles." On personnel, the armed services were authorized to maintain up to 5 million people in uniform, far more than any defense planner had contemplated since 1945. The one exception to these generalities was military construction. Mindful of the federal pork barrel, the armed services committees insisted on the right to authorize most individual construction projects. Construction, however, constituted only a tiny portion of defense spending and did not entail first-order decisions on defense policy and military strategy.[7]

Over a twenty-four-year period (1959–1983), the armed services committees gradually extended the scope of their annual authorizations. The committees also began to take their authorization of person-

TABLE 2-1. Fiscal Years in which Annual Authorizations Were First Required for various Appropriations Titles*

Year	Appropriation title
1962	Procurement of aircraft, missiles, and naval vessels
1965	Research, development, testing, and evaluation†
1967	Procurement of tracked combat vehicles
1969	Personnel strengths of the reserve components
1971	Procurement of "other" weapons‡
1972	Procurement of torpedoes and related support equipment; active-duty personnel strengths
1982	Operations and maintenance
1983	Procurement of ammunition and "other procurement"§

*There are separate titles for each (or several) of the armed services for many of these appropriations; such as procurement of aircraft, army; procurement of aircraft, navy.

†An "emergency fund," accounting for only 0.2 percent of the research and development budget, was omitted until 1967.

‡This title includes artillery, air defense weapons, small arms, and crew-fired weapons.

§"Other procurement" includes electronics and communications gear, support equipment, and so forth.

Sources: Robert J. Art, "Congress and the Defense Budget," in Barry M. Blechman and William J. Lynn, eds., *Toward a More Effective Defense* (New York: Ballinger, 1985), p. 133; Brent Baker, "National Defense and the Congressional Role," *Naval War College Review* 35 (July/August 1982): 11.

TABLE 2-2. Percentage of Defense Budget Requiring Authorization, 1961–1983*

Fiscal year	Person-nel	Operations & maintenance	Procure-ment	Research, development, test & evaluation	Construc-tion	% of total requiring authorization
1961	0	0	0	0	90	2
1962	0	0	75	0	90	27
1965	0	0	74	100	94	37
1967	0	0	63	100	93	32
1969	4	0	55	100	93	29
1971	6	0	70	100	94	31
1972	100	0	71	100	94	63
1982	100	100	73	100	93	91
1983	100	100	100	100	94	100

*By appropriations title and total.

Source: Office of Management and Budget, *Budget of the U.S. Government* (Washington, D.C., various years).

nel strengths more seriously, specifying annual limits by service and reserve components, as well as changes in salaries and benefits. These actions gave the armed services committees effective control over the entire defense budget, matching the power of the appropriating committees. The history of this extension of the legislative committees' budgetary role is shown in Table 2-1.

The resultant growth in the share of appropriations requiring annual authorizations is shown in Table 2-2. As will be seen, the committees' annual jurisdiction grew from two percent in 1961 to nearly one hundred percent in 1983. Procurement appropriations received the committees' initial attention, followed by funds for research and development. Military personnel appropriations were not authorized until 1972 (and then only indirectly); operations and maintenance funds remained unauthorized until 1982. This growth in the armed services committees' jurisdiction reflected a radical change in the legislative committees' perception of their rightful role, as well as in their willingness to challenge both the Pentagon and the appropriating committees on defense budgetary issues.

Reforms in the 1970s

The primary impetus behind the growing congressional role in defense budget making was the sharp change in the attitudes of many members toward defense and the military that resulted from the Vietnam War. The new congressional role was made possible by the sudden "democratization" of Congress, and specifically of congressional committees. Until the late 1960s and early 1970s the defense committees had been notorious for the autocratic styles of their chairmen, almost all of whom had come from the South, and many of whom had ruled for extremely long periods of time: Congressman Mahon chaired the House Subcommittee on Defense Appropriations for thirty years; Carl Vinson of Georgia chaired the House Armed Services Committee for nearly three decades. He was succeeded by a South Carolina Democrat, L. Mendel Rivers, and then in 1970 by a Louisiana Democrat, F. Edward Hebert. None of the three was prone to question the Defense Department too closely, except with regard to why additional facilities could not be located in their home districts. Rivers was particularly notorious for this; observers joked that Charleston would fall into the sea with the weight of concrete being poured for military bases there.

Nor were the chairmen inclined to permit their colleagues to ask questions. According to Congressman William L. Dickinson (R.-Ala.), currently the ranking minority member of the Armed Services Committee, "Junior members didn't have diddly squat to do." Congressman Bill Nichols (D.-Ala.) put it even more clearly: "Very seldom did I get to talk." According to Samuel S. Stratton (D.-N.Y.), also a longstanding member of the House Armed Services Committee, Rivers especially ran the committee as his private domain: "If you did not go along with him, he'd see that certain things were taken away."[8]

The chairmen were able to enforce this discipline due to the autocratic organization of the House itself; the rules gave extraordinary powers to committee chairmen. Things began to break in the 1970s, though, when Hebert practically revolutionized the House Armed Services Committee by establishing a rule that permitted each member five minutes to question witnesses.[9]

Hebert's innovation was actually a rearguard action to prevent more radical change. It was both too little and too late to satisfy the large number of younger, more liberal members of Congress elected to the

House of Representatives in the antiwar classes of 1968 and 1970. The new members forced passage of the Legislative Reorganization Act in 1970, and in 1973 caused the House Democratic Caucus (the association of all Democratic members of Congress that is used to formulate rules and floor strategy, select the party's leadership in the House, and make committee assignments) to adopt a Subcommittee Bill of Rights. Together, the two measures greatly limited the power of committee chairpersons, gave greater authority (and resources) to subcommittees, ensured more choice assignments for junior members, and opened up committee hearings and votes. Hebert did his best to ignore the new democratic spirit and as a result was deposed by the caucus in 1975. His successor, Melvin Price of Illinois, probably leaned as favorably toward the Defense Department as did his predecessors, but recognized the new political realities within the House and acted accordingly.[10]

Similar legislative and procedural changes took place on the Senate side. Senator John C. Stennis (D.-Miss.), who chaired the Armed Services Committee throughout this critical period (1969–1980), not only implemented the reforms enthusiastically, but by all accounts took the lead in devolving the committee's highly centralized structure. According to Senator Carl M. Levin (D.-Mich.), who joined the committee in 1978, "Stennis was very open and sensitive to new members, ensuring fair debate, giving them plenty of speaking time, encouraging junior members to play a central role."[11]

Stennis understood the realities. He recognized that the congressional tide of antidefense sentiment blamed the traditional congressional leadership, committee structure, and procedures as much as the Pentagon for what was seen as the Vietnam catastrophe in U.S. defense policy. By cooperating fully with the reform movement, Stennis hoped to regain credibility for the Armed Services Committee and may have avoided more far-reaching changes in the committee's perquisites.[12]

The appropriations subcommittees also responded to the tides of reform sweeping the Congress, but only defensively. More demanding standards in evaluating defense requests came only in response to the armed services committees' more critical pose and with the knowledge that cuts either would be made by the subcommittees or would be imposed on the floor. Squeezed between the legislative committees and the floor, the appropriators had to act preemptively to retain their authority, making sure that the defense bill that reached the floor was fundamentally acceptable to a majority of the members.

Other structural changes in congressional procedures in the 1970s also had major effects on defense issues. Most importantly, the 1974 Congressional Budget and Impoundment Control Act created for the first time a process through which the Congress was required to consider the overall effect of individual decisions on federal revenues and expenditures. The new process made clear the tradeoffs between spending on defense and spending on domestic programs, the impact of both spending categories on the federal deficit, and the need for new tax revenues. It also created two new committees, the Budget committees, which also gained some authority over the defense budget. The process of drawing up each year's Budget Resolution makes clear the impact of defense spending on other priorities and has had a sobering effect on the Armed Services committees' claims on resources.[13]

Reforms in the 1980s

Since the mid-1970s, the Congress's role in defense oversight has continued to become more comprehensive, and there has been a continuing tendency for an ever larger number of members to take active stances on defense questions. Assertive congressional involvement in defense issues did not fade with the first wave of anti-Vietnam sentiment. Sustained initially by prodefense conservatives of both parties who sensed a popular backlash against defense cutbacks before the Carter administration got wind of the change, congressional involvement gained even greater momentum in the mid-1980s, when the Reagan administration proved unable to modify its initial defense program to accommodate the rapidly changing economic and political situation.

Jimmy Carter ran for president on the wave of antidefense sentiment that followed Vietnam. Competing in the early stages of the campaign against Congressman Morris K. Udall (D.-Ariz.), Senator Frank Church (D.-Idaho), and other liberals for the support of the party's dominant left wing, he proposed, among other things, to withdraw U.S. troops from Korea, to cancel the B-1 bomber, and to reduce defense spending by $5–7 billion per year. Antidefense sentiment had crested in 1975, however, with the fall of pro-American governments in Phnom Penh and Saigon, leaving those politicians on the curl of the antidefense wave increasingly high and dry. Carter's opposition in the later primaries came from the more conservative side of the party—Senators Henry "Scoop" Jackson (D.-Wash.) and Hubert H. Humphrey (D.-Minn.). And he barely maintained a rapidly diminishing lead against a ridiculed, but even more conservative incumbent, Gerald Ford, to limp into the presidency.

President Carter attempted to implement the defense cutbacks promised in the campaign, even though popular support for these initiatives was rapidly diminishing. By 1978, when the Carter administration had completed a major review of naval missions and force structure, denying as a result the navy's request to include funds in the fiscal 1979 budget for a new aircraft carrier, the Congress was ready to assert its more accurate understanding of the nation's growing uneasiness about the United States's diminishing military capabilities. The carrier request came to symbolize the administration's mistaken priorities and antidefense bias. Funds for the carrier were added to the Defense Authorization bill in committee and, after a hot debate, retained on the floor. Although the president vetoed the bill and was able to make the veto stick, the dispute renewed congressional assertiveness in setting defense budgetary priorities.[14]

The 1980 election of Ronald Reagan and a Republican Senate on a tide of prodefense sentiment temporarily stilled the Congress. For three years the Congress enthusiastically endorsed the very sharp increases in defense spending requested by the administration. The defense budget grew sixty-eight percent between fiscal 1980, the last Carter budget, and fiscal 1983. By 1984, however, public opinion had swung against further increases, and the Congress reacted accordingly. Gallup polls showed that advocacy of increased defense spending dropped forty-nine and fifty-eight percent in two 1980 polls, to about twenty percent in 1982. In 1984 pollsters were reporting that fewer than one in five Americans wished to spend more for defense.[15]

The very size of the increase in defense spending in the early 1980s caused some of the decline in support for higher defense budgets, but other factors were at work as well. The federal deficit skyrocketed in response to the tax cuts mandated by the 1981 Economic Recovery Tax Act, and it was clear that neither increased revenues promised by supply-side economics nor cutbacks in domestic programs were going to be large enough to make up for continuing defense increases. A consensus subsequently emerged that reductions in defense expenditures had to play a role in curtailing the nation's fiscal deficit.

More to the point as far as popular opinion was concerned, a series of defense-related scandals rocked the country. News of extraordinary prices for equipment and spare parts ($7,000 coffee pots, $400 hammers, $74,000 ladders) and prosecutions of numerous defense contractors for financial irregularities grabbed the headlines. They also raised serious questions—even among conservatives—about what the Defense Department had been doing with the huge sums of money the Congress had allocated to it. By 1985 Senator Charles E. Grassley (R.-Iowa), for example, elected on a prodefense platform in 1980 over John Culver (then one of the leading defense critics in the Senate), was singlehandedly leading the charge against the administration's alleged incompetence in defense management:

> You can learn a lot from watching pigs. They lie around and eat all you feed them, but the end result is good eating and an efficient use of food. Defense Department procurement officials are a lot like pigs. They eat all you feed them, but the end result is $700 toilet seats. Pigs will be pigs, whether they wear three-piece suits or mud. . . . Congress can and must change the eating habits of the Pentagon pig. When they find the courage to change that diet, the Pentagon pig will squeal loud and clear. All it takes, however, is a little courage.[16]

Secretary Weinberger's management style and personality greatly aggravated the administration's problems and contributed measurably to the Congress's willingness to take the initiative in defense planning. Knowing that the Congress would make some reductions whatever the administration's request, Weinberger fought within the executive branch for the largest possible amount and then refused to compromise with the Congress, either publicly or privately. While this tactic might have gained a few extra dollars for defense in the atmosphere of the early 1980s, by mid-decade, the Congress was barely paying attention to the Pentagon's continuing requests for extraordinary increases. Congressman Les Aspin (D.-Wis.), for example, chairman of the House Armed Services Committee, called the fiscal 1987 request "dead before arrival," while Senator Mark O. Hatfield (R.-Oreg.) labeled Weinberger "a draft dodger in the war on the federal deficit."[17]

Weinberger's stubbornness was legendary. In the spring of 1983, for example, he induced the president to turn down a negotiated compromise on the budget, which would have given defense a seven-percent real increase, holding out for ten percent. Weinberger's intransigence forced congressional Republicans into the uncomfortable position of having to choose between their two favorite issues: fiscal responsibility and defense growth. In the end, defense received only a five-percent increase that year.

By the end of his tenure, Weinberger had thoroughly enraged the members of Congress, including such prodefense administration stalwarts as Senator Dan Quayle (R.-Ind.). Quayle said of the Defense Department: "They're like a little kid playing marbles. If they don't win, they pick up their marbles and go home." [18]

Weinberger was blamed for not adjudicating the requests of the armed forces and for not establishing priorities in defense needs. He was blamed for incompetence in the management of defense resources and for not gaining control of the defense procurement scandals quickly enough. Most importantly, Weinberger was blamed by prodefense conservatives, particularly those of his own party, for handing an issue—the efficient management of the Defense Department—to the Democrats, and for putting the Republican leadership into the uncomfortable position of choosing between inaction on the deficit and cuts in defense spending.

By the time Secretary Weinberger left office in late 1987, many members of the Congress sighed in relief, some quite openly. By refusing to take economic realities and political sensitivities into account in composing defense requests, and by resisting any changes in defense organization and procedures, even though the most junior members of Congress realized that something had to be done (if only to reassure the public), the secretary had contributed decisively to yet another reassertion of congressional decisionmaking on defense issues.

This time, the defense committees were not able to contain the new congressional activism, particularly on the House side. Beginning in the mid-1980s, the House Democratic Caucus moved to exert control over relevant committee chairmen. The caucus did this not only to ensure greater power sharing with more junior members, as in the 1970s, but to make certain that the defense committees' chairmen followed a correct policy line as well.

In the early 1970s, the caucus had become a distinctly liberal organization, and it liberalized House procedures accordingly. Although the caucus's political coloration moderated somewhat later in the decade, the conservative victories of 1978, and especially 1980, in the words of Congressman Norman D. Dicks (D.-Wash.), "had shocked and clarified the minds of the members, causing us to recognize that we are in the land of the enemy." The caucus consequently disciplined itself to act with far greater cohesion.[19]

In 1985 the caucus deposed Chairman Price of the Armed Services Committee, replacing him not with the next most senior member of the committee, as they had done when Price had replaced Hebert, nor with the third-, fourth-, fifth-, or even sixth-ranking member. They passed over six conservative Democrats to elect Les Aspin, a relatively young activist elected in the major anti-Vietnam class of 1970, who had made a name for himself by challenging the Pentagon with a nearly weekly press release panning some aspect of defense management. Over the years, Aspin had become more moderate and more selective about the issues he chose to contest but retained a liberal image. During his first two years as chairman, however, Aspin veered from caucus-supported positions on key defense issues such as the MX missile and Contra aid; as a result, he was deposed. When the caucus met in January 1987 to organize for the 100th Congress, Aspin was not renamed as chairman of the Armed Services Committee. He regained the office a few weeks later, but only after a concerted political campaign featuring commitments to toe the caucus's policy line. This commitment has circumscribed his positions ever since.[20]

The caucus also dominated the Defense Appropriations Subcommittee. When Bill Chappell, Jr. (D.-Fla.), was appointed chairman of the subcommittee in 1986, after Joseph P. Addabbo (D.-N.Y.) died, key Democratic leaders made it clear that Chappell's continued tenure would depend on his willingness to keep the subcommittee close to the party's mainstream; Chappell agreed and was reelected as chairman in 1987. When Chappell lost his congressional seat in 1988, as a result of his implication in a Defense Department scandal, he was replaced by John P. Murtha of Pennsylvania, a member often disposed to challenge Pentagon decisions.

The tight limitations that the Democratic Caucus now imposes on its chairmen were never made more clear than in the conferences on the Defense Authorization bill in 1986 and 1987. In those years, as in 1985, the House added amendments to the bill, requiring certain actions by the administration with respect to arms control (see Chapter 3). In 1985 none of the amendments survived the conference with the Republican-controlled Senate, an outcome attributed to the greater conservatism of most senior members of the House Armed Services Committee, including the new chairman, Les Aspin, than of the majority of House Democrats. To avoid a similar problem in 1986, the Speaker of the House appointed special conferees from outside the committee to observe how hard committee members fought for the arms control amendments. In 1987 the House conferees were divided, with only the special representatives from outside the committee authorized to negotiate on the arms control amendments. While unusual, the rules do give this unappealable authority to the Speaker, with only the proviso that conferees should be people who generally support the House position. By taking this action the Speaker and the caucus made clear that the leadership of the Armed Services Committee no longer represented the mainstream of House Democrats and that it would no longer be permitted to dominate the resolution of highly politicized defense issues.

On the Senate side, as is usually the case, the changes in defense budgetary procedures have been instituted much more on an individual basis than along organized party lines. The Senate tended to lag behind the House in the 1980s because it remained in Republican hands for the first six years; committee chairmen and other leaders had clear incentives not to challenge administration policies and came under considerable pressure to support them. Even so, as the nation's fiscal problems deepened, conservative Republicans found themselves torn between the conflicting priorities of fiscal responsibility—perhaps the most stalwart party position—and the demand for a stronger defense posture (which had gotten many of the younger members into office). As political cartoonists and late-night television comedians had a field day with the armed forces' coffee pots and toilet seats, Republican senators increasingly chose to disassociate themselves from the administration on defense budgetary and management issues.

Senator Dave Durenberger (R.-Minn.), for example, not a member of either the Armed Services or Defense Appropriations Committee, issued a 200-page document in 1983 entitled "America's Defense: A Plan for the 1980s." Membership rose sharply in the Military Reform Caucus, an informal bipartisan organization aimed at bringing about fundamental change in the nation's military establishment. Debate on the Defense Authorization bill on the Senate floor increased considerably. From a yearly average of two or three days of floor debate between 1976 and 1981, the annual debate averaged nearly ten days between 1983 and 1987. The number of amendments to the defense bill rose even more impressively: from a low of 6 in 1977, they rose to 17 in 1981 before starting a sharp climb—58 in 1982, 68 in 1983, 108 each in 1984 and 1985.[21]

Nor was the budget the only focus of congressional defense activism. More than 250 pieces of legislation were introduced in the Congress in the 1980s to reform procurement practices. In 1985 and 1986, first the House and then the Senate passed landmark legislation to reorganize the nation's military establishment. Sponsored in the Senate by Barry M. Goldwater (R.-Ariz.) and Sam Nunn, then-chairman and ranking minority member of the Armed Services Committee, the legislation drew determined opposition from Secretary Weinberger's Pentagon. So convinced was the soon-to-be-retired chairman that the legislation was desperately needed, however, that when the administration tried to delay the bill's passage in committee, he suspended all other committee business—including usually routine approvals of budget reprogramming notifications and officer appointments and promotions.

Dimensions of the Congressional Process in the Late 1980s

Taken together, these successive waves of congressional reforms have greatly increased the length and depth of the Congress's budgetary review process. Hearings held by the Armed Services committees and subcommittees increased from roughly sixty days per year in the late 1960s to an average of one hundred days yearly between 1980 and 1987. Pages of testimony roughly doubled, to 10,000 per year. The annual reports of the committees have grown from about 100 pages to more than 1,000 pages. Activities of the two Houses' appropriations subcommittees have increased comparably. Between the late 1960s and late 1980s, for example, the two Defense Appropriations subcommittees' reports increased from about 130 pages to more than 700.

These figures reflect the much greater degree of congressional initiative and modification of administration budgetary requests that has become commonplace. The data in Table 2-3 demonstrate the extent of this increase. Perhaps the most telling statistics are the final ones: the number of budget line items actually altered by the Congress. The

TABLE 2-3. Congressional Initiatives on the Defense Budget, 1970–1988

Type of action	1970	1976	1982	1985	1988
Requested studies and reports	36	114	221	458	719
Other mandated actions	18	208	210	202	n.a.
General provisions in law	64	96	158	213	179
Number of programs adjusted					
in authorization	180	222	339	1,315	1,184
in appropriation	650	1,032	1,119	1,848	1,579

Sources: Data for 1988 from Comptroller, Office of the Secretary of Defense; all other data from *Congressional Record*, October 1, 1985, p. 25351.

increase in "intrusiveness" in the authorizing process has been relatively greater than in the appropriating process, although the latter continues to result in a greater number of budgetary alterations. The degree of congressional involvement rose even more sharply in the late 1980s than in the 1970s. The number of programs adjusted by either or both pairs of committees increased ninety percent between fiscal 1982 and 1988, as compared to fifty-one percent between 1970 and 1976. Congressional activity died down somewhat in fiscal 1989, for reasons discussed later (and in Chapter 6).

Participating in, and responding to, the congressional process is time-consuming for executive branch officials and a source of recurrent complaints. The greatest resentment of Pentagon officials concerns the repetitiveness of the process. Secretaries of defense have appeared before the defense committees as often as ten and eleven times in a single year; the chairman of the Joint Chiefs of Staff and the secretaries of the military services appear at least four times each year— once before each of the committees. Lesser officials may be burdened even more, as they must appear before a variety of subcommittees. All told, something like 300 individuals make about 500 appearances before the four committees each year; two-thirds of the individuals are executive branch officials who make nearly three-quarters of the appearances.

Officials must also respond to written requests for information; long lists of questions are often taken back to the Pentagon from these committee appearances, or submitted separately to witnesses by individual representatives and senators. In almost all cases the questions are intended primarily to get information on the record, to commit the department publicly to certain courses of action. The questions are constructed and reviewed by congressional staff; the members themselves have very little interest in them. In fact, they often serve only the most trivial whim of the most junior staff members, but the cost to the nation of responding is quite significant.

In recent years the Defense Department has also been required by the Congress to produce an extraordinary number of reports. (The enormous increase in this requirement is shown in Table 2-3.) Preparation of testimony, answering written questions, and completing reports are all elaborate exercises involving dozens of officials. Documents must usually be approved by every bureaucratic component with an interest in the subject.

Along with, and contributing to, the successive waves of reform in the way the Congress approaches the defense budget has been a substantial increase in the resources and expertise available to facilitate the process.

The Budget Reform Act of 1974 created the Congressional Budget Office (CBO), a counterpart to the Office of Management and Budget, and a source of objective and informed analyses of defense budgetary issues. The CBO has about twenty-five professionals working on defense issues, a number that has remained relatively steady since 1978. The inspired leadership of the CBO's first director, Alice Rivlin (1975–1983), created an image of seriousness, impartiality, and nonpartisanship—enabling the organization to function effectively in the highly politicized defense arena.

A second new institution is the Office of Technology Assessment (OTA), created in 1972 to help the Congress grapple with increasingly complex technical questions. The number of people assigned to defense issues by OTA is difficult to estimate, as the institution works on a project-by-project basis, supplementing its small nucleus staff with expert consultants as necessary.

The number of professional defense specialists at older congressional agencies has grown as well during the past twenty years. The staff of the General Accounting Office increased by almost fifty percent between 1969 and 1978, dropped slightly the following year, and held steady throughout the 1980s. The defense-related professional staff of the Congressional Research Service grew from seven in 1969 to eighteen in 1978 to twenty-eight in 1987.[22]

Professional staffs of the defense committees in both Houses have also grown impressively, as shown in Table 1-1, although their numbers remain small in comparison to the thousands of individuals helping to prepare the budget in the executive branch. All told, the four committee staffs increased more than fourfold, from twenty-one in 1969 to ninety-two in 1988.

Due to the expansion of defense-related analytic capabilities available to it, the Congress has been able to identify problems in existing or proposed defense programs, and also to outline practical alternatives to solutions favored by the executive branch. Importantly, those expanded capabilities also have given members greater confidence to challenge the defense budget. At the same time, the existence of these congressional experts, whose own job satisfaction and career advancement lie in an independent and assertive congressional role in defense budget making, strongly suggests that the new congressional role would be difficult to roll back.

The Politics of the Defense Budget

The macropolitics of defense are simple enough. Virtually all Americans favor a "strong defense"; the political liability of being perceived as "weak" on defense, had it not been evident as a result of the 1980 election, was made brutally clear by the rout of Michael Dukakis in 1988. As a result, American politicians are reluctant to advocate cuts in defense in the absence of a politically acceptable, higher-ranking objective. In the 1986 congressional elections one such acceptable objective was to reduce "waste, fraud, and abuse in defense spending." In the 1988 congressional elections an acceptable alternative objective was "to reduce the burden of deficit spending on future generations of Americans." Circumstances determine the relative ranking of these objectives. In the wake of the Soviet invasion of Afghanistan in 1980, being for a strong defense was far more important than being against waste, fraud, and abuse. In the wake of the October 1987 stock market crash, acting to bring about smaller deficits became much more important than building strong defenses.

It is precisely in these simplistic slogans that the national dialogue on defense is carried out in political campaigns. The substantive issues—whether or not to build strategic defenses, the efficacy of the "Maritime Strategy," how to maintain survivable strategic forces— are the stuff of innumerable white papers and learned articles intended mainly for the attentive elite. They set the stage for the broader debate by helping columnists and other opinion makers to frame their arguments, but they rarely enter into the perceptions of most voters. In the 1980 election, for example, the vast majority of the electorate could not name which weapon systems President Carter had actually canceled, and they were certainly not aware that he had increased overall spending on defense. All they knew was that he was "weak" on defense and, as a result, that Americans were being pushed around in various foreign countries. They also knew that Ronald Reagan was for a "strong" defense.

Given the loose parameters within which these images are formulated, and their dependence on circumstance, public relations, and rhetoric, they have little direct impact on congressional decisions on the defense budget. Most members wish to be seen as supportive of a strong defense, but an able politician can create and sustain such an image while still voting for substantial reductions in defense spending. By making speeches on patriotic themes and favoring strong defenses and increased defense spending in principle, a "prodefense" position is assumed. When a vote is cast against a particular weapons program, a skillful politician can make certain that what is cut is perceived to be wasteful, fraudulent, or abusive. Or if the weapon is not one of those three pariahs, then the ill-fated program can be portrayed as an unfortunate, and no doubt temporary, sacrifice on the altar of fiscal responsibility. The macropolitics of defense leave members of Congress with too much maneuvering room to influence specific budgetary choices decisively.

Instead, congressional decisions on the defense budget tend to be determined on far more pragmatic grounds. Defense, after all, is business—big business. The defense budget accounts for more than five percent of the gross national product; the defense work force, military and civilian, direct and indirect, accounts for some five percent of the nation's employment. Decisions on defense spending can affect the economic fortunes of hundreds of major corporations, and tens of thousands of smaller companies that supply materials, services, and components for defense goods—to say nothing of the millions of their shareholders, employees, and dependents. Rare is the congressman whose district is not measurably affected by trends in defense spending.[23]

Defense influences politics in other ways as well. The armed services are among the oldest and most powerful institutions in the country. Their members—serving and retired—have important, traditional ties to political leaders and a variety of levers to bring to bear on congressional decisions. Associations of retired military officers influence defense decisions on both the national and the local levels. Military reservists, and particularly National Guard organizations, which are integral parts of state governments (and can put pressure on state delegations in the Congress), are a particularly important channel of political influence. Veterans' organizations are also influential, mainly on personnel questions, but sometimes on hardware issues as well.

Political forces can also work against defense spending. Nuclear weapon systems attract particular negative attention, as do other military programs, like major construction projects, that threaten environmental damage. Moreover, a variety of citizen groups in recent years have devoted considerable public education and lobbying efforts to improving the efficiency of the defense posture and to ensuring that defense takes its fair share of deficit-related budget cuts. Whenever these causes gain popularity, as in the early 1970s and early 1980s, more House members and senators will see political advantage in opposing certain defense programs.

The mechanics of the budgetary review process itself help to determine congressional decisions. The sheer size of the defense budget and the technical complexity of so many of its issues restrict the Congress's freedom of action. As a consequence, the greatest single influence on congressional choices, by far, is the administration's preferences. But the second greatest influence is that of the congressional staff, which plays an extremely important, independent role in the making of congressional decisions.

How the Review Process Works

To understand the role of congressional staffs, their relationships to members, as well as the importance of other strengths and weaknesses of the congressional review process, it will be instructive to look at the passage of a specific piece of legislation. The Senate's version of the fiscal 1988 Defense Authorization bill is a good illustration, despite differences between the House and Senate and between the authorizing and appropriating processes. The illustration makes clear the patterns of behavior of the players—the relationships that are relevant in broad terms to all aspects of the Congress's defense budget review.[24]

COMMITTEE ACTION

The fiscal 1988 defense authorization process began in late January 1987 with submission of the president's budget. In a departure from then-recent practice, the proposed defense budget was relatively realistic, envisioning a modest three-percent real increase in defense appropriations. Still, in view of overriding concerns about the size of the budget deficit, the president's adamant stand against revenue increases, and the bipartisan congressional consensus that reductions in expenditures should not come exclusively from domestic programs, it was clear that defense would have to be cut substantially. Moreover, the Democrats had just regained control of the Senate, a shift that accentuated important differences between the executive and legislative sense of defense priorities.

Following the usual hearings on the proposed budget in the winter, the new chairman of the Armed Services Committee, Senator Sam Nunn, took the Democratic members and majority staff to a country club for dinner. In a highly unusual session, the members discussed the fiscal situation and budgetary priorities. One staffer termed the conversation "exciting." The staff subsequently prepared a paper outlining alternative budgetary macrostrategies. The choices were briefed to members individually, and a second meeting of committee Democrats was convened. At this point, a broad approach to the budget was decided: programs that contribute to the readiness of forces for battle would be protected, modernization of conventional forces would be stressed at the expense of nuclear programs, and production lines for weapons already being delivered would be maintained at efficient rates, at the expense, if necessary, of longer-term development programs.

The Senate Armed Services Committee is divided on a functional basis into six subcommittees: (1) Readiness, Sustainability and Support; (2) Strategic Forces and Nuclear Deterrence; (3) Conventional

Forces and Alliance Defense; (4) Defense Industry and Technology; (5) Manpower and Personnel; and (6) Projection Forces and Regional Defense. Based on the discussion at the two meetings and on individual consultations, Chairman Nunn established savings targets for each of the subcommittees. With this guidance and the broad priorities of the adopted budgetary strategy, the committee staff set to work, preparing for each subcommittee a document known as the "staff package," recommending dollar amounts for each line item in their portion of the budget. The subcommittees deliberated on the package, and each voted to adopt the package in place of the president's budget. As the president's proposal was unrealistic financially, it indeed was, in Congressman Aspin's words, "Dead before arrival." The committee's and subcommittees' subsequent actions, known as the *mark-up*, consisted solely of debate over changes in the staff package.

How did the staff decide what to include in each package? Members' interests were the overriding concern, most importantly members of the relevant subcommittee, then other Armed Services Committee members, and then other senators, with some—such as members of the Defense Appropriations Subcommittee—being more equal than others. Senators themselves sometimes spoke to the relevant committee staff member directly, or they dispatched their personal staffers to make their preferences known. In other cases, experienced committee staffers simply were aware of members' favorite programs and the futility of trying to cut them; these projects are known as "pet rocks."

For the most part, senators' initiatives were intended to protect, or to add to, constituents' special interests ("pork" in the vernacular). They each tended to involve relatively small amounts of money (that add up to large sums). According to one senator's estimate, in the fiscal 1988 mark-up, when the authorizing committees cut roughly $30 billion from the administration's budget proposal overall, congressional initiatives still added something like $4–5 billion to the budget.

The committee staff had relatively little contact with representatives of defense companies themselves, as lobbying tends to be done through senators' personal offices. (The tradition on the House side is different; there is more contact between lobbyists and committee staff.) Obviously, not every initiative of every senator could be accommodated by the staff, but the overriding criterion was to satisfy members' interest—especially members of the relevant subcommittee, especially members of the majority party. Certainly, each subcommittee chairman's interests were satisfied, as he had to approve the "staff package" before it could be tabled.

During the subcommittee mark-up, amendments were offered primarily by the minority, largely reflecting efforts by the administration to undo those changes to its budget proposal that the Defense Department found most objectionable. Reportedly, very few such amendments were offered in 1987. The staff did not make any recommendation on some of the most controversial questions, such as the level of funding for the Strategic Defense Initiative or whether to build the MX missile. Several of these controversial questions were deferred by the subcommittees as well; they were left to the full committee to decide.

The "staff packages," as amended by the subcommittees, became the basis for the full committee mark-up. There are typically many more amendments at this level (perhaps 100–150 in 1987), primarily because of the larger number of senators who do not have much direct input to some of the original staff packages. Again, most amendments deal with pork. In 1986, for example, Senator Edward M. Kennedy (D.-Mass.), then a relatively new member of the committee who until that point had essentially ignored both the subcommittee and full committee mark-ups, took the committee floor to save the Fort Devens, Massachusetts' marching band from the sharp pencil of the budgeteers.

The inclination in full committee, as in subcommittee, is to accommodate members' interests (Senator Kennedy saved the band). More than eighty percent of the amendments offered in committee passed in 1987. Senators recognize the requirements of their office, and they act to protect one another on these issues—with only rare exceptions, regardless of party, regardless of ideology. If nothing else, care is taken to ensure that proper process has been preserved. It is deemed essential that all members believe their concerns have been treated fairly, that—at a minimum—they can return to their constituents and report honestly that they did their best and that the constituents' interests received a full and fair hearing.

Policy issues are also aired in the full committee mark-up; indeed, the tradition is that the most controversial questions are finally resolved in this forum. These amendments also tend to be successful; they are designed to be. If a senator knows he does not have the votes to pass a substantive change on a policy issue, he will phrase the amendment so that it can be passed even if it then requires only a report from the Defense Department or a warning of future budgetary changes. The policy amendments that do not pass tend to be those intended to make a statement, making it possible for members to report that they pressed the issue, even if they were unable to move the majority.

ACTION ON THE FLOOR

As noted, floor debate on the Defense Authorization bill has increased in recent years, reflecting greater political involvement in the subject. In 1987, some 114 amendments were introduced on the Senate floor. The vast majority (ninety) were passed; only two were defeated outright, the rest were tabled or withdrawn. To be sure, the bulk of the amendments mandated very little in the way of tangible action. The success rate demonstrates again the members' inclination to support their colleagues, as well as senators' abilities to gauge the limits of their colleagues' tolerance. (Virtually all the failed amendments were symbolic protests against administration policies introduced by "hard-right" conservatives.)

About sixty percent of the amendments addressed broad policy issues (such as arms control, foreign trade, or the allies' defense burdens) or technical questions of defense management. The remaining forty percent were divided more or less evenly between specific programmatic issues and the particular interests of specific constituencies. Many of the latter concerned military personnel; others, the acquisition of military land by local communities. Virtually all of these amendments attempted to add funds to the committee's bill or otherwise protect constituents' interests. All but four of them passed.

(On the House side, amendments to most legislation are restricted severely by the "rule" that accompanies every bill to the floor. The Defense Authorization bill is an exception, however, being considered under one of the most open "rules." One hundred twenty-four amendments to the fiscal 1988 Defense Authorization bill were introduced on the floor of the House in 1987; three-quarters of them were passed.)

Despite its length (and heat), the floor debate on defense bills is played largely to the galleries—in Washington and in home districts. A few special interests that were somehow overlooked in committee gain a new lease on life, but the floor debate is largely an opportunity for members to make points for the record, by recording encomiums, by requiring reports on various topics, or even by going down to defeat on key issues. The real action is in the committees, and particularly in the subcommittees, not on the floor. The only exceptions are certain broad policy issues, particularly in arms control. But here, as will be discussed in Chapter 3, the defense budget is being used as an instrument to force change in the administration's approach to certain treaties and negotiations; the budget debate is the medium, not the message.

CONFERENCE

The differences between the House and Senate versions of the Defense Authorization bill are resolved in secret, in a special conference. The conferees meet in Room 406 in the center of the Capitol—midway between the two legislative bodies. The room was the home, years ago, of the Joint Atomic Energy Committee. It also serves for special meetings of the intelligence committees and is considered to have the best security arrangements on Capitol Hill.

Room 406 has little else to commend it. The Senate Armed Services Committee sent twelve of its members to the conference in 1987, leaving eight at home; this was the first time not all members of the Senate committee participated. The House sent a veritable army of sixty-six, including twenty-eight from the committee and thirty-eight outside conferees for special issues. The room is far too small for this many people. It is also too hot, too noisy, and too smoky. It has no facilities for side meetings, no copying machines, a small table, and far too many chairs. The physical arrangements are so poor that, when asked how he would improve the congressional defense budget review process, the initial response of Congressman John M. Spratt, Jr. (D.-S.C.), was to recommend the construction of special conference facilities.

Quite often in recent years, the conference committee meetings have proceeded through the night, leaving members tired, irritable, and confused. With differences on literally thousands of programs to be resolved, most members cannot even remember what was decided, much less why.

The issues that are considered thoughtfully depend more on circumstance and members' idiosyncracies than their intrinsic merits. The 1987 conference, for example, devoted three full hours to a minor issue of a military base in Hawaii, while thousands of other issues involving billions of dollars were resolved by staff and never discussed by the members.

One of the few amenities in the conference room was jars of M&M candies; the late Congressman Dan Daniel (D.-Va.) used to arrange for this local product to be distributed. In moments of boredom conferees have been known to debate the relative merits of peanut-filled versus plain M&Ms. One year a member had army field rations delivered. Caffeine and empty calories are poor sustenance for the seriousness of the decisions being taken.

Most of the programmatic differences between the two bills are resolved by the two committees' staffs. According to participants, of roughly five thousand differences in program elements in 1987, more than ninety percent were resolved in this manner. How does staff reach decisions? Much is determined by the structure of the budgetary situation. In 1987 the Senate bill was considerably higher than the total for defense ultimately agreed upon in the overall budget compromise; Senate staff thus had to give way on many issues. In previous years the House bill often had a total that members and staff understood was much lower than the president would accept; House conferees thus had to give way more often.

Again, staffers are well aware of their members' most important interests—and fight hard for them. They are willing to trade a victory on one of these key issues for concessions on two or three others. Everyone recognizes the nonnegotiable issues and cooperates to protect them. Not all interests can be protected, of course, and again a hierarchy reigns, depending on the sponsor's position in the committee and the congressional leadership.

In 1987 most residual issues not settled by staff concerned broader policy questions. These were worked out by subpanels of the members, an innovation started by Les Aspin when he took over the chair of the House committee. Assignments to the key panels are obviously decisive. Previously, the chairmen would take one or two of the most interested individuals to one of their private offices and work out a deal. The technique has not been entirely abandoned: the most controversial issues in 1987 were resolved by private meetings of the chairmen and ranking minority members of the two committees.

Perhaps the most extraordinary thing about the House/Senate defense conference is the tight secrecy in which it is cloaked. Despite all the Congress's rhetoric about freedom of information, despite repeated invocations of the public's "right to know," despite frequent criticism of the Defense Department's abuse of secret, or "black," programs, the most decisive phase of the Congress's defense budgetary process takes place behind closed doors, in total secrecy, with such an obsessive concern for security that the meetings can be held only in the most secure room of the Capitol.[25]

The Role of Staff

The Russell Building, on Constitution Avenue, is named after Senator Richard Russell (D.-Ga.), who was chairman of the Armed Services Committee from 1951 to 1968 (with a two-year hiatus when the Republicans gained control of the 83d Congress). The building is one of the most elegant and dramatic office buildings in Washington. Its 300-foot-long corridors filter the outside light in such a way that approaching figures are seen only as shadows, larger than life. Its seventeen-foot-high ceilings give sound a special quality, lending importance to the most trivial remark. Its columns, the rotunda, its expanse of marble, the huge mahogany doors to most offices and committee rooms conspire to intimidate all but the strongest egos.

The elegance evaporates once inside a suite. The explosion of congressional staffs had long ago required the division of these handsome rooms into much smaller cubicles. In each is a desk, the inevitable computer monitor, a bookshelf, a chair or two for visitors, and piles of documents and reports. The suite of offices on the first floor of the Russell Building that houses the staff of the Armed Services Committee is no exception. But what the twenty-five men and four women of this staff may lack in appointments, they are more than compensated for in terms of influence and responsibility.

As the description of the fiscal 1988 Defense Authorization process makes clear, the annual review of the budget of the Department of Defense, like most business of the United States Congress, is accomplished largely by staff. Staff does not make final decisions, nor does it resolve important issues of policy. It operates, moreover, under clear guidelines determined by the chairman and the members of the committee. Still, the sheer size of the defense budget, and the technical complexity of so many of the issues, ensures a major role for staff, with numerous opportunities to inject their own preferences and prejudices into decisions determining the allocation of billions of dollars.

Given their small size, staffs of the subcommittees on Defense Appropriations, in particular, have enormous responsibilities. For example, one person reviews virtually the entire research and development budget for the Senate subcommittee. Les Aspin was once asked at a meeting in the early 1980s to name the most influential person in developing the nation's defense posture. Expecting to hear John Stennis, or Melvin Price, the audience was startled by the congressman's response. "Peter Murphy," he replied, without hesitation. Aspin went on to explain that at the end of the congressional review process, when the appropriators usually had to pare the budget by some substantial amount to reconcile it with the overall budget resolution, Subcommittee Chairman Addabbo would turn to Murphy, the key committee staff member, who would, "sharpen a pencil and adjust literally hundreds of programs by small amounts until the requisite total was in hand."

Who are these people? Judging from available biographies, a typical committee staffer is likely to be in his forties ("his" is not inappropriate here; in 1988, for example, only fifteen of the eighty-nine committee staffers were women), and very likely to have come to the committee after having served in the armed forces. If not, he is likely to have worked for the Defense Department as a civilian or for a defense think tank. Transfers from personal staffs or other congressional organizations (such as the Congressional Research Service) are another favored career route. Many of the committee staffers are graduates of the military academies; no other academic institution stands out as a favored source of staffers. Committee staffs tend to be older than personal congressional staffs. They also tend to stay on the job longer. A very large proportion have been working for the Congress for at least five years; a considerable number have been there ten years or more.[26]

The independent role of committee staffs is not decisive on either broad policy or aggregate fiscal questions, and their degree of influence on individual programs is constrained by members' preferences. Still, they have an extremely important impact on thousands of decisions determining the pace and extent of the nation's defense programs. In the heat of the 1987 conference on the Defense Authorization bill, Congressman Ronald V. Dellums (D.-Calif.), upon hearing that issue after issue had already been resolved by staff, is reported to have exclaimed in exasperation, "If I have even one life after this, I hope to God I return as a committee staff member."

The staff members of the House and Senate Armed Services committees and the Defense Appropriations subcommittees are extraordinarily competent and hardworking people; they have considerable expertise and substantial experience that compares very favorably to the knowledge and competence of bureaucrats in the executive branch. But they are vastly outnumbered and have neither the time nor the resources to learn as much about specific defense programs as do responsible officials in the military services and in the office of the secretary of defense. There is no good reason for them to play as decisive a role as they do now.

Reforming the Congressional Process

During the past twenty years, and most importantly during the 1980s, legislators' attitudes toward their rightful role in the defense budget process changed appreciably. The members and staff interviewed for this book see little prospect of a return to the Congress's previously less assertive role. As Senator Carl Levin put it, "Having tasted the power and seen few problems as a result, they [the Congress] will not hesitate again." [27] More responsible administration budgets might induce the Congress to retreat a bit, as happened in 1988 (see Chapter 6). But a real disengagement from the details of the budget will come, if ever, only over the long term and never with regard to highly politicized issues like nuclear weapons.

The Congress generally acted constructively in the 1980s in asserting its will on the defense budget. It constrained total spending to a level that was supportable politically and economically. It helped redirect priorities from nuclear to conventional programs, from the navy to the army. It increased the production rates for many weapons to more efficient levels, thus decreasing the cost per unit of equipment. It slowed certain advanced development programs to reduce the demand for budgetary resources in future years.

Still this observer, among many others, remains uneasy with the new congressional role. It asks too much of the Congress. There are too many complex issues; the time members can devote to them is too limited; their backgrounds are inappropriate. The staff is too small. There are too many opportunities for parochial interests to be given precedence at the expense of national objectives. Most importantly, the nonhierarchical organization of the Congress means that it is virtually impossible for it to establish an overall military strategy and broad set of policies, and then derive a coherent set of programs to implement them.

The Congress clearly was a better budgeteer than the Defense Department during the mid- and late 1980s. But that was because Secretary Weinberger did not impose priorities and realistic limitations on the military services' individual budget requests. In that sense, Weinberger replicated in the Defense Department the organizational flaws inherent in the Congress. But a new secretary can always reassert his prerogatives and regain control of the budget, as did Weinberger's successor, Frank Carlucci, in 1988. The Congress's problems are structural. The legislature will always be limited by its fundamental institutional organization.

The congressional process concentrates power in the hands of very few. The locus of decisions is overwhelmingly in the subcommittees and committees and in their conferences. The defense committees reflect the will of each House on broad fiscal and policy questions, but in recent years, with only rare exceptions (such as the MX missile), the fates of specific defense programs have been determined largely by the members and staffs of the relevant subcommittees.

The criteria applied in congressional decision making are often inappropriate from a national perspective: the overriding criterion in congressional deliberations necessarily is to protect the interests of constituents. This often means that dollars allocated for defense are used inefficiently.

The Congress is incapable of making hard choices in defense. Because of members' predisposition toward accommodation, stopping an ongoing program is virtually impossible. There are few successful examples. One occurred in 1986 when the air force announced plans to terminate the T-46 aircraft, scheduled to be built on Long Island, in the district of the normally skeptical, if not antidefense, Congressman Thomas J. Downey (D.-N.Y.). He was able to mobilize the New York delegation and a good part of the Democratic leadership in a last-ditch attempt to save it, but the effort was unsuccessful because Senate Armed Services Committee Chairman Barry Goldwater, in his final congressional action, resolved to kill it. According to a colleague, "It took a heroic effort on Barry's part, and it really left scars. It took something out of him." Members not about to retire, and not in such a position of strength as Goldwater, are unwilling to take on such battles with their colleagues.

The more common congressional decision is to preserve programs, even those unwanted by the military services and the secretary of defense. Congressman Mahon, for example, kept the production line for the A-7 aircraft open for years after the services no longer perceived a need for the plane. Every defense secretary since Robert S. McNamara has wanted to shut large numbers of defense installations to reduce the department's overhead, but has been prevented from doing so by congressional resistance. Indeed, during the 1980s, Secretary of the Navy John F. Lehman, Jr., turned the traditional base-closing game on its head. His "strategic homeporting" program sought to expand the number and locations of naval facilities around the country, ostensibly to help the navy survive a nuclear war. It passed handily, judiciously spreading the federal largess associated with naval facilities to new constituencies on all three coasts, thus increasing the base of support for naval shipbuilding programs. Taxpayers will be footing the bill indefinitely.

Confronted with a need to cut defense spending, the Congress's response inevitably is to spread the pain across the board. Instead of canceling a single weapons program, dozens of them are slowed. The net results are typically reductions in the armed services' operating accounts, inefficient rates of production (and thus higher unit costs), and delays in putting new types of weapons into the field.

There is nothing wrong with congressmen acting this way. Our system of government is built on this play of local interests in the Congress; but from the perspective of the national interest in an efficient defense posture, there is a price to be paid for the supremacy of parochial interests in congressional decision making. As the Congress's role in defense budget making has expanded, that price tag has multiplied.

There is one final problem in congressional decision making on defense issues—its lack of consistency. Members rightly point out that they are much more responsive to changes in public opinion than the executive branch. But there are drawbacks as well as benefits when support for sharply rising defense budgets turns around, or vice versa. Sharp changes in any federal program, up or down, bear a price. There are start-up costs and inefficiencies as programs begin, just as there are termination costs and inefficiencies on the way down. Between fiscal 1979 and 1988, the defense budget increased in real terms by about fifty percent. But, as shown in Figure 2-1, the preponderance of the increase occurred in the early 1980s; the trend later in the period was downward. Had the defense budget grown at a steady five-percent annual rate, the rough average in any event, and had this course been predictable at the start of the decade, the nation would have received a much greater return on its dollar.

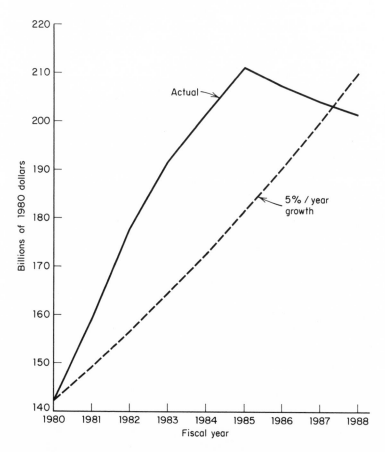

FIGURE 2-1. Defense Department Budget at Constant 1980 Prices

But the Congress inevitably responds in an exaggerated way to changes in constituents' moods. Politicians must get out in front of these swings in opinion if they are to appear to be leading them—and, indeed, if they are to be able to direct them in constructive directions. "Getting out front" inevitably leads to exaggeration and excess. Thus the national mood supporting a defense buildup in the early 1980s was translated in the Congress to wholly uncritical support for proposed budget increases that everyone in the business knew had not been well thought through and could not possibly be spent efficiently. Similarly, national concern with defense procurement practices in the mid-1980s often led to rhetorical excess, as well as to more than 250 pieces of legislation to reform defense management—some well thought through, the majority ill considered.

Proposals for Congressional Reform

There are a number of things the Congress could do in the near term to improve the effectiveness of its budgetary process. For one, it should add staff. The staffs of relevant defense committees are not large. For example, currently only thirty-nine staffers work for the House Armed Services Committee, while eighty-six work for the House Energy and Commerce Committee and fifty-nine for the Post Office and Civil Service Committee. As Congressman Spratt pointed out, constituent interests always receive first priority. Larger staffs would mean more resources to evaluate programs seriously.

The placement of senators and House members on the defense committees might also be reconsidered. The Democrats in the House and the Republicans in the Senate make committee assignments almost exclusively on the basis of seniority. At the beginning of each session, the most senior members decide whether to retain or change their assignments, and depending on the number of seats available to the party that session, new members are assigned. Members who choose the defense committees are no doubt motivated by an interest in military affairs, but there is clearly an added incentive for members from districts with major defense installations.

The Senate Democrats have a different system, which might be emulated by the others. The Democratic Steering Committee recommends committee assignments based on seniority as well as geographical and ideological balance. Attention is also paid to providing some opportunity to newcomers, so that younger members' perspectives are represented. The point is both to ensure that the committee represents the mainstream of Senate Democrats and also to reduce the concentration of individuals on the committees with major constituent interests in defense, thus giving a boost to national perspectives on defense issues. As Congressman Spratt, who has almost no defense industry or military facilities in his district, said: "I can be much more objective and independent in my votes. Efforts to ensure more equal representation on the committee to all parts of the country could make a difference."[28]

Beyond relatively small changes like these, the Congress is in no mood to consider serious reform of its approach to the defense budget. Justifiably proud of its performance in recent years, it is content to leave things as they are. President Reagan's veto of the Defense Authorization bill in the summer of 1988 (in order to create a defense issue in the presidential campaign), and the bitter partisan fight over John Tower's nomination to be secretary of defense in 1989, confirmed the Congress's determination not to give ground on the budget process.

It will take several years of more responsible executive branch behavior for the Congress again to look objectively at the burdens and drawbacks of its current system. At such a time, two major fundamental reforms could greatly enhance the Congress's ability to make decisions on defense in the national interest.

First, it would be desirable to redirect the legislative committees' annual review of the defense budget, a process that has come to duplicate the work of the Appropriations committees. There is somewhat more of an emphasis on policy issues in the legislative committees than in appropriations, a distinction accentuated recently by Chairmen Nunn and Aspin, and there is somewhat less stress on the details of program management. But these are differences of degree, not kind; essentially, under the current system, the Congress reviews each year's defense budget twice—holding the same hearings, questioning the same witnesses, applying the same criteria to decisions.

There is no substantive reason why the Armed Services committees need to focus their annual review process on the budget itself. Instead, they might concentrate on the "Five Year Defense Program," the primary force planning document within the Department of Defense. This document specifies in detail, on a functional basis, the planned force posture as well as the personnel, operations, and development programs to modernize those forces. The so-called FYDP is currently made available to the Congress each year, but no action is taken on it.

Under this proposal, the Armed Services committees would review the Defense Department's five-year program each year and enact legislation authorizing both the program and the budgets necessary to implement it. A methodology would have to be developed to translate decisions on the FYDP into budgetary terms, but such "crosswalks" already exist within the Pentagon and no doubt could be adapted readily to congressional requirements.

The annual review would concentrate primarily on the newly proposed fifth year of the plan. The committees, and of course the full Congress when the legislation came to the floor, would have the option of modifying elements in the first four years according to emerging developments. In the absence of compelling reason, however, programs would remain intact for four years. This added stability could contribute significantly to the efficiency of the defense program as well as to the efficiency of the Congress by reducing the burden of the review process.

Most important, this change in the focus of the legislative committees could lead them to concentrate on broader questions of the purposes and objectives of the U.S. defense program. They could review the relevant military and budgetary strategies as well as the longer-term financial and military implications of current decisions. They could spend less time on the fine points of program management, and more on the longer-term implications of current decisions.

Indeed, legislative enactment of the FYDP would cause the Pentagon itself to take the "out years" of its program more seriously. As things now stand, given the large percentage of elements that are substantially altered during the first two years of the program, construction of the third through fifth years is largely an empty exercise. Congressional review of the FYDP could be an extraordinarily important improvement in the stability, efficiency, and effectiveness of the U.S. military posture.

Second, the appropriating committees should consider enacting two-year budgets. The arguments for this change are compelling: there is too much turmoil in government programs when every item in the budget is reviewed every year, and the burden of annual budgets on both branches of government is too great. While economic and other circumstances may change over a two-year period, there is nothing intrinsic in the concept of two-year appropriations that would prohibit modifications midway.

It has been suggested, in fact, that any potential problem caused by the need for midcourse corrections could be avoided by creating a relevant legislative vehicle that would come up automatically in the second year of each session.[29] This midperiod Appropriations Adjustment Act would enable the administration to propose any changes and would provide the Congress with a suitable vehicle to debate modifications. Congressman Les Aspin, for example, has proposed that if the Congress appropriated a two-year budget during the first year of each session, it might wish to consider military personnel appropriations and pay raises during each second year. The pay bill would provide a legislative vehicle in committee and on the floor for members concerned about any element in the budget to suggest amendments. Moreover, because of its subject matter, the bill would be virtually veto-proof, and the Congress would not have to worry that by shifting to a two-year budget they had effectively ceded one-half of their leverage to the executive branch. The administration, no doubt, would have amendments of its own to suggest during the second year, and many midcourse changes in the budget could be made. Still, the presumption would be that programs would not change in the absence of compelling reason, and the majority of the budget would likely remain intact.

It is the understandable reluctance of congressmen to yield power, or even the appearance of power, which prevents two-year appropriations from being enacted. As Senator John Warner put it, ''Members want their constituents to know every year that they have voted to preserve 'Fort Useless.' '' Privately, almost every member interviewed for this book admitted that the shift would be a good idea. The greatest resistance will come from the members of the Appropriations committees themselves. There is an old adage in the Congress to the effect that no appropriator has ever not been reelected. Naturally, the members who have secured these sought-after assignments are not going to give up their power easily.[30]

Congressman Norm Dicks, a member of the Defense Appropriations Subcommittee, suggested three conditions that might make two-year defense appropriations feasible: (1) it would have to be part of an overall budgetary reform package—the domestic budget would have to be extended to two years as well; (2) the party caucuses would have to insist on the change against the protests of the members of the appropriating committees; and (3) it would have to be part of a bargain with the executive branch, in which the latter made changes in its budgetary procedures desired by the Congress. Still, Dicks said, "It would be tough, not impossible, but very difficult to accomplish politically.[31]

Implementing these two fundamental reforms in the congressional defense review process would require enlightened and inspired leadership in both branches of government. The likelihood is that they seek too great a change to be realistic. If the reforms could be accomplished, however, they would greatly aid the development and implementation of effective and efficient defense programs while preserving the recently expanded and essential role of the Congress in the management of the nation's defenses.

|3|

Arms Control

For all its closer attention to weapon programs and military spending, the Congress's role in U.S. defense policy has changed most dramatically with respect to efforts to control arms. As Vietnam stimulated greater congressional activism in defense policy in the 1970s, the stalemate in nuclear negotiations at the start of the 1980s led to renewed congressional initiatives. The analogy is striking. In both cases, growing popular concerns about international events catalyzed grassroots political movements that, in turn, induced the Congress to change executive branch policies. In both cases, the popular political pressures overwhelmed the bureaucracy's resistance.

Although specific congressional initiatives had only limited effects, their passage made clear the power of the political forces behind them, as well as the growing political liability of continued opposition. Presidential administrations in both the 1970s and the 1980s reluctantly came to recognize the foolhardiness of continuing to appear recalcitrant, and reversed policies in important ways that went far beyond the specific demands of the Congress. In both cases, these policy reversals came too late. By the time these administrations responded to the political dynamic, the Congress had carved out new procedures and acquired new resources to ensure that the legislature's more intrusive role would continue.

In the 1970s the U.S. involvement in Vietnam induced radical changes in the Congress's view of its proper role with respect to U.S. military interventions abroad. New procedures and new institutions were established to ensure that Congress was aware of, and would thus influence, all forms of involvement of U.S. military power abroad—from "covert" paramilitary operations to full-scale military engagements (see Chapters 5 and 6).

Similarly, in the 1980s the seeming failure of administration efforts to control nuclear weapons induced the Congress to take a much more active role in the formulation ot U.S. arms control policy. To achieve this, the Congress turned to its most unambiguous and powerful weapon—the power of the purse. In effect, it began "to appropriate arms control," a move that meant some reordering of its internal distribution of power: the House of Representatives acquired unusual importance in what is essentially an issue of foreign affairs. Moreover, within each chamber, real authority on arms control matters shifted from the Foreign Affairs to the Armed Services committees.

By linking demands for specific arms control initiatives to military appropriations, the Congress forced the Reagan administration, against its own preferences (1) to continue to abide, more or less, by the terms of the much-scorned SALT II Treaty limiting offensive strategic arms; (2) to continue to restrict testing of new technologies potentially useful for strategic defense systems within a traditional, narrow interpretation of the 1972 treaty limiting antiballistic missile defenses; and (3) to maintain a moratorium on tests of antisatellite weapons. The Congress even came close to imposing a moratorium on most tests of nuclear weapons, perhaps the item on the arms control agenda most strongly opposed by Reagan administration officials.

This chapter examines the causes and consequences of this remarkable change in the congressional role in arms control.

Traditional Instruments Found Wanting

The Senate's power to advise on, and consent to, treaties, combined with past demonstrations of the Senate's willingness to utilize this authority to destroy major executive branch initiatives, has put the upper chamber in a position to command considerable respect in the conduct of the nation's foreign relations.

Throughout its history, the U.S. Senate has approved about ninety percent of the roughly 1,500 treaties that have been submitted to it. Only seventeen treaties have been turned down explicitly by the required "one-third-plus-one" minority. The most famous was the Treaty of Versailles, ending World War I and creating the League of Nations, in 1919. There have been only five such explicit rejections since then; most recently, a Protocol to the Warsaw Convention on International

Air Travel, proposed in 1975. Forty-three additional treaties have been approved by the Senate with such contentious reservations that they proved unacceptable, either to the president or to the other signatories, and never went into force. These agreements, rejected de facto, have largely been bilateral treaties on such technical matters as income taxation, arbitration, and extradition. (Roughly 200 additional treaties also included reservations, but none so onerous as to prevent the agreement from being implemented.)

An additional eighty-eight treaties that were submitted to the Senate were withdrawn when the upper chamber failed to take final action on them. (Again, these pertained largely to technical matters.) And another twenty-nine treaties have remained pending before the Foreign Relations Committee for more than three years, either because the committee itself has held them up or because the president, believing that they would fail on the floor, caused them to be delayed. A number of arms control agreements fall into these last two categories, including the 1974 Threshold Test Ban Treaty and the 1976 Treaty on Peaceful Nuclear Explosions, as well as the 1979 Strategic Arms Limitation Treaty (which actually was withdrawn by the president before it could be killed).[1] To paraphrase Senator Alan Cranston (D.-Calif.), finding thirty-four senators willing to oppose an arms control treaty—for reasons of conviction, or only election—has sometimes proved not even a sporting game, far less an insurmountable chore.[2]

Throughout the period of Strategic Arms Limitation Talks (SALT) from 1969 to 1980, and into the Reagan/Bush period of Strategic Arms Reduction Talks (START), individual senators and senatorial institutions have attempted to capitalize on this ultimate (ratification) authority in order to carve out a role for themselves in the negotiating process. Their reasoning is clear: the choice at the time of ratification is essentially accept or reject; there is little leeway for modifications. Amending a document as complicated and tightly drawn as a modern arms control treaty, which requires years of effort including the repeated attention of the highest executive authorities to negotiate, is often functionally equivalent to rejecting it outright. The more substantive the proposed change, the likelier it is that the act would be rejected. At the time of ratification, therefore, the real choice facing senators lies between accepting an agreement that may contain unpalatable provisions, or rejecting it all together.

It is difficult for any member of the president's party to vote against an arms control treaty. Even members of the opposition usually have trouble standing up to a president's pleas, or threats, when confronted personally. While a handful of senators—Jesse A. Helms (R.-N.C.) is the obvious example—have crafted images of obstreperous naysayers, which play well to home audiences, most senators prefer to cultivate a positive image of getting things done. This basic political bias strongly favors the president.

Treaty opponents, therefore, often voice misgivings, thunder against specific provisions, and demand strong safeguards in the way of compensatory actions or programs, but are much less likely to actually vote against an agreement. Final treaty votes may be very close, but those margins are deceptive. Presidents understand political needs and are quite willing to tolerate up to thirty-three senators voting against their treaties. There is no serious reward for a larger margin, and presidents—like any other politician—seek to conserve their capital. For example, although the Panama Canal Treaty barely squeaked through with sixty-eight votes, and then only after extensive negotiations on the Senate's reservations and understandings, President Carter is reported by one of the key White House lobbyists to have had two or three additional votes in his hip pocket, if he had really needed them.

Even when the political atmosphere is skeptical of arms control, the broad pragmatic center of the Senate, incorporating most members of both parties, prefers not to reject arms control pacts. The unpopular SALT II Treaty, for example, passed through the Senate Foreign Relations Committee in 1979 without any so-called disabling amendments and, until spared the test by the Soviet invasion of Afghanistan, was expected by both administration officials and congressional insiders to barely pass on the floor, despite a very well funded and organized opposition, only lukewarm support from the pro–arms control constituency, and a political operation on the part of the White House that impressed almost no one in either conception or implementation. Similarly, despite great protestations prior to its actual submission, the more recent Treaty on Intermediate-Range Nuclear Missiles sailed through the Senate's review with only limited opposition from the far Right.

The real battle in the Senate on arms control treaties is fought out in less apocalyptic terms. The Senate has developed a variety of means to fudge the difficult choice between ratification and rejection. If their personal objections to the agreement, and the political forces bearing on their positions, are felt only weakly, senators can always express substantive reservations or special interpretations in floor speeches, in committee during the ratification hearings, or less officially to the media. Those senators who are members of the Foreign Relations Committee can insist that their positions be incorporated into the committee's report on the treaty, thus emphasizing their concerns. To make more of an issue, a senator can work to incorporate an "understanding" into the "resolution of consent," the legislative vehicle used to bring the treaty to the floor. Such an action does not usually affect the treaty itself at all. Even more pointed is adding a "reservation" to the resolution of consent that actually changes an obligation contained in the treaty. Such reservations must be conveyed to the treaty's other signatories but, if phrased carefully, do not necessarily require the others' concurrence and therefore do not necessitate renegotiation.

Still short of rejection, the Senate can amend the treaty itself, an action that does require renegotiation, but the wording of amendments conceivably can be "cooked," with the administration acting as middleman between the Senate and other signatories to ensure that the outcome is successful. Such a process reportedly took place during the Panama Canal Treaty debate, for example, with the Carter administration brokering a deal between Senator Dennis DeConcini (D.-Ariz.) and Panamanian leader Omar Torrijos. This is a risky undertaking, however, if one's purpose is not to kill the agreement altogether.[3]

Senators' motives in working for these various types of actions vary. Starting with the most aboveboard:

TO INFLUENCE FUTURE AGREEMENTS

There have been cases in which senators have had serious concerns about an agreement presented for ratification but either were unwilling or believed themselves unable to persuade thirty-three other members to reject or amend the treaty. In such situations, a reservation expressing concern can serve both to satisfy political forces seeking to destroy the treaty and to put the administration on notice that it had better pay more attention to such concerns in future talks. By pursuing such reservations, opponents of the treaty in effect are giving up on the current agreement but want to either camouflage that fact for political reasons or influence the terms of the next round of battle.

The so-called Jackson amendment to the SALT I agreement (named after its sponsor, the late Senator Henry Jackson) is the most famous reservation. Only advisory in nature, it called upon the president "to seek a future treaty that, *inter alia,* would not limit the United States to levels of intercontinental strategic forces inferior to limits provided for the Soviet Union.''

Several similar reservations were presented to the 1987 Treaty on Intermediate-Range Missiles with the purpose of influencing the final terms of a second treaty, on central strategic forces, then under negotiation. The most important was introduced by Senators Frank H. Murkowski (R.-Ak.) and Dan Quayle. Adopted by voice vote on May 25, 1988, the resolution, among other things, declared that future strategic arms limitation agreements should not restrict deployments of cruise missiles armed with conventional explosives. The purely symbolic nature of the action was made clear in the following colloquy between Senators Quayle and J. James Exon (D.-Neb.).

EXON: This is a sense-of-the-Senate resolution, is it not?

QUAYLE: Yes.

EXON: So it is obviously not binding on anyone. It is merely expressing the sense of the Senate on this particular matter. I just wanted to clarify that.[4]

TO ENSURE "SAFEGUARDS" AGAINST CHEATING OR ABROGATION

Other senators have sought to ensure that administrations initiate and pursue certain actions to safeguard against cheating or sudden termination of an agreement. These actions, taken during ratification debates, often express concerns of the military or other hard-liners within the administration itself. In ratifying the 1963 Limited Test Ban Treaty, for example, key senators, reflecting the views of the Joint Chiefs of Staff, sought and received President John F. Kennedy's assurances that the United States would maintain a standby capability to conduct atmospheric nuclear testing, and also would improve U.S. capabilities to monitor nuclear testing and detect violations of the agreement. (A third test ban assurance, that the administration would pursue a vigorous program of underground nuclear tests, better represents the third type of senatorial purpose, to be described later.)[5]

Debate on the 1987 Intermediate-Range Missile Treaty also led to improvements in U.S. intelligence capabilities. In its report on the treaty's verifiability, the Senate Intelligence Committee indicated that current surveillance systems would be stretched to their limits and would eventually not be sufficient for the necessary monitoring. Committee

Chairman David L. Boren (D.-Okla.) met with the president and elicited an "understanding" that necessary improvements in U.S. collection systems would be funded. One specific satellite system, codenamed Indigo-Lacrosse, was apparently the focus of the discussion. When the administration delayed in seeking the necessary funding, Boren threatened a filibuster against the treaty that would prevent its approval in time for the upcoming summit meeting in Moscow. According to Senator Alan Cranston, Boren was "not trying to hold the Treaty hostage," he was only "trying to get the administration's attention." The tactic apparently worked.[6]

TO LOCK IN COMPENSATORY ACTIONS

On several occasions, senators have sought to offset weaknesses they perceived in a treaty, or in the circumstances surrounding its negotiation, by demanding compensatory actions from the administration. Although expressed as nonbinding reservations to the consent resolution, the sponsors of such arrangements often withhold a commitment to vote in favor of the treaty until the administration has agreed to the desired action.

Prior to the Soviet invasion of Afghanistan, for example, Senator Sam Nunn and others demanded that the defense budget be increased in real terms by five percent per year to offset weaknesses they believed to exist in the U.S. defense posture. They made such a commitment by the administration a prerequisite for their support for SALT II. While no final agreement was reached, the administration fully intended to fulfill the demand, as Nunn's consent to the treaty was believed critical.

Although a number of compensatory actions concerning the military balance in Europe were discussed early in the ratification debate on the Intermediate-Range Missile Treaty, none were added to the resolution of consent. This may have been because the Joint Chiefs of Staff were united in their unconditional support of the agreement, and treaty opponents thus found little military support for contentions that the treaty would have adverse effects on the military situation in Europe.[7]

TO "DISABLE" THE AGREEMENT

Recognizing the difficulty of convincing most senators, in the end, to vote "point blank" against a treaty, opponents may seek to "disable" the agreement by amending it, thus requiring its renegotiation, or by passing reservations to the consent resolution that, if conveyed to other signatories, would cause them to demand renegotiation. The fight over these so-called killer amendments is the real nub of the ratification debate. By fighting the battle on these grounds rather than the final ratification vote, treaty opponents ostensibly accept the disadvantage of needing fifty-one votes, rather than only thirty-four, as they must gain a majority to pass an amendment. In fact, their loss is considerably less: with only forty-one votes, plus determination and astute parliamentary tactics, they can tie up the Senate with filibusters and other delaying methods until the majority bows to their view. In any event, by offering senators the option of a vote that is the equivalent of rejecting the treaty but that can be characterized as only seeking to improve an ostensible major flaw in the agreement, they presumably have eased the opposition's primary problem—the reluctance of most members to be seen to be defying the president (and history) by voting to kill a treaty outright.

In theory, the use of killer amendments can persuade senators who oppose a treaty, but who fear the political consequences of being seen as naysayers, to vote with the opposition. Although the White House always makes clear which are the killer amendments, senators who want to stop a treaty prefer to vote to amend rather than to reject. Use of the device thus is pervasive.

In the Intermediate-Range Missile Treaty ratification debate, for example, Senator Jesse Helms—perhaps the treaty's most virulent critic—introduced a series of amendments, both in committee and on the floor, any one of which could have killed the treaty. Helms's amendments included efforts to keep the treaty from going into effect until the president certified the accuracy of the Soviet Union's count of SS-20 missiles—a task known to be virtually impossible—and to add an additional type of missile to those prohibited by the treaty. Senator Larry Pressler (R.-S.Dak.) also sought to delay implementation of the treaty indefinitely, until North Atlantic Treaty Organization (NATO) and Warsaw Pact conventional forces in Europe were in parity.

POLITICAL POSTURING

Debates on arms control treaties have also been used to advance personal or party political agendas. As the Treaty on Intermediate-Range Missiles neared completion in 1987 and entered the ratification process, some Democratic senators (including the majority leader, Robert Byrd), who had previously criticized the administration for not moving ahead more rapidly on arms control, suddenly expressed reservations about the prospective agreement. They recognized a virtually risk-free way to modify the Democratic party's image of "peace at any price" by expressing caution about even an agreement negotiated by Ronald Reagan. The virulency of most Republican senators' attacks on SALT II in 1979, to cite another example, was motivated at least in part by their (correct) understanding that, given the nation's political mood, the debate was further weakening the Carter presidency and helping to ensure Republican victories in the 1980 election.

Personal objectives enter into ratification debates as well as political motives. By positioning oneself shrewdly in the debate, and particularly by taking a leading role, there is considerable opportunity for media coverage and the cultivation of public images. Some senators may seek attention for their pro–arms control stance; others for disabling, curtailing, or compensating for alleged weaknesses in the agreement and the nation's defenses. In the 1988 debate, for example, Senator Steven D. Symms (R.-Idaho) introduced five amendments that would have delayed implementation of the Intermediate-Range Missile Treaty until the president had certified that the Soviet Union was complying with five previous arms control agreements. Because President Reagan had already charged the Soviet Union with violating these agreements, the amendments were clearly not going anywhere, and were defeated overwhelmingly on the floor. Symms had made his point to the extreme right-wing constituency, however—the base of his financial support.

Personal objectives ordinarily pertain to reelection campaigns but may also involve aspirations for future congressional roles, such as committee assignments, or may even reflect presidential ambitions. In addition, a senator may express reservations about a treaty to be in position to extract something completely unrelated from the president in return for an eventual positive vote. If skillfully done, senators can put themselves among the "swing" votes—thus increasing the price they can extract for eventual backing.

During the Carter administration, for example, the late Senator Edward Zorinsky (D.-Neb.) was notorious for coupling unrelated demands with both the Panama Canal Treaty and SALT II. One White House lobbyist described a meeting between President Carter and Zorinsky on the canal treaty as beginning with a long discourse by the president on the strategic importance of the agreement and ending with the promise of enormous federal housing subsidies for Omaha; Zorinsky is reported not even to have mentioned Panama. To cite a second example, Herman Talmadge (D.-Ga.) tied his support of the Panama Canal Treaty to the farm bill.[8]

Deciphering the reasons why senators adopt particular positions is always difficult. When it comes to issues as serious as arms control treaties, the vast majority of them act primarily on the basis of substantive beliefs and objectives. That is not to say that they are not aware of the political implications of their actions, but their basic positions are sincerely determined. There have clearly been cases, however, in which senatorial behavior during ratification debates has been dominated by personal objectives and the national interest be damned. Moreover, as arms control issues have become increasingly more salient politically, the temptation for such behavior has no doubt increased.

The debate over ratification of arms control treaties is thus rather more complicated than a simple vote up or down. Through a variety of instruments, individual senators seek to achieve a variety of substantive and political objectives, while the president—utilizing all the instruments of influence at his disposal—seeks to construct, at the least cost, the coalition necessary to push through the agreement free of disabling amendments.

From the Senate's perspective, the instruments at its disposal during the ratification process are far more valuable for achieving political and personal objectives than for achieving substantive goals. The give and take on substance greatly favors the executive branch. Killer amendments that actually change the terms of a treaty and thus require its renegotiation are very difficult to pass, while reservations requiring certain actions in the future are primarily face-saving devices that cannot really be enforced.

Even the Jackson amendment to the SALT I agreement had only limited effects. Both the Ford and Carter administrations, in the 1974 Vladivostok and 1979 SALT II agreements, respectively, found ways to interpret Jackson's demand for equality in future agreements that were not too constraining (and that did not please Senator Jackson and his supporters). In retrospect, Gerald Ford and Jimmy Carter may have been better advised to have interpreted the amendment more closely, but short of rejecting SALT II, which it appears to have been unprepared to do, the Congress had neither the timely information, nor the legislative devices, to impose Senator Jackson's view.

Consultative Process

Because of the limited choices at the time of ratification, senators clearly prefer to influence the terms of a treaty during the policy formulation and negotiating processes. If they are successful, they reason, they will either be able to support the completed treaty or prevent those concessions required for completion that they oppose, and thus avoid the debate on ratification altogether. If unsuccessful, they are at least no worse off at the time of ratification. In fact, their leverage should be greater.

When arms control is popular politically, as in the 1980s, participation in the negotiating process bears additional cachet. It boosts the member's credibility on defense issues generally ("I've sat across the table from the Russians and let me tell you . . ."; or, "I've discussed this issue with the secretary of state and the president's national security adviser and persuaded them . . ."). Participation in the arms control process provides a politically positive image of working for peace and toward a reduced risk of nuclear war. It also yields trips to European capitals during legislative recesses, journeys that can bring a variety of personal and political rewards.

The struggle for a real consultative process between the executive and legislative branches on arms control issues, and for congressional participation in the negotiation process, has been going on for nearly twenty years. In the beginning, little progress was made by the Congress.

On November 12, 1969, for example, one week before the start of the SALT negotiations in Helsinki, the White House canceled the planned first testimony of chief negotiator Gerard Smith before the Senate Foreign Relations Committee's Subcommittee on Arms Control. Smith's appearance was intended to "brief" the subcommittee members, in secret, on the administration's initial negotiating position, but even this limited form of cooperation was considered unnecessary by Henry Kissinger, then the president's national security adviser. The first serious congressional briefing did not take place until the spring of 1970, prior to the second round of talks, when eight senators and seven congressmen were invited to the White House to hear the administration's position. Unprepared and unsupported by expert help, the members had little choice but to receive the brief without comment. The symbolism of the lawmakers going to the White House, rather than executive branch officials appearing in congressional committee rooms, was not unimportant either.[9]

Senator John Sherman Cooper (R.-Ky.) tried repeatedly in the early 1970s to persuade the administration to permit senators to participate in the SALT talks, perhaps as observers, but these efforts were rebuffed. Cooper's argument that such participation might ease problems during ratification carried little weight. Kissinger made an exception for Senator Jackson, the Democrats' foremost defense expert, who was kept well apprised of the negotiations for a treaty on antiballistic missile systems. But even Jackson was apparently cut out of the information loop during the six months prior to the conclusion of the treaty in 1972. Richard Perle, Jackson's key aide during those years, commented, "Kissinger never felt a responsibility to engage in what you might call 'real consultation.' "[10]

The practice of excluding senators from the negotiating process continued through the final moments of the SALT I talks. Kissinger then rejected the suggestion that Senators Cooper, Jackson, Michael Mansfield (D.-Mont.), and Stennis attend the 1972 Moscow summit at which the SALT I accords were to be signed, as a demonstration of congressional–executive cooperation (and to better the prospects for senatorial consent).

Legislative–executive consultations did increase during the second Nixon administration and during the Ford years. The main reason for this was the Watergate scandal, which drastically curbed the president's power in all fields. The other reason was Kissinger's appointment as secretary of state in 1973. In his drive to defuse opposition to his nomination, Kissinger pledged repeatedly a new era of openness with the Congress. And like Charlie Brown and the football in the "Peanuts" comic strip, the innocents fell for it yet again. In 1974, when the substance of the Vladivostok agreement became known, it was clear that the Congress in fact had been no more informed than any man-or-woman-in-the-street.

The agreement was criticized from both the Right and the Left; it pleased no one. Vladivostok demonstrated to both executive officials and the Congress that the consultative process had to be improved.

Jimmy Carter took the lesson to heart—perhaps too much so. Upon taking office, Carter decided not to turn the Vladivostok principles into a treaty, as had been his predecessor's objective, but to reach for a more ambitious agreement. In crafting the terms of that proposal, he specifically sought to satisfy Senator Jackson's concerns, figuring that "Scoop's" support would carry a broad, bipartisan, centrist coalition with it. David Aaron, the deputy national security adviser, and Leslie Gelb, chief arms control adviser to Secretary of State Cyrus Vance, met several times with Richard Perle during this period.[11]

The resulting proposal, which Secretary of State Cyrus Vance took to Moscow in March, satisfied Senator Jackson, but was totally unacceptable to the Soviets. They not only resented Carter's abrupt dismissal of Vladivostok, an agreement that they had negotiated in good faith, but found specific elements in the new proposal, such as its one-sided emphasis on large, land-based missiles, totally abhorrent. The Carter administration soon returned to a position not far from the Vladivostok accord, and eventually turned it into the SALT II Treaty, but valuable time—and the initial momentum of a new administration— had been lost.

In retrospect, the decision to cultivate Senator Jackson was a major mistake; it cost Jimmy Carter the opportunity of depositing a ratified arms control treaty during his term in office. It was a lesson ignored by his administration, however. Throughout his term, such leading advocates of arms control in the Senate as Senators Claiborne Pell (D.-R.I.) and Charles McC. Mathias (R.-Md.) complained of neglect by an administration far more concerned with placating its enemies than building on its strengths. This resentment led directly to the lack of enthusiasm on the left for SALT II; a few liberals, George McGovern (D.-S.Dak.), for example, went so far as to oppose the treaty.

For all its efforts at consultation, however misdirected, the Carter administration in the end faced a still-hostile Right, and an unsupportive and distinctly unimpressed Left that was unwilling to stick its neck out politically in the treaty's defense. But a pattern of more frequent, more substantive, and more serious consultations between the executive and legislative branches on arms control negotiations had been initiated.

The Carter administration also broke with prior practice in May 1977 when Paul Warnke, director of the Arms Control and Disarmament Agency, asked congressional leaders to designate several members of each chamber as advisers to the SALT II delegation. He stated that they could "attend as observers the plenary sessions of the Delegations and also attend intra-U.S. Delegation meetings where their comments and advice would be solicited." Congressional advisers were even permitted to read and discuss the joint draft text of the emerging agreement. The arrangement, by all accounts, worked fairly well, and members expressed satisfaction that their views were being heard by the executive branch. The Congress, however, continued to be excluded from the intra-agency groups that really established negotiating strategy (the meetings in Geneva dealt largely with tactical measures), and some supporters continued to believe that the administration was more determined to placate its enemies than to keep its friends on board.[12]

Hearings on arms control subjects became more frequent during President Reagan's tenure: briefings and informal meetings proliferated. As the politics of arms control heated up throughout the late 1970s and early 1980s, the executive branch began to pay attention to the House of Representatives as well as the Senate. In the Senate, the Armed Services Committee began increasingly to discuss arms negotiations, eventually supplanting Foreign Relations as the primary focus of congressional influence. At the same time, in the House, members began to make greater use of congressional spending powers to seek direct influence over the U.S. position in the strategic arms talks.

In late 1984, when it appeared likely that arms negotiations—interrupted in 1983 by a Soviet walkout—would soon resume, Senate leaders moved quickly to establish a formal observation mechanism, and legislation was enacted in time for the first round of the renewed talks in March 1985. Responding to the political salience of arms control and the benefits of appearing "involved" in the process, the Senate established the bipartisan Arms Control Observer Group. The group visited the talks in Geneva two or three times each year between 1985 and 1989, meeting informally with the principal U.S. and Soviet negotiators to discuss key issues. When the U.S. negotiators returned to Washington between rounds, they often briefed the Observer Group on the latest developments. The House of Representatives was not totally excluded from this process; in 1987 a group of about thirty "Congressional Observers" paid a visit to the Geneva talks. In recognition of its limited constitutional authority in this area, however, the House did not establish a formal observational mechanism.[13]

The formal executive–legislative consultative process on arms control improved greatly during the 1980s, primarily through the creation of the Senate Observer Group. This initiative established a pattern of regular contacts and a relationship of some confidence and trust between the branches. The Senate observers also played useful roles in the arms talks themselves, encouraged by the administration to reinforce certain U.S. positions in private conversations with Soviet negotiators. Most importantly, though, creation of the Observer Group established a core of knowledgeable individuals in the Senate who were "up to speed" on the latest twists in the talks and felt involved in the process. This connection provided a modicum of sympathy within the Senate for the negotiators and their problems, and gave the executive the beginnings of a base upon which to build to promote a favorable outcome for any treaty eventually submitted to the legislature for approval.

Even so, the Senate Observer Group has been only a pale reflection of what might be possible if the two branches were truly to cooperate. There are clear limits on the ability of the Congress to influence arms control negotiations through the consultative process alone, no matter how elaborate and frequent the meetings may become. The Observer Group consists of a set of individuals who are neither empowered to act collectively nor to speak for the Senate as a whole. Moreover, the House is virtually excluded from the process, an omission that led to greatly understating the importance of the antinuclear movement as a political force in the early 1980s.

Most importantly, as long as the administration's interest in the congressional consultative process is primarily to remove the unnecessary political frictions caused by denying the Congress a visible role, or to identify issues that might prove disabling in any ratification debate, the process does not translate into real congressional power. Given the disinclination of either the Carter or Reagan administration to actually heed congressional views, the real decisions on arms negotiations continued to be made solely by the executive branch.

Additional Traditional Instruments of Influence

Two additional, traditional means used by the Congress to influence executive behavior also failed to confer real authority on the legislature. The Senate's constitutional mandate to advise and consent on the appointments of senior officials, and the legislature's ability to request reports from the executive branch, were both used by the Congress to gain some leverage in arms control policy, but neither proved decisive.

The constitutional requirement that the Senate provide advice and consent on executive branch appointments offers opportunities for senators to adopt high profiles on arms control issues. These opportunities can be used both to caution the administration on substantive issues, and also for political and personal objectives. Both pro– and anti–arms control factions have made use of the device.

The first such occasion took place in 1973, when Senator Edmund S. Muskie (D.-Maine), among others, attempted to use the nomination of Fred C. Ikle as director of the Arms Control and Disarmament Agency (ACDA) to air concerns about the administration's policies—but with no visible effect. The 1977 debate over the nomination of Paul Warnke to be both director of ACDA and the chief arms negotiator for the Carter administration was more successful. Warnke's nomination touched on a number of old disputes—including whether a single individual should hold both posts—as well as on some specific personal concerns. The debate was particularly bitter. Although Warnke sailed through the Foreign Relations Committee's hearing, the Armed Services Committee, in an early foray into the arms control process, held ''informal'' hearings that turned out to be the best theater in Washington since the Watergate hearings three years before. Senator Jackson was the chief inquisitor, apparently judging his substantive differences with Paul Warnke and the Carter administration to be more important than the comity that normally would be dictated by common party allegiance.[14]

When Warnke's appointment as chief negotiator was supported on the floor by only fifty-eight senators (more than enough to confirm the nomination, but insufficient to ratify a treaty), the incident was interpreted as demonstrating the clout of Jackson and the anti–arms control forces. It thus helped rally those forces, encouraging further organization and activities, as well as encouraging Republicans to take positions increasingly hostile to arms control. The Warnke vote reconfirmed the administration's political weakness on defense issues, hinted at even earlier in the term, when it withdrew the nomination of Theodore Sorensen to be director of the Central Intelligence Agency. It also contributed to the Carter administration's misguided decision to seek Senator Jackson's support for its first SALT initiative.

The pro–arms control forces tried to return the favor six years later, in 1983, when Ronald Reagan nominated Kenneth L. Adelman to direct ACDA. By then the political atmosphere had changed totally. Fear of nuclear war had supplanted fear of the Soviet Union as the nation's foremost national security concern, and the Congress was reacting accordingly. Pugnacious and outspoken, Adelman had spent the previous two years as Ambassador Jeane Kirkpatrick's deputy at the United Nations. Considerable controversy preceded the hearings, based primarily on the nominee's past writings and the administration's own rhetoric about nuclear war and nuclear arms control. The action this time came in the Foreign Relations Committee, where the pro–arms control forces dominated. Democratic Senators Cranston and Paul Tsongas (D.-Mass.) were the chief opponents, although Republican Larry Pressler played the role of Brutus for a while (rather less well than Jackson had in 1977). Despite an unfavorable recommendation from Foreign Relations, Adelman was eventually approved by a vote of 57 to 42.

Again, the political effects of the controversy were important. The near victory provided encouragement to pro–arms control organizations, reinforced the growing tendency of politicians to take this constituency more seriously, and raised, in the minds of many members of Congress and other political actors, a growing conviction that nuclear arms control provided an issue with considerable potential for inflicting defeats on the once seemingly invincible Reagan administration.[15]

As in the debate on Paul Warnke, the Adelman nomination provided an opportunity for individual senators to advance their party's and their own electoral interests by drawing attention to their participation in a politically salient issue. They wanted voters to know clearly which side of the arms control issue they, and their opponents, were on. For example, asked shortly before the floor vote what had been gained by Adelman's opponents, Senator Tsongas replied, "We've made arms control an issue. . . . If someone wants to sign up with Adelman's views, I want his constituents to know that. . . . If it makes someone more vulnerable in 1984, that's all right with me."[16] Arms control was already an issue, of course, particularly in the senator's home state of Massachusetts, where the nuclear freeze movement had originated. Planning to run for reelection in 1984, it no doubt suited Tsongas to demonstrate his own activism on the issue, as well as to make Republicans vulnerable.

A second traditional instrument through which the Congress has attempted to influence arms control policy is its ability to elicit reports from the executive branch. In 1974, for example, the Congress passed legislation requiring the administration to provide a yearly report on the impact of all nuclear weapon programs (and all conventional programs meeting certain cost criteria) on existing arms control agreements and negotiations.

In theory, these mandated reports would enable the Congress to consider the potential effects of new weapon programs and would force the executive branch to take account of any possible adverse consequences (they would surface in the preparation of the reports). In fact, the Congress was asking the administration to provide the ammunition for its own defeat. It was requiring officially sanctioned arguments against new weapons at precisely the same time that the administration was requesting that funds be appropriated for them—a political nonstarter if there ever was one. As a result, most "arms control impact statements," as they are called, blandly state that all programs are fully consonant with all arms control obligations and prospective agreements. When the Carter administration made a more serious effort to comply with the law, the statements presented all sides of all relevant issues, and concluded that, on balance, it was in the national interest to fund the new weapon.

It is hard to find any effects of arms control impact statements. There was an attempt to hold up funding for enhanced radiation weapons (neutron bombs) in 1977 on the grounds that an arms control impact statement had not been filed, but this resulted only in three mid-level officials staying up all night to satisfy the requirement in a pro forma way. Few members were willing to settle such a serious issue on the grounds of a violation of a technical reporting requirement.

More effective use of reporting requirements has been made by political conservatives with respect to alleged Soviet violations of existing arms control agreements. By forcing the executive branch to express positions on possible violations, and by making the report public, opponents of arms control hoped to constrain the administration's flexibility in ongoing negotiations and to poison the political atmosphere for future agreements. According to Senator Symms, for example, ". . . arms negotiations now must first be focused upon ending [Soviet] violations of existing treaties, before there can be further progress toward new agreements."[17]

Soviet cheating on SALT, for example, was alleged almost before the ink was dry on the 1972 agreement. By 1978, the charges had become so commonplace that the Carter administration, responding to a request by the Senate Foreign Relations Committee, released a white paper, "SALT Compliance and Verification," intended to refute the allegations. Conservatives apparently found the paper unpersuasive, however, as the 1980 Republican party platform pledged to end the "Carter cover-up" of Soviet violations.

Most Reagan administration officials came to appreciate the uncertainty of the data pertaining to alleged infractions, as well as the difficulty of inducing the Soviets to end them (at least without taking radical measures), and thus did not want to go on record as clearly charging violations. Two exceptions were David Sullivan and Michael E. Pillsbury, fervent anti-Soviet and anti–arms control propagandists. They headed the ACDA transition team for President-elect Reagan, but were too radical for the director-designate, Eugene Rostow, and were let go in early 1981. With their departure, the main keeper of the flame on Soviet cheating became the General Advisory Committee (GAC) on Arms Control, a committee appointed by the president with the advice and consent of the Senate under the terms of the Arms Control and Disarmament Act (the law that established ACDA). A GAC report alleging systematic Soviet cheating on arms control agreements was circulated within the executive branch in November 1983.[18] In 1984, Senator James McClure (R.-Idaho), Sullivan's most loyal patron, got the administration to release the report.

Sullivan and Pillsbury returned to work on Senate staffs from where they attempted to move the administration to the Right. Mandating reports on Soviet compliance with arms control was one weapon in their arsenal. In 1983, at the initiative of Senator McClure, the Arms Control and Disarmament Act was amended to require the administration to prepare classified and unclassified reports on Soviet compliance (or noncompliance) "with the letter and spirit" of arms control agreements. In 1985 the Congress institutionalized the reporting requirement, amending the Defense Authorization bill to require annual classified and unclassified reports on Soviet arms control compliance.

The requirement forced the administration to confront a whole range of allegations of Soviet cheating that are hard to resist. Refuting them because of ambiguities in data exposes bureaucrats to charges of being "weak" on the Soviets. Politicians find it even more difficult to resist the charges, as the popular American image of the Soviets had long included an assumption that they cheat on treaties.[19] By enshrining the charges in official reports, conservative sponsors of the reporting requirement sought to make it more difficult to reach new agreements, particularly by stiffening the administration's position on measures of verification. Commenting in 1983 on a letter he and thirty-three other senators had sent to President Reagan, Senator McClure noted,

> we cautioned the President that until current Soviet violations of SALT I, and SALT II, and the other arms control treaties are dealt with successfully, and either Soviet compliance is enforced or the U.S. abrogates, this group of thirty-four will continue to have significant reservations about whether a new START or INF [Intermediate Nuclear Force] treaty can receive the advice and consent of the Senate needed for ratification.[20]

The number of signatories to the letter, of course, was not an accident. And although the threat turned out to be empty (the INF Treaty was ratified overwhelmingly without substantive modification), its potential effect on bargaining within the executive branch, on the U.S. position on verification provisions, for example, cannot be discounted.

The compliance issue also served more blatant political motives. It was used as part of the concerted campaign to discredit the Carter administration's security policies—as witnessed by the Republican party's 1980 platform. Although Ronald Reagan's reputation (and rhetoric) protected him from similar charges (even though his administration behaved virtually no differently from the previous one while the instances of alleged Soviet violations multiplied), treaty compliance became an important undercurrent in intra-Republican politics in 1987 and 1988, with Secretary of State George P. Shultz and other "moderates" serving as proxy targets for the then-emerging presidential campaign of Vice President George Bush.

Internal Organization of the Congress for Arms Control

The much greater political importance of arms control in the 1980s led the Congress to supplement its regular committees and staff by expanding several internal organizations to include experts in the field. The four party-based organizations—the Democratic Study Group and the Republican Conference (through its research arm, the House Republican Research Committee) in the House and the Senate Democratic and Senate Republican policy committees—each acquired two staff members to work exclusively on arms control subjects.

Two nonparty-related groups—the National Security Caucus and the Arms Control and Foreign Policy Caucus—also have grown in the 1980s. The National Security Caucus was founded in 1979 as the Coalition for Peace through Strength, with the purpose of defeating the SALT II Treaty; it has a staff of six. The Arms Control and Foreign Policy Caucus was founded in 1959 as an informal breakfast discussion group. It hired its first staff member in 1966, grew significantly in the 1980s, and now has four people working just on arms control issues.

Membership in these two caucuses is voluntary and ostensibly nonpartisan, although the former is overwhelmingly Republican and the latter overwhelmingly Democratic. Members join both because they support the organization's policy objectives, and to convey a political message to constituents. The Military Reform Caucus, for example, grew sharply during the spare parts scandals in the mid-1980s when there was a political premium on concern about Pentagon practices.[21]

The precise impact of any of these organizations is hard to assess. They help prepare their members for debates and help "educate" nonmembers by writing papers, arranging meetings and seminars, circulating articles, and providing summaries and analyses of pending legislation. They sometimes also try to coordinate floor strategy; the National Security Caucus, for example, in 1988 named four legislative "whips" for this purpose.

Members of Congress tend to dismiss the effectiveness of the two nonpartisan organizations either as influences on policy preferences or as planners of legislative strategy. The sense is that they are not really in a position to forge the coalitions necessary for effective legislative action. They serve more as spokesmen for specific, and usually extreme, positions than as effective articulators of the compromises necessary to pass legislation. Indeed, members tend to see these organizations rather cynically, referring far more to their political importance than to their policy or legislative roles.

The four party-related organizations tend to be taken more seriously. They can serve as forums for the discussion of policy alternatives or even as crucibles for forging party consensus positions on specific issues. Crafting and managing legislative strategy are not their strong points, however; these functions reside with individual senators and representatives, and with the formal leadership of the two Houses.

The Antinuclear Movement

In the late 1970s, Senator Alan Cranston summarized the Congress's influence in arms control as follows:

> Congress can perhaps serve its most effective role as a public forum for new ideas and as a catalyst between the public and its president. Individual members of Congress . . . can play a creative, constructive part. And Congress can serve as a collective point-man and help lead, or push, the president toward control and reduction of weapons arsenals. . . .[22]

Given the political weight of the antinuclear movement in the 1980s, and the widespread concerns of ordinary Americans about the dangers of nuclear war, this modest perspective on congressional influence was no longer sufficient. The demands being made on members by their constituents far exceeded these indirect functions; the people wanted action. Nor were these functions sufficient to take advantage of the political opportunities presented by the emergence of a true grass-roots movement to limit nuclear arms. The Congress had to find a more direct way to impose a more positive approach to arms control on a reluctant executive branch.

Between 1981 and 1983 the nation was virtually enveloped by a fire storm of spontaneous local activism directed at a variety of antinuclear objectives, most importantly at the achievement of a ''nuclear freeze.'' The activities were motivated by the Carter administration's withdrawal of the SALT II Treaty from the Senate prior to ratification, the virtual termination of arms control negotiations, and the rhetoric of the new Reagan administration. There seemed to be a common belief that the possibility of nuclear war was not only real, but rising.[23]

Although the antinuclear movement has always been loosely organized, impelled more from below than directed from above, the landmarks of its accession and decline are clear. In March 1981 the first National Strategy Conference of the Nuclear Weapons Freeze Campaign was convened to set out the movement's overall approach and organizational structure. By November local activities had reached impressive proportions. As coverage of mass protests in Europe against the deployment of intermediate-range missiles played on American television alongside glib statements by U.S. officials about the feasibility of fighting and surviving nuclear war, increasing numbers of Americans began to worry that the new administration might not have its bearings on the essential issue of arms control. A profusion of organizations emerged (doctors, lawyers, clergymen), most of which centered on specific geographic constituencies (cities, states, congressional districts). On Veterans Day 1981, meetings, teach-ins, and marches were held across the country, some involving thousands of participants. Politicians and commentators took notice.

Drafts of congressional resolutions calling for a freeze on nuclear weapons began to circulate in "Dear Colleague" letters on Capitol Hill early in 1982. Congressman Edward J. Markey (D.-Mass.) drafted the first one. (In fact, he appears to have jumped the gun on the freeze movement itself, which was hoping to stimulate widespread bipartisan support before taking formal action.) Congressional interest was piqued when Senators Edward Kennedy and Mark Hatfield decided to sponsor a comparable resolution in the Senate; similarly worded concurrent resolutions were introduced in both Houses in March. Kennedy's backing gave the proposal a certain legitimacy with some powerful political constituencies. His prominence gave the freeze movement a national, "big-league politics" flavor for the first time; and his support meant that his Senate office, which runs a very effective political and media operation with contracts throughout the country, could be leveraged for the cause. Running hard for the presidency at the time, the senator no doubt expected to gain considerable political advantage from being identified with this popular movement in its early stages.

The nuclear freeze movement soon made its way up to the top of the nation's issues agenda. It peaked as a public force with the June 1982 demonstration by 700,000 people in New York City.

The freeze was an issue in many parts of the country in the 1982 election, with resolutions on scores of municipal and state ballots, and many candidates for even local elections hard-pressed to avoid taking a position. The administration opposed the proposal in every manifestation, arguing that a freeze was not really arms control or arms limitation, that it was unverifiable, that it would fix the status quo and therefore favor the Soviet Union, and even suggesting that the movement was probably inspired and guided by Moscow as a means of disrupting the U.S. military buildup.

Despite the president's opposition, the antinuclear movement did very well in the 1982 elections. Even though the freeze resolution itself had been defeated narrowly on the floor of the House in August, local initiatives passed handily in seven of the eight states and thirty-six of the thirty-eight municipalities and counties in which they appeared on the ballot; polls showed that upward of two-thirds of Americans supported the concept. How important the freeze may have been in determining the results of individual elections, however, is difficult to gauge. Congressman Markey's office claimed that the freeze had become an important issue in forty-seven House races, thirty-eight of which were won by freeze supporters. Considering all changes in the House, due to both electoral losses and voluntary retirements, Markey's staff aide Douglas Waller estimates that the freeze movement gained twenty to thirty seats in the Congress that took office in 1983.[24]

Not surprisingly, Waller's estimate brackets the partisan change in the House: Democrats gained twenty-six seats. While there were important exceptions in both parties, the freeze was very much a partisan issue. Democrats found it an effective instrument to bash Republicans—and especially the president—for their unresponsiveness, even active resistance, to the popular impulse for nuclear arms control. Some Republicans, particularly those from conservative districts, found "freeze-bashing"—talk of its alleged KGB origins, and so on—to be equally rewarding in electoral terms. The political dynamic, however, favored Democrats, leading many Republicans who were running for office to distance themselves from the administration on the issue of arms control. If they did not come out and support the freeze, they at least declared a firm commitment to the objective of controlling nuclear weapons and to alternative proposals toward that end.

Unburdened by an administration perceived as being unresponsive, the Democrats had it a great deal easier. To ride the freeze wave, they needed only to support the concept loudly, repeatedly, and vigorously. Details ("mutual," "verifiable") were expressed much less vocally and were scarcely noticed by the public, which received only the intended message: this candidate would work to reduce the threat of nuclear war and end the arms race.

Just how nuanced Democratic support actually was, however, became clear just four months after the election. Put on a fast track by then-Chairman of the House Foreign Affairs Committee Clement Zablocki (D.-Wisc.), the Freeze Resolution was taken up for the second time in March 1983. It passed the full House this time, but only after a long and rancorous debate, and in a heavily amended form. Virtually everyone was confused about what really had been passed, and who actually had won the debate. In any event the resolution died quickly in the still-Republican-controlled Senate, and its passage in the House seemed to dissipate the antinuclear movement's energies. A few weeks later, the House voted to release funds for the MX missile that had been sequestered from the previous year's budget. Some fifty Democratic congressmen who had voted for the Freeze Resolution also voted for the MX. The antinuclear movement seemed unable to mount a serious lobbying effort against the MX so soon after the massive freeze effort, and in any case representatives were able to argue that in its final form the resolution did not really preclude support for this new, controversial, and most destructive U.S. missile.

Passage of the Freeze Resolution in the House thus marked the political high point of the antinuclear movement. The compromises necessary to squeeze the resolution through, even in the overwhelmingly Democratic House, antagonized the organizations that had originated the concept and fractured the loose alliance with more centrist organizations. In the eyes of the true believers, House approval of the MX before the ink was dry on the Freeze Resolution demonstrated the cynical way in which the Movement's idea, and its political strength, had been expropriated.

The antinuclear movement never recovered. Its influence on the 1984 presidential and congressional elections was negligible. The rebirth of the arms control process in the fall of 1984, with then-Soviet Foreign Minister Andrei Gromyko's surprise visit to Washington, and the relatively rapid progress that was subsequently made in a range of negotiations, undermined the earlier centrist support for the freeze. Senator Nancy Kassebaum said of the influence of the antinuclear movement in her state since the mid-1980s:

> Concern about nuclear issues is not broadly based. There is a small group of activists whose influence is disproportional, but still not very great. There is a larger group, but still a minority, that opposes arms control in principle. Most people are relatively indifferent; they will follow the lead of the president and other political leaders.[25]

The antinuclear movement can hardly be termed a failure, however, even if it never came close to achieving its primary objective. The popular response to the Reagan administration's attitudes toward arms control and nuclear war, and the freeze movement, which channeled those sentiments into politically relevant activities, radically altered the political landscape. Politicians who in 1980 denied ever saying a positive word about arms control, in 1982 worked hard to make their commitment clear. The administration also did a turnaround from its original position of eschewing all arms negotiations in favor of an unprecedented nuclear buildup. In the fall of 1981 President Reagan moved toward talks for the total elimination of intermediate-range missiles in Europe and, in the spring of 1982, toward negotiations for "deep cuts" in central strategic forces. Neither substantive developments nor a personal epiphany led to this reversal; politics did.

In fact, the White House's perception of the political benefits that would accrue by expressing support for the fundamental objective of the powerful antinuclear constituency led Ronald Reagan to propose the most extreme initiative ever attempted in this area. In a televised speech on March 23, 1983, the president proposed to "render nuclear weapons impotent and obsolete" by deploying advanced technologies in space—the Strategic Defense Initiative (SDI)—to defend the United States against nuclear-armed missiles. While this so-called Star Wars program had been pressed on a receptive president since the start of his term by a small group of devoted believers, it is clear that the timing of the speech—premature in many respects, but coming on the eve of the vote on the Freeze Resolution in the House of Representatives—can be understood politically as just another means of seeking to capture the antinuclear vote.[26]

What was the Congress's role in all this? Congress responded, it did not initiate. It carried the message of the antinuclear movement to the administration. It conveyed the concerns that had sprung unexpectedly, and inchoately, in constituencies throughout the country. Congressmen and senators sought to associate themselves with the popular mood, many because they shared the popular concerns, other for cynical political reasons; most from a mixture of motives, some personal and selfish, others generous and public-minded.

The antinuclear movement had a secondary and lasting effect similar to that of the anti–Vietnam War movement of the 1970s: it galvanized the Congress to gain greater leverage on arms control policies. It caused senators, and especially representatives (because of the need to renew their mandate every two years and because they were effectively shut out from decisions on arms control policy), to devise new means of influencing executive branch decisions. On the Democratic side of the aisle, some members wanted to advance the freeze; others wanted to advance centrist alternatives to it. All, however, wanted to leverage the movement to isolate the president and other Republicans, thus hoping to set the stage for future electoral victories. On the Republican side, some members wished to save the administration from itself and edge it toward a more popular stance on arms control, thereby helping to defuse the political consequences of the antinuclear movement. Others, no doubt, wished primarily to save themselves by declaring an independent stance and working to compel positive actions by the executive branch.

Regardless of motive, the Congress needed real power to accomplish these goals—not just the show of power afforded by consultations, ratification debates, nomination confirmations, and reporting requirements. They needed to be able to force concessions in arms control policies and at the negotiating table. The Congress found that power in their one unassailable constitutional authority—the power of the purse.

Appropriating Arms Control

Clearly the Congress was always aware of the potential of its authority over spending for compelling changes in arms negotiations. Until the remarkable growth of the antinuclear movement in the 1980s, however, there was little political necessity to connect these seemingly disparate subjects. Attempts to force the Nixon administration to negotiate a ban on deployments of multiple independently targetable reentry vehicles (MIRVs) are instructive in this regard.

In March 1970 the Senate overwhelmingly passed a resolution (10 to 0 through committee, and 72 to 6 through the full Senate), calling on the president to declare a moratorium on MIRV flight-testing and to negotiate an agreement with the Soviet Union that would freeze MIRV development at the level already achieved by the United States. Such a "sense-of-the-Senate" resolution, however, is only advisory and compels no specific action by the executive branch. (The 1982 Freeze Resolution would have been similar.) As President Nixon subsequently said at a press conference, "I think the Resolution really is irrelevant to what we are going to do."[27]

Eventually the Nixon administration did propose a MIRV ban (in response to a variety of pressures), but in a form that it knew would be rejected by Soviet negotiators. The cynicism of the move was revealed in testimony by William Van Cleave, a member of the negotiating team. The proposals, he said, "were not set forth for bargaining as can be seen by the rapidity with which they were dropped. . . ." They were made, instead, ". . . to provide a record—for the United States Congress and public—that at least the United States tried to get MIRV limitations."[28]

The lesson of the MIRV resolution was taken to heart by Senator Hubert Humphrey. In a prototype of a legislative initiative to be seen frequently in the 1980s, in September 1971 Humphrey attempted to amend the Defense Authorization bill to place all funds for MIRV deployments in "escrow" until such time as the president and the Congress jointly determined that Soviet testing and deployment of its own MIRVs necessitated U.S. deployments. Humphrey's move was premature, however, and considered too radical an encroachment on executive privileges even in the antimilitary atmosphere of the Congress in the early 1970s. His amendment was soundly defeated, 39 to 12.[29]

The first successful congressional initiative of this type came early in the 1980s. The leverage was provided by the administration's difficulty in securing congressional approval of the MX missile. The Defense Department's continuing inability to come up with a credible scheme to protect the missile from a Soviet first strike, together with the widely held perception that the weapon was either intended for a U.S. first strike or would be perceived as such by the Soviet Union (and was thus destabilizing), tightly circumscribed its appeal. The missile was in perpetual jeopardy throughout the Reagan presidency.

In 1983, however, a group of key Democratic congressmen—most importantly, Les Aspin, Norm Dicks, and Albert Gore, Jr. (D.-Tenn.)—had the idea that instead of just attempting to kill the budget request for the first fifty MXs, it might more judiciously be held hostage to elicit concessions from the administration on related issues. From a Democratic perspective the strategy had the political advantage of avoiding an action that Republicans could point to as further evidence of the Democrats' weakness on defense. In addition, it eliminated the political liability of allowing the administration to use the denial of MX funds as an excuse for failing to negotiate new arms control arrangements, thereby blunting the antinuclear vote in the 1984 election.

The price extracted by the House members was a commitment by the administration to develop a smaller, mobile intercontinental ballistic missile—the so-called Midgetman. Proposed by the bipartisan Scowcroft commission in the spring of 1983 (but fiercely resisted by the air force because it correctly understood the missile to threaten funding for the MX), the Midgetman was seen by centrist House Democrats as the basis both of a more secure strategic posture and a more constructive (and less politically vulnerable) Democratic approach to military issues.

The key congressmen subsequently forged an alliance with two leading senators, William S. Cohen (R.-Maine) and Sam Nunn, to ensure that the proposal would pass the upper chamber as well. The senators extracted an additional price, however—a commitment to include the so-called build-down proposal in the U.S. negotiating position at the strategic arms talks. In a truly amazing concession to congressional power, the administration not only accepted the proposal, but even agreed to accept an individual nominated by the key legislators as an observer at the talks to make sure that the proposal was tabled accurately and pursued with diligence.[30]

The arms control part of the deal was forged in an uncomfortable negotiating session in the White House with then-Chief of Staff James A. Baker III. It produced an agreement that the president would write a letter to the senators agreeing to the desired commitments. The deadline for receipt of the letter was the day scheduled to mark up the Defense Appropriations bill in the Senate committee. The letter arrived the day prior to the deadline, but it fudged on the negotiated commitments; the senators returned to the White House late at night to renegotiate. At the last moment on the next day a new letter was brought to the committee room by courier, and the MX missile was approved a few minutes later.

The deal was almost immediately overtaken by events. The Soviets walked out of the talks in late 1983, protesting the first deployments of U.S. Pershing missiles in Europe. When the talks resumed in 1985, much more ambitious proposals were negotiated and obscured the build-down concept. As for the Midgetman, although the missile continued to be developed at the insistence of the House of Representatives, both it and the MX remained controversial within both branches of government. With growing pressure on the defense budget, it seems likely that aside from the fifty MXs approved in 1983, neither missile will ever be deployed. Nonetheless, precedents for effective congressional action on arms control through the power of the purse had been established; the administration had been compelled to adopt a specific negotiating position. Subsequently, three additional and more ambitious applications of these powers were attempted. They are described below.

ANTISATELLITE WEAPONS (ASATS)

The United States began to develop a modern antisatellite weapon in response to Soviet testing of a system with limited capabilities in the late 1970s. By the early 1980s the Soviets had ceased their tests after a mixed record of successes and failures, while the U.S. system was nearing operational testing and deployment. American experts believed the Soviet Union would then attempt to build a system of comparable sophistication, at which point it no longer would be possible to negotiate a verifiable ban on these weapons.

Given the two great powers' growing reliance on satellites to direct military operations and for other military functions, the existence of operational ASAT capabilities would provide an incentive for both sides to strike first in the event of crisis and could make the termination of conflict more difficult. Arms control activists thus sought to compel the administration, which believed an ASAT agreement to be both impractical and unwise, to curb the U.S. program short of testing and deployment. They argued that such unilateral action would encourage the Soviet Union to maintain its own moratorium on ASAT tests and perhaps facilitate negotiations for an eventual ban on these weapons. The anti-ASAT forces were unable to budge the administration. They then turned to the Congress, especially the House of Representatives, and particularly to the Congress's power of the purse.[31]

The initiative actually began in January 1983 when Congressman Joe Moakley (D.-Mass.), a liberal Democrat from South Boston who had introduced the House's first anti-ASAT legislation the previous year, established what became known as the Space Policy Working Group. This informal organization brought together members, congressional aides, lobbyists from the Federation of American Scientists (FAS) and the Union of Concerned Scientists (UCS), and representatives of other pro–arms control groups. It provided a channel for scientists to help educate politicians about space issues, and for politicians to help scientists think politically. Following President Reagan's Star Wars speech (March 1983) with its emphasis on uses of space for military purposes, the working group gained new importance. The number of participants grew sharply; appearances by congressmen became more frequent.

An amendment to the fiscal 1984 Defense Authorization bill that had been introduced in June 1983 by Congressman George E. Brown, Jr. (D.-Calif.), would have cut $19.4 million from the ASAT program, the amount designated for initial procurement. The measure was defeated on the floor (243 to 177) but anti-ASAT forces were pleased that this first binding initiative received as much support as it did. Encouraged, they tried again later in the summer—this time utilizing the Defense Appropriations bill as the legislative vehicle.

Their initial effort focused on finding a sponsor on Appropriations in order to incorporate the amendment in the legislation that emerged from the committee—a major advantage. They convinced Congressman Matthew F. McHugh (D.-N.Y.), whose district includes Cornell University, to be the sponsor. At McHugh's suggestion, the lobbyists then persuaded Congressman Lawrence Coughlin (R.-Pa.) to cosponsor.

The next problem was to find the language that would have the best chance of gaining a majority. Lobbyists from the UCS visited six members of Appropriations seeking support. Norm Dicks was sympathetic but reluctant to support a cut in the appropriation, as his district included facilities and employees of the Boeing Company, an important subcontractor on the ASAT project. He suggested instead an amendment that would provide the full appropriation, but deny use of the funds to test the system as long as the Soviets continued to adhere to their moratorium. The lobbyists agreed, and Dicks agreed to cosponsor.

In the committee, Congressman Mickey Edwards (R.-Okla.) objected vociferously to the proposal. He suggested alternatively that the test moratorium be dropped, but that the $19.4 million for initial procurement be withheld until forty-five days after the president submitted a report on ASATs and the prospects for ASAT arms control—a proposal that was adopted. (In theory, if the president's report was unpersuasive, the 45-day delay provided time for a new effort to stop the program. If the anti-ASAT forces had been stronger, however, they would have insisted that a second vote be held after the president's report but prior to the release of the $19.4 million, thus shifting the burden of persuasion to ASAT proponents.)

The Senate bill was amended on the floor by Senator Paul Tsongas to require a similar report, but his measure did not include a delay of the expenditure of funds. (Tsongas had also sponsored nonbinding legislation the previous year.) The compromise reached in conference was to withhold the procurement money until a report was submitted to the Congress, which had to occur no later than a certain date. The bill was signed into law on December 8, 1983.

As expected, the president's report (submitted in spring 1984) found that an ASAT test ban would not be in the United States's interest. But it provided an opportunity for members of the Space Policy Working Group to interrogate administration witnesses in committee hearings and thus educate their colleagues about anti-ASAT views. Moreover, following submission of the report, the anti-ASAT lobby decided to concentrate on building a broad bipartisan coalition to support a test moratorium.

The issue was drawn when the fiscal 1985 Defense Authorization bill came to the floor, as the House Armed Services Committee had approved the requested ASAT appropriation without condition. Brown and Coughlin cosponsored the amendment, this time prohibiting the use of funds for testing the ASAT against objects in space (considered essential prior to the weapon becoming operational), until the president certified that the Soviet Union or any other foreign power had conducted a test of its own ASAT system. Coughlin delivered an unexpected thirty-five Republicans in favor of the test limitation. After relatively close votes to defeat weakening amendments, the Brown–Coughlin bill was approved overwhelmingly.

The Senate, meanwhile, had passed a measure that again simply required a presidential report prior to funds being expended. To ensure a strong defense of their position in conference, given the Armed Services Committee's support of the program, leaders of the anti-ASAT movement in the House persuaded Speaker Thomas P. ("Tip") O'Neill, Jr. (D.-Mass.), to appoint Congressman Brown as a special conferee. Brown disappointed his supporters, however, by accepting a compromise that permitted two of the four proposed tests, as long as the president first certified that the United States was endeavoring in good faith to negotiate the "strictest possible," verifiable limitations on ASATs with the Soviets. The certification requirement would clearly be no hindrance, because the president had already stated that no ASAT limitations were verifiable.

Brown's concessions caused an uproar among House liberals. His reasoning was based on the conclusion that because of the ASAT program's severe technical problems two tests would be far from sufficient to check out the system and it would, therefore, still be possible to negotiate restrictions in the event of a new administration in 1984.

At this point, what had been the most professional and effective pro–arms control lobby fell apart as a result of dissension in the Space Policy Working Group. A number of radical, single-issue groups had sprung up in the wake of the Star Wars initiative. These new organizations resented the UCS's and FAS's dominance of the group and its chairman, John Pike, who was forced to resign. Their second target was the pragmatic sense of compromise that had worked so well. "Better right than successful" seemed to become the new philosophy.

The new tensions affected efforts to stop SDI but did not hurt the anti-ASAT forces, largely because the House had already carved out its position. The Brown–Coughlin test moratorium was added to the Defense Authorization bill again in 1985, as in 1984. In the Senate the effort to constrain the ASAT program with reporting requirements was retired along with Senator Tsongas. His successor, Senator John F. Kerry (D.-Mass.), was joined by Republicans John H. Chafee (R.-R.I.) and Charles Mathias in sponsoring a measure similar to the Brown–Coughlin test moratorium. It was defeated by a lopsided margin, 51 to 35. The Senate thus entered conference with no limitations on the ASAT program.

The conference again bitterly disappointed the anti-ASAT members. Les Aspin, the new chairman of the Armed Services Committee, believed himself to be in too weak a position to force the majority of the House conferees—senior members of the committee who generally were more conservative than most of the Democrats in the House—to stick with the Brown–Coughlin moratorium. He accepted a compromise that imposed a testing moratorium for five months, after which it permitted three tests against objects in space. Given that Aspin had retreated or struck weak compromises on several other controversial issues (chemical weapons, SDI spending levels, the MX missile, and procurement reforms), his performance on ASAT contributed importantly to the subsequent effort to unseat him.

The anti-ASAT forces finally hit pay dirt a few months later, however, when the Continuing Resolution for Fiscal 1986 was considered. (The Continuing Resolution was an omnibus spending bill that was repeatedly used by the Congress in the mid-1980s to appropriate funds, in place of individual appropriation measures.) The two chambers entered conference on the resolution with more or less the same irreconcilable positions on ASAT testing as during the Defense Authorization debate. This time, however, two of the House conferees, Norm Dicks and Les AuCoin (D.-Oreg.), were determined to obtain the moratorium. AuCoin especially believed that it was now or never for ASAT negotiations. If tests of the U.S. system were not stopped, he argued, the Soviets would have every incentive to start testing again, and any possibility of a verifiable ban on deployments would be lost.

Circumstances aided Dicks and AuCoin, as well. The chairman of the House Defense Appropriations Subcommittee, Joe Addabbo, was in failing health and did not take part in the conference. Acting Chairman Bill Chappell, who wished to succeed Addabbo, recognized that he was considered too conservative by many members of the Democratic Caucus. He was well aware, moreover, of the disappointment with Aspin's performance and aware that he would be judged harshly if the House did equally poorly on the Continuing Resolution.

The House conferees made clear their determination to persevere on ASATs. Congressman John P. Murtha (D.-Pa.), for example, is reported to have said, ''I can't imagine the House supporting a conference report without the ASAT provision.'' The Senate chairman, Ted Stevens (R.-Alaska), had other more pressing priorities and decided to trade the test moratorium for House concessions on other issues (SDI funding and the production of chemical weapons). It was probably Stevens's priorities that negated the president's effort to lobby against the ASAT test moratorium, which included calls to the conferees' homes at 7 A.M. on the morning of the decision. The final bill ''prohibited the obligation or expenditure of funds'' for ASAT testing against objects in space ''until the President certifies to Congress that the Soviet Union has conducted . . . a test against an object in space of a dedicated antisatellite weapon.''

After two and one-half years, the House had succeeded. The test moratorium was never seriously challenged after that, and was enacted into law again in 1986 and 1987. In 1988 the Defense Department decided to terminate the ASAT program as part of a major effort to reduce defense costs.

Again, circumstances favored the congressional effort to terminate

ASAT tests. The Soviets maintained their moratorium throughout the period. The U.S. program did not fare well in development, experiencing huge cost overruns and repeated technical problems. The constituency for the program was small to begin with. Although an air force program, the ASAT's greatest supporter was the navy, which wanted a capability at the onset of a war to destroy Soviet satellites intended to track U.S. warships. Yet even in this context it was an uphill fight.

The anti-ASAT side won in the end because of two factors. First, the lobby was extremely effective. The UCS and FAS were uniquely qualified to explain the highly technical issues related to ASAT deployments, and they had great credibility on the Hill. Their approach was moderate, moreover, being willing to compromise in order to obtain the support of key members. Their approach was pragmatic, striving for small gains, taking a longer-term view than is usually the case on these issues.

Second, the anti-ASAT effort was the first arms control issue taken up seriously by liberal House Democrats, thereby creating a sense of precedence and loyalty among its proponents. With each small victory came the prospect of "winnability" and the momentum of success. In the mid-1980s members were eager to show positive results to their pro–arms control constituents. They were also eager for victory for personal reasons as well; enthusiasm can be maintained for only so long in the face of repeated defeat. House Democrats thus banded together to make the ASAT test moratorium their highest arms control priority. As political tides shifted, it became virtually inevitable that they would achieve their goal.

ENFORCING ADHERENCE TO THE SALT II TREATY

When the Carter administration withdrew the SALT II Treaty from senatorial consideration in 1980, it announced that its policy would be not to "undercut" the agreement as long as the Soviets exercised similar restraint. This was taken to mean that it would adhere to the quantitative limitations on forces included in the text, and that it would take no action, such as the flight-testing of a type of weapon prohibited by the agreement, which would nullify a treaty provision. In March 1981 the Reagan administration announced that it was reviewing arms control policy but that in the meantime it would not "undercut" existing agreements, again providing that the Soviets did the same. In May 1982 President Reagan personally endorsed the "no undercut" policy.

Given the new administration's repeated denunciations of SALT II as fatally flawed, there was considerable concern in the Congress in the early 1980s over the durability and rigor of these commitments. Given the growing strength of the antinuclear movement, there was also congressional interest in promoting SALT II as means of playing to this newly vocal constituency, particularly by members who were reluctant to support the Nuclear Freeze Resolution. In late 1981, for example, Senator John Glenn (D.-Ohio) sought on the floor to amend the Defense Appropriations bill with a nonbinding measure calling on the administration to maintain the "no undercut" policy. Glenn's sponsorship of the amendment was particularly ironic, as he had been a persistent critic of SALT II during the Carter administration, and was one of the last Democratic holdouts, considered likely to vote against ratification. His turnaround between December 1979, when the treaty was withdrawn from Senate consideration, and December 1981, when he introduced the "no undercut" amendment, reflects the rapidly growing political strength of the antinuclear movement during this period.[32]

A variety of additional, usually nonbinding measures in support of the "no undercut" policy were introduced prior to 1986, some as free-standing resolutions, others as amendments to the Defense Authorization bill. Some passed, others did not. All measures that would have enforced the SALT II agreement by withholding appropriations were unsuccessful during this period, however. (An amendment to the fiscal 1983 Defense bill that would have prohibited the use of funds for any program that would undercut existing arms control agreements, for example, was passed by the House in 1982, but failed in conference.)[33]

The situation changed greatly in May 1986 when the president announced that, in view of what the administration considered Soviet violations of the SALT agreement, the United States would abandon its informal compliance. Scheduled deployments of cruise missiles on B-52 bombers suggested that the United States would breach the SALT limit on the total number of MIRVed systems toward the end of the year. Two measures were introduced in the House; Congressman Dicks successfully moved to amend the Defense Authorization bill to bar the use of funds for deployments in excess of certain specified SALT limits as long as the Soviets behaved similarly; and the House Appropriations Committee acted to require the navy to dismantle two additional missile-carrying submarines. (This latter measure would have had the effect of preserving the threatened limit on MIRVed systems without mentioning SALT II by name.)

The Senate, however, passed no binding SALT restrictions in 1986 and appeared determined to defeat House initiatives in conference. The upper chamber is more conservative on these issues, but its position was determined primarily by institutional prerogatives. As one Senate staffer put it, "The Senate just isn't going to be prepared to see the other body get involved in treaty ratification."[34]

Early meetings of the conference committee suggested a compromise along the lines of the House Appropriations measure: an initiative that did not mention the treaty, but that required specific reductions in U.S. forces sufficient to maintain compliance with the agreement. This would fulfill the House's arms control objectives (and yield the political benefits associated therewith), but preserve at least the appearance of the Senate's traditional prerogatives pertaining to treaties. The conferees apparently intended to change the type of forces that would be restricted—from Poseidon submarines to cruise-missile-armed B-52 bombers—but the entire issue became moot on September 30, when plans for the Reykjavik summit were announced.

If they had continued to insist on their position, House Democrats would have been in the politically awkward position of appearing to tie the president's hands on the eve of his meeting with the Soviet leader, and only six weeks before the election. Accordingly, political prudence carried the day. The House Democratic leadership accepted the fig leaf of nonbinding SALT language and some vague promises on nuclear testing in exchange for backing off binding language on SALT II and accepting compromises on several other arms control issues.

The failure of the Reykjavik summit, and efforts by the administration to ease out of its commitments on the testing issue, guaranteed congressional action when the 100th Congress convened in January 1987. This time, House activists stated their intention, if necessary, of putting binding SALT language on every available budget measure: the supplemental Defense appropriation for fiscal 1987, the Defense Authorization and Appropriation acts for fiscal 1988, even the Continuing Resolution for fiscal 1988. When the Senate, with the Democratic majority that resulted from the 1986 election, passed its own binding measure to enforce SALT limits (a floor amendment by Senator Dale Bumpers to the Defense Authorization bill), the Congress was poised to act decisively.

The compromise in conference, like that contemplated prior to the Reykjavik announcement, did not mention the treaty, requiring instead the retirement of a strategic submarine to keep the United States close to the SALT II limits. The conference report also stated the Congress's intention to continue forcing the retirement of submarines as they came due for overhauls—an action justifiable both as a SALT-compliance measure and as a sensible cost-saving step. (Given the rate at which new strategic systems were being deployed, the retirement of older submarines was not sufficient to keep the United States strictly in compliance with SALT, but it at least kept the rate of divergence from growing too rapidly.)

The House was only partially successful in enforcing SALT constraints because the issue received a secondary priority until 1986, when the administration announced its intention of breaching the treaty's limitations. Given that the administration was following a no undercut policy up to that point, there was little reason for the pro–arms control forces to expend much political capital on the cause. By the time SALT limits became important, however, ASAT test restrictions had gained a higher priority among the House arms control demands.

Enforcement of SALT II was also hampered by political liabilities. First, the treaty itself had been so thoroughly discredited during the 1980 campaign that many members, otherwise supportive of arms control, were reluctant to embrace it. Second, House action on SALT II provoked spirited opposition from the Senate just on institutional grounds; there simply was no way that the upper chamber was going to concede an explicit role in treaty matters to their colleagues in the House. For the Senate to grant the House an explicit role concerning a treaty would be like the House permitting the Senate to initiate a tax bill. Few things are guarded more jealously in the Congress than the respective prerogatives of the two chambers.

NUCLEAR TESTING

Despite repeated efforts throughout the 1980s, the House failed to force the administration to move toward a comprehensive nuclear test ban.

Nonbinding resolutions calling on the administration to submit two partial test ban treaties to the Senate for ratification and to resume negotiations for a comprehensive ban on nuclear testing died either in committee or in conference from 1982 to 1985. Reasons included the administration's unrelenting hostility to any restrictions on nuclear testing and divisions among the measure's sponsors in the House, specifically between Congressmen Berkley Bedell (D.-Iowa), the resolution's initial sponsor, and Edward Markey, a later adherent who sought to capitalize on the test ban's political appeal in Massachusetts.[35]

In addition, even normally pro–arms control members were willing to invest only limited energy on behalf of the test ban measures, which would be nonbinding in any event and likely to be ignored by the administration. There were clear similarities between the test bill and the ill-fated Freeze Resolution; indeed, the idea was generated by staffers who had been heavily involved in the Freeze effort and wanted to salvage what they could. Many members were reluctant to go down to another defeat.

The environment for a test ban changed importantly in August 1985 when, on the fortieth anniversary of the bombing of Hiroshima, Soviet leader Mikhail Gorbachev announced a unilateral moratorium on all nuclear tests and called upon the United States to follow suit. This encouraged Congresswoman Patricia Schroeder (D.-Colo.), until then unenthusiastic about the nonbinding resolution, to introduce a bill that would have denied all funds for nuclear testing after a certain date, provided that the Soviet Union continued its own moratorium. Schroeder's move was not well received by the backers of the nonbinding resolution, who believed it was essential to put the Congress on record in support of negotiations prior to seeking binding legislation. The issue was fought out in the so-called Wednesday Morning Group, an informal organization of members, staff, and outside lobbyists, similar to the Space Policy Working Group.

Having legislative precedence, the nonbinding resolution (designated H.J.Res. 3 by the leadership) was taken up first. It was passed by the full House in February 1986, clearing the way for consideration of Schroeder's proposal. Encouraged by several extensions of the Soviet moratorium (the last a ploy intended to deflect attention from the Chernobyl nuclear accident), Schroeder (and cosponsor Tom Downey) attempted to attach their restriction to the fiscal 1986 supplemental appropriation bill, but were defeated by procedural problems.[36]

Congressman Bill Green (R.-N.Y.), a liberal New York Republican, then attempted to amend the Department of Energy's (DOE) appropriation to deny funds for weapons testing, as he had the previous year. (Funds for nuclear weapons development and testing are administered by DOE.) In a naked partisan power play, Downey persuaded the Rules Committee to rule Green's amendment nongermane, even though it was worded strictly as a modification of the funding proposal. Downey had two purposes: first, he did not want to see Democratic leadership on the issue diluted; second, he wanted the measure attached to the Defense Department authorization to force Les Aspin's hand on the testing issue. Downey believed Aspin's performance on this would help make clear whether the new chairman deserved the continued support of the Democratic Caucus. These partisan and intraparty complications obviously did not help the test ban cause. Congressman Green is reported to have been particularly bitter; Les Aspin was not pleased with Downey's maneuvering either.

Sponsors of the nuclear test ban subsequently sought to gain centrists' support through modifications in the amendment's language. Tests with explosive yields below one kiloton were excluded, for example, and elaborate verification requirements were included. However, Aspin, the key to a group of moderates, continued to vacillate until late June, when he defied the House Democratic leadership to vote for Contra aid. The ensuing cries of betrayal prompted two members of the Armed Services Committee—Charles E. Bennett (D.-Fla.) and Marvin Leath (D.-Tex.)—to announce that they would contest the committee's chairmanship when the new Congress convened in 1987. Downey and others made clear to Aspin that his support of the testing prohibition was essential if he expected to gain any liberal backing.

Aspin signed on in mid-July, immediately bringing two other key moderates, Richard A. Gephardt (D.-Mo.) and John Spratt with him. The latter was particularly important, as he had a reputation as one of the most thoughtful members on security issues and, indeed, ended up crafting the changes that permitted the measure to pass. In the following weeks, Aspin and his colleagues worked diligently to gain centrists' support, and on August 8 the test ban was passed by an astonishingly large margin, 234 to 155.

The Republican-controlled Senate was not nearly as enthusiastic. Even so, the by-then year-long Soviet moratorium was having its effects. In August the Senate passed another nonbinding resolution, sponsored by Republican Charles Mathias, calling for submission of the two partial test bans and the beginning of negotiations for a comprehensive test ban (CTB).

The House entered the 1986 Authorization conference determined to reverse the previous year's results and gain victories in each of the five contentious arms control issues, nuclear testing included. Chairman Aspin certainly had the incentive to work hard for these measures, given his upcoming struggle to remain in the chair. To be certain, Speaker O'Neill named key Democratic leaders on arms control issues as "special conferees," including AuCoin, Bedell, Brown, Dicks, Downey, Dante B. Fascell (D.-Fla.), who was chairman of the Foreign Relations Committee, Vic Fazio (D.-Calif.), Gephardt, and Markey. The House conferees constituted such a large group that Barry Goldwater, chairman of the Senate committee, refused to begin the conference. "Who are these Hottentots? Who are these animals?" he is reported to have said. He then threatened to have Senator Jesse Helms, a virulent opponent of arms control, appointed to the Senate team. Aspin held tough, though, and the senator relented.

In the end, the House position was undercut by announcement of the Reykjavik summit. Reportedly, the outlines of a compromise had been made clear. The prospective agreements on SALT and ASAT have already been noted. Differences between the two chambers on SDI funding and chemical weapons were split more or less down the middle. On nuclear testing, a proposal by Senator Gary Hart (D.-Colo.) to limit expenditures for testing to permit only six tests per year seemed likely to carry. Not bad on an issue for which the House only one year before had been unable to pass even nonbinding limitations.[37]

The effort to constrain nuclear testing peaked with this aborted compromise. In 1987 the House again amended the Defense bill to prohibit all tests above one kiloton, but circumstances had changed by then, and the political momentum behind the move was less compelling. The Soviets had resumed nuclear testing, and there was progress in talks on both intermediate-range missiles and central strategic forces. More to the point, the Soviets had accepted the administration's position on testing, agreeing to talks on strengthening the verification provisions of the two partial test limits. (For their part, the Soviets gained only some language suggesting the relevance of the two older treaties to a comprehensive test ban.)

All in all, this congressional effort to influence arms control policy could not be judged a success. Valuable time was lost with nonbinding measures and in squabbles among members with similar objectives. The lobbyists on the test ban issue tended to be more strident and extreme in their policy demands than the anti-ASAT lobbyists, and less willing to compromise. The greater political salience of the testing issue tempted members to make use of it for partisan and intraparty political purposes, even at the expense of substantive progress. Whereas the anti-ASAT lobby courted bipartisanship, Democratic advocates of testing limits at times sought deliberately to undermine a visible Republican position.

The limited progress made on the testing issue in 1985 and 1986 was due largely to the coincidence of two factors. The first was that the Soviet testing moratorium was extended from four to eight to twelve to nearly eighteen months and thus became more and more credible. Political pressures for a positive U.S. response increased accordingly, peaking with the near compromise to limit the number of U.S. tests in September 1986. The second was Congressman Les Aspin's struggle to maintain his chairmanship, which guaranteed his vigorous participation in the effort to constrain nuclear testing.

The New Politics of Arms Control in the House of Representatives

Given the size of the Democratic majority, politics in the House of Representatives is first of all the politics of the Democratic party. As with most other foreign policy issues, the party is divided on arms control issues. Perhaps one-quarter to one-third are committed liberals and can be counted on to support most pro–arms control measures. Their leaders, many of whom entered the Congress in the post-Watergate classes of 1974 and 1976, are now in positions of rising influence. This liberal faction is confronted on many issues by a smaller group of Democratic conservatives—including the so-called Boll Weevils (largely southern representatives who sided with the Reagan administration on many votes in the early 1980s) and remnants of the older conservative Democrats who dominated the House until the mid-1970s. This older group continues to hold key subcommittee chairmanships and other important posts, but many are on the verge of retirement.

The more important challenge to the liberals comes from the emergence of a moderate, centrist bloc, responsive to antinuclear pressures and personally committed to achieving what might be called progressive arms control objectives, but above all, pragmatic. Responding in part to the Democrats' defeats from 1978 to 1984, they seek to forge policy positions that might help the party regain its former hold on the center of the U.S. political spectrum. As compared to the liberals, they tend to favor a strong military posture, and have been more skeptical about the possibilities for very rapid progress in arms control and U.S–Soviet relations.

This centrist bloc has been the key to effective action in the House on arms control. According to one member, perhaps forty to sixty Democrats are the major players. If they can be swung behind a position, it can usually be sold to liberals who are pressing for more far-reaching limitations as well as to conservatives who remain skeptical of arms control. Support of the centrist bloc in the House is also essential if the position is going to have a chance of being accepted by the more conservative Senate.

House Democrats exhibited a great deal more discipline and cohesion on arms control issues in the mid- and late 1980s than they did earlier in the decade. According to Congressman Dicks, "The political context in which we are operating is much less emotional, much less bitter and divisive."[38] Credit for this is given in part to the leadership, particularly to Congressmen James C. Wright (D.-Tex.) and Tony Coelho (D.-Calif.) when they held leadership positions. Their willingness to put pressure on key subcommittee chairmen is said to have been particularly important. Procedural reform also was beneficial: beginning in 1986, whip task forces were formed for arms control issues on which there was a consensus position. Members of the task forces were appointed on a regional basis, and their job was to make clear to members the preferred positions, priorities, and legislative strategy of the leadership.

The task force process is very informal. Initiatives arise from individuals or groups of congressmen. Informal, nonpartisan organizations combining members, staff, outside experts, and lobbyists, such as the Space Policy Working Group, can help to educate members on the substance of issues, craft strategy, and find outside sources of influence on key congressmen. Initiatives may be discussed in meetings of the Democratic Caucus, or the Democratic Study Group, but neither group is central in the formation of positions. A whip task force will be organized by the leadership only after it is made clear that the basis for successful pursuit of a consensus position exists. The steps necessary to demonstrate such potential are accomplished through informal networks of members; the key players in each faction who can speak authoritatively for their colleagues are well known.

The critical legislative change in both the House and the Senate has been the shift from the Foreign Affairs and Foreign Relations committees, the traditional focus of congressional activities concerning arms control, to the Armed Services Committee. According to Les Aspin, "To gain leverage over the executive branch, we needed something which the president wanted to sign, a bill which he considered essential." [39] Nothing falling within the jurisdiction of the Foreign Affairs Committee met this requirement. The Congress goes years without approving a new foreign aid bill, the largest appropriation coming under the committee's jurisdiction, mainly because there is virtually no constituency for it. (A threat to hold up foreign aid would be laughable.) Foreign Relations also authorizes the State Department's appropriation, but it is a very small bill and also lacks political support.

The Defense Authorization and Appropriation bills, however, are among the most "veto-proof" measures taken up by the Congress. There are no absolutes in the legislative business, of course, and presidents have vetoed defense bills in the past, most recently in 1988, but—particularly if it is near the start of the new fiscal year—they are reluctant to risk any disruption in military operations. More to the point, presidents are generally unwilling to appear to be trifling with the nation's security because of what the public might perceive to be a quarrel with the legislature.

There are other reasons for the shift in the locus of arms control authority to the Armed Services committees. As noted, the process began in the Senate in the 1970s with experiments like the Humphrey "MIRV escrow" proposal and the Armed Services Committee's "informal' hearings on the Warnke nomination. One reason the shift in the upper chamber was possible was because the leadership of the Foreign Relations Committee has been extremely weak, ever since the retirement of William Fulbright (D.-Ark.) in 1974, particularly when the Democrats were in the majority.

A similar situation prevailed in the House, but without the power either to ratify treaties or to confirm nominations, there simply was no basis for the Foreign Affairs Committee to have any real influence on arms control. What is important in the junior chamber is not so much a shift between committee jurisdictions as the achievement, through the Armed Services Committee, of only meaningful role in arms control decisions. On a number of issues the House has been able to grab the lead from the Senate and dominate the debate.

Circumstances—external and domestic—determine the boundaries of what is feasible in congressional initiatives on arms control. Within those boundaries, however, success or failure continues to depend importantly on the new politics within the House of Representatives.

Executive–Congressional Cooperation in Arms Control

The Congress's new role in arms control has some serious problems. It is hard enough for the U.S. government to negotiate arms control treaties with foreign governments; if it must first negotiate with a hostile and suspicious legislature, largely in public, the task gains added complexities that even a Metternich would have found daunting. The Congress's new intrusive role also shares the debilities of its excessively detailed participation in other aspects of defense policy: few House members and senators are knowledgeable enough to speak authoritatively on the complexities of the issues on the table in these negotiations. Establishing broad guidelines on the need for verification procedures, for example, is one thing; determining the degree of uncertainty associated with a particular verification scheme is quite another.

When the Congress becomes involved in the details of decision making, there are too many opportunities for parochial interests to dominate; in the area of arms control, calculations of political advantage can be particularly distressing. The debate too often accords political interests a greater priority than substantive analyses of the national interest. There is also a degree of trendiness; the Congress, especially the House, reacts directly to prevailing political forces. Senator Glenn's shift between December 1979 and December 1981 from fervent opposition to the SALT II Treaty to equally fervent support may illustrate this phenomenon more than any other single event, but the short if enthusiastic lifetime of the Freeze Resolution is a close second.

The Congress carved out its new role in arms control in response to the administration's failure to satisfy the popular demand for progress in nuclear arms negotiations. A more responsive administration can cause the Congress to back off, as it did in 1987 and 1988, when movement in arms talks led the Congress to push its own measures less determinedly. Activists continued to promote their initiatives, but the context was no longer conducive to the formation of the centrists' coalition so essential for effective congressional action.

Still, having discovered its ability "to appropriate arms control," the Congress, and especially the House of Representatives, seems unlikely to abdicate its new power totally. We may return episodically to something akin to the balance of power between the branches that existed in the mid- to late 1970s, but never to the congressional passivity that characterized the pre–Vietnam War period. Future administrations will have to come to terms with the Congress's ability to utilize the power of the purse to achieve arms control objectives.

From a national perspective, the struggle between the branches for power over arms control policy, particularly in its partisan implications, is extremely harmful. The country benefits when it can show a united face, especially to its potential adversaries. The discord that has dominated the national dialogue on nuclear weapons and nuclear arms control for the past twenty years has led to repeated embarrassments for successive administrations and caused both friends and foes to be wary of our apparent unreliability as a negotiating partner. The ability of future presidents to pursue policies that can effectively protect the nation's interests could be jeopardized. It may be too late for the national nuclear debate to be muted in significant ways, but some modifications are possible and much to be desired.

As pointed out by Richard E. Messick, former chief counsel of the Senate Foreign Relations Committee, the current understanding of the requirement that the Senate provide "advice and consent" on treaties is far from the process envisioned by the Constitution's framers. They intended that the Senate provide its advice during the course of negotiations, advice that the president would be under some obligation to accept. Presuming that he did so, the Senate would be obliged to consent to the completed treaty. This collaborative process, however, did not make it through the first administration. Messick reports,

> Washington tried this approach. Early in his first term he met with the Senate to discuss a planned treaty with the Creek Indian tribe. But he quickly grew exasperated with the Senate's penchant for postponing de-

cisions. He came back a second day, only to see the matter referred to a committee . . . Washington stormed out of the Senate's chambers vowing he would be damned if he would ever return.[40]

Washington never did return. Instead, he began submitting completed treaties on a "take it or leave it basis." And the Senate, for its part, began to approve treaties only on the condition that certain changes be made in them. Thus was born the current system of amendments, reservations, safeguards, and understandings.

As noted, with regard to arms control, a formalized consultative process during the course of negotiations has evolved as a means of ameliorating the problems that otherwise might develop at the time of senatorial consideration of a completed treaty. Even so, administrations tend to view the consultative process primarily as a nuisance, as something intended to give the appearance of considering congressional viewpoints, thus satisfying political requirements and flattering congressional egos. At most, consultation has been seen as a means of learning the limits of congressional tolerance as an administration tries to push its treaty down the throats of the Congress.

Administrations willing to shape their negotiating objectives and positions in true collaboration with the Congress are rare. Messick points to one modern exception—the consultations between Under Secretary of State Robert Lovett and Senator Arthur Vandenberg (R.-Mich.) in the late 1940s on the question of postwar relations with Western Europe. Together, the two men shaped a resolution that reflected a true consensus of the overwhelming majority of the Senate. The resolution was brought to the floor of the Senate, debated, amended, and eventually approved. It then provided the basis for the international agreement that established NATO, an eminently successful U.S. policy that has been sustained for forty years, bringing peace and prosperity to Western Europe, and, more recently, freedom to Eastern Europe, while safeguarding the nation's own security interests in the bargain.

The far more frequent experience is illustrated no better than in the conflict over the interpretation of the 1972 Treaty Limiting Anti-Ballistic Missile Systems. In October 1985 the Reagan administration suddenly revealed a new, looser interpretation of that treaty's limitations on the development and testing of new types of ABMs. The disclosure of this break with the view and practice of the previous three administrations, including the one that negotiated the treaty, surprised virtually everyone, including key members of the Senate. The ensuing confrontation between the executive and the legislature was as spirited as any on arms control issues. The administration's position outraged no member as much as Senator Sam Nunn, the generally conservative chairman of the Armed Services Committee and a keen and shrewd defender of the Congress's prerogatives.

Despite the obvious political liability of antagonizing Senator Nunn, the administration was not dissuaded. It fought bitterly for nearly a year to prevent the Senate from obtaining the negotiating record of the ABM treaty talks. It then fought over the principle of which branch had the right to interpret the agreement. Having reviewed the record, Nunn concluded that the negotiators understood that strict limitations had been placed on testing, and that the Senate had given its consent to the agreement on the basis of that understanding. Nunn wrote to the president: ". . . absent due consultation, a unilateral executive branch decision to disregard the interpretation of the Treaty which the Senate believed it had approved when the accord was ratified in 1972 would provoke a Constitutional confrontation of profound dimensions."[41]

To enforce this view, Senators Nunn and Carl Levin amended the 1988–1989 Defense Authorization bill to require explicit congressional approval prior to the testing of those types of systems that were in contention. Later in the year, the administration announced that it was abandoning the battle over the principle of interpreting treaties, and that it would seek approval of tests on a case-by-case basis. But the damage to executive–congressional cooperation—and to the administration's own agenda on both ABM development and negotiations—had been done.

How much better it would have been had the administration consulted Senator Nunn and others prior to deciding on a new interpretation of the ABM treaty. Instead, a centrist–liberal coalition emerged strong enough to force the administration to back down. It embarrassed the president and damaged the U.S. position in the negotiations.

It was the procedural issue raised by the sudden treaty reinterpretation that galvanized the effective antitest majority over SDI. Genuine consultations almost certainly would have resulted in an arrangement permitting implementation of the administration's plans for ABM research, thus upholding the administration's negotiating position with the Soviet Union while protecting senatorial prerogatives. The basis for a lasting policy, gaining the support of majorities of both parties, might well have been laid.

It is difficult for officials of the executive branch to concede a role in defense policy to the Congress—habits and egos get in the way, to say nothing of the arrogance of "expertise" and the vested interests of the bureaucracy. Congress, however, will no longer be excluded. The real choice is between a congressional role imposed by a hostile legislature against the executive's will, usually long after negotiating positions have been tabled and defended publicly, and a congressional role defined in the course of establishing policy. The benefits of collaboration over confrontation are evident.

| 4 |

Arms Sales

To the foreign policy professional, the evaluation of arms sales involves complicated calculations of military, political, and economic pros and cons. Arms sales are business ventures, of course—big business. They are said to be indirect means of ensuring the nation's defense, making it possible for friendly nations to defend their security (and, presumably, American interests) without risk to American lives. Arms sales are also instruments of diplomacy, used either to develop closer relations between the United States and foreign nations or to avoid their deterioration. Sometimes there are direct military benefits of arms sales, as when the United States agrees to make available a certain value of weapons in exchange for the lease of military facilities abroad, but more often the benefits are more subtle. Arms sales are said to buy influence and unseen leverage, which is banked for use at critical times when the United States needs the support of foreign powers.

Rare is the congressman who finds these complex political/military/ economic trade-offs of arms sales an interesting or intellectually stimulating subject. Evaluating the risks/benefits of weapons transactions is not an exercise to which the overwhelming majority of members had ever given a thought prior to entering the legislature. One former senator estimated that only twenty-five members of the House and ten senators have anything resembling expertise on the issue. Moreover, there are few occasions when arms sales would attract most members' attention. These transactions generally pass unnoticed by the public; with rare exceptions, the issue is simply not salient politically. As a result, the typical congressman is likely to defer to the executive branch, generally assuming that arms sales are beneficial—bringing jobs and profits to U.S. companies, security to U.S. allies, and influence to the United States.

There are a few exceptions: for a very small number of congressmen, arms sales imply moral judgments; they believe it is wrong to sell weapons abroad. A more important source of opposition is ethnic politics—specifically, the Greek lobby, which sometimes has sought to restrict weapon exports to Turkey, and the very effective Israeli lobby, which often has sought to modify U.S. weapon sales to Arab nations. For the most part, however, arms sales elicit little interest.

Until the mid-1970s the Congress had been content to leave decisions on the export of weapons wholly to the executive branch. Two trends came together at that time to produce restrictive legislation— the sudden prominence of arms sales as an instrument of U.S. defense policy, and a movement by the Congress to curb the traditional independence of the executive branch in defense matters.

The 1974 Nelson amendment, modified in 1976 by the Arms Export Control Act, was the result of this new congressional initiative. The amendment required the president to notify the Congress thirty days prior to enacting major weapon sales, during which time the Congress was empowered to veto the transaction. Both the value and the characteristics of U.S. weapons being sold abroad were changing enormously in the mid-1970s, primarily because of the Nixon doctrine's emphasis on providing the means for allies to defend themselves (rather than risking American lives to defend them). In addition, arms sales skyrocketed because of the far greater financial resources available to Middle Eastern nations in the wake of sharp increases in the price of oil. Yet arms sales threatened to bypass the Congress's newly defined influence over defense policy, as enshrined in the War Powers Act, restrictions on covert operations, and other then-recent legislation. Legislation governing arms sales was required to extend congressional authority over what was becoming the hottest means of maintaining and extending U.S. military influence abroad.

In practice, the Arms Export Control Act has turned out to be a little-used instrument of congressional involvement in defense policy; there are only a handful of instances in which the Congress has forced changes in prospective sales, either directly or indirectly, by threatening to invoke the act. Nevertheless, there is little penchant to yield this piece of political turf, as the Reagan administration learned quickly when it considered abolishing the legislation early in its term. While the executive branch finds the mere existence of the legislation to be a damaging intrusion on the president's ability to conduct the nation's foreign relations, a small group in the Congress led by Senator Joseph R. Biden (D.-Del.) and Congressman Mel Levine (D.-Calif.) would like to strengthen the act. In 1987 they introduced legislation that would have replaced the potential veto of the Arms Export Control Act with a requirement that the Congress vote on, and approve, most sales prior to their enactment.

In general, however, the Congress is not inclined to take part in arms sales—the issues are too complicated and too far removed from constituents' interests. In most cases there is virtually nothing to be gained by voting against sales, except perhaps some promise of future rewards from party leaders or colleagues. Yet, with rare exceptions, the benefits of siding with the executive are similarly elusive.

The old "merchant of death" image clearly retains some political liability because most members prefer not to be known as enthusiasts for weapon sales abroad. Even the economic gains from arms sales tend not to motivate congressmen. In the absence of special circumstances, therefore, most members would prefer to leave the decisions, and the responsibility for any adverse effects, to the executive. They rather reserve for themselves only the right to intervene when a prospective sale antagonizes important constituents.

In those few instances in which the Congress has challenged the executive branch on arms sales, the politics have been fascinating. Challenges are difficult to defend to constituents. In the words of former Senator John Culver:

> Most members do not want to engage on these issues. There has to be something that makes it salient—makes it fit into the bread and butter of routine political business. . . . It's a briar patch. You have to be nuts to take on a proposed arms sale.[1]

But the political calculus can change when control of the executive and the legislature is held by different parties. In 1981, for example, the Democratic House leadership seized on a prospective arms sale to Saudi Arabia to demonstrate the president's potential vulnerability on an important issue. The partisan showdown was seen as important by House leaders to secure a stronger bargaining position for other issues and to curry favor from specific interest groups. On this and similar occasions, the basic divisions are along party lines, but odd alignments result from crossovers by members responsive to special interests such as the aerospace industry or unions or relevant ethnic groups. Members with strong opinions on the propriety of weapon sales per se may also desert their party positions.

Arms Sales in U.S. Defense Policy

Arms sales are big business. Rising steadily from approximately $4 billion in 1971, the value of U.S. weapons delivered abroad had doubled to $8 billion by 1977, a level exceeded in every subsequent year. Indeed, in 1983 the value of weapon deliveries peaked at $15 billion. Annual receipts are currently running between $9 billion and $10 billion, and contracts already concluded virtually guarantee comparable revenues well into the 1990s, despite recent declines in new orders (due in part to congressional actions). Weapons are one of the leading exports of the United States, accounting for nearly five percent of total annual sales abroad. Moreover, the U.S. arms industry is one of the few manufacturing sectors that held its own in the 1980s. Weapon sales have provided as much as eleven percent of U.S. exports of manufactured goods in recent years.[2]

But decisions on arms sales are not driven by economic considerations. Denials of aircraft and missile sales to Arab nations in 1985–1988 shifted more than $30 billion in potential business from U.S. to European companies, with commensurate effects on jobs, but caused hardly a ripple of complaint. One of the leading opponents of these sales, Congressman Mel Levine, represents a district with probably the largest concentration of aerospace and electronics companies in the country, including Hughes, Northrop, Rockwell, and TRW.

The fact that the economic aspects of arms sales are not considered by most members of Congress was testified to by the aerospace industry's chief lobbyist for exports, who complained woefully:

> Increasingly, one of my objectives is to try to interest some of the pro-trade Members in understanding that defense exports are a trade as well as a security issue. If Congress's [1985] rejection of F-15s for the Saudis had been grain, the farmers would have been plowing up the Mall in protest.[3]

The primary engine behind arms sales is not economics, but politics—international politics. The executive branch considers arms sales to be an extremely important instrument of U.S. defense policy. A decision to export weapons to a given country suggests implicit approval of the buyer's policies, or at least of its general stance in world affairs, and is understood in those terms by friends and foes alike. The selling of arms is a serious matter, different from other commodities. The late Israeli defense minister Moshe Dayan put the matter very clearly in expressing indignation at a proposed 1978 sale of F-15 aircraft to Egypt and Saudi Arabia: ". . . these are killing machines, they are not washing machines, and who are they going to use these killing machines against?"[4]

The sale of arms represents the taking of sides by providing the means for one nation to make war on another. In this sense, a sale represents the tacit beginnings of an alliance and the first step toward the establishment of a defense commitment. Sometimes this is done deliberately, as in the U.S. efforts beginning in 1979 to inculcate a military relationship with China. The objective was to exert strategic pressure on the Soviet Union so that Soviet officials would come to believe that, in the event of war, U.S. and Chinese military forces might fight together.

While there is nothing automatic about the process of building such an alliance, that is the implicit result—deliberate or not; arms sales are simply not clean, one-time transactions. They tend to result in a multiplicity of relationships between the United States and the purchasing country, including U.S. involvement in both the regional and domestic politics of the recipient.

Typically, arms sales take place in a broader military context of consultations between high-level officials, ceremonial port calls by naval warships, and exchanges of visits by air force or army combat units. Formal, bilateral consultative mechanisms to plan weapon sales—so-called joint military commissions—are becoming increasingly common. U.S. and foreign officials meet annually or semiannually to discuss the purchasing country's military "requirements," mutual security concerns, and so forth. The United States has established such arrangements with just about every major recipient of military assistance, involving the United States in the military planning of perhaps twenty nations, quite apart from its formal treaty allies.

In almost all cases the United States provides military training to countries that purchase weapons from U.S. firms. Teams of military officers and civilian technicians are sent to tutor indigenous forces in the use and maintenance of the specific equipment, and sometimes to tutor the country's armed services in modern warfare. Officers from the purchasing country may be enrolled in U.S. military schools, or U.S. advisers may serve with military units in the receiving country. Purchases of U.S. military equipment also initiate an extensive logistics train: munitions, spare parts, and repair equipment will all have to be purchased to keep the weapons operational; U.S. personnel— uniformed or civilian—will be required for many years to keep the weapons in working order. In fact, the organization and efficiency of this logistics effort are what often cause foreign nations to opt for U.S. equipment.

In some cases, the U.S. presence in a foreign country can attain massive proportions. In 1978, for example, the year before the fall of the shah, there were approximately 45,000 Americans in Iran; 9,300 of them were associated with the U.S. military sales program in one capacity or another, either as U.S. servicemen (fifteen percent), or as civilians (usually retired military officers) hired by the shah to maintain his military hardware and to train Iranians in its operation. At present, there are more than 4,000 Americans in Saudi Arabia carrying out similar activities.[5]

Clearly, these in-depth relationships have consequences. When the recipient of U.S. arms is a democratic, peaceful government with foreign policy views compatible with our own, weapon sales serve both U.S. interests and those of the recipient. When it is an unpopular and perhaps unstable regime, however, as in Iran under the shah, the backlash against the United States can be considerable. The shah's enormous expenditures on high-tech weapons came to symbolize for many Iranians the excesses of his rule, and the United States's very prominent role in support of those purchases caused us to be seen as his primary mainstay, with adverse consequences when he was overthrown.

Weapon sales and their ensuing logistics and training networks inherently suggest support for the purchasing country, automatically antagonizing neighboring states. There are many examples of this, one of which was the deterioration of U.S. relations with moderate Arab nations during the 1960s and early 1970s, when U.S. sales of advanced military equipment to Israel was first initiated.[6]

In a sense, these arms sales relationships are the modern-day equivalent of formal defense treaties. The defense commitment implied by the relationship is ambiguous, but the interaction between the armed forces of the two states makes it appear that such a commitment exists—or might exist, should push come to shove. The issue is not whether these relationships benefit the United States or not, but rather that these commitments occur almost unconsciously; they are rarely debated within the executive branch, and they are certainly not put before the American people or their elected representatives for approval. Who decided that the American people should be committed to the defense of Oman, the Sudan, Kenya, or Morocco? The Senate never gave its advice and consent to such treaties, yet the reality of the military relationships between the United States and these nations—of which arms sales are a central element—makes it appear that this is the case.

When a foreign nation significantly dependent on U.S. arms becomes involved in a military conflict, it can force the United States into difficult choices. At the extreme, weapon sales have implicated the United States in regional military conflicts leading to U.S. confrontations with the Soviet Union.

At such times, continuing the supply of weapons, or just the munitions necessary to support the weapons, directly implicates the United States as a belligerent nation. If the regional conflict turns into a sustained military engagement the United States may face requests for the expedited delivery of equipment or even the involvement of U.S. personnel in supporting roles. While it may have served U.S. interests at different times to have been seen to side with Morocco against Algeria, Ethiopia against Somalia, or Pakistan against India, who determined that that would be the case? When the Soviet Union was supplying military equipment to the opposing local state, the consequences of peacetime military relationships became more risky. U.S.–Soviet confrontations occurred in the Middle East, for example, in 1967, 1970, and in 1973, when there were even veiled threats of a nuclear crisis.

The alternative is to discontinue military support to a recipient of U.S. arms when a crisis occurs. Such a decision, however, would constitute a very clear signal to the nation directly involved—a signal more clear than is usually desirable in international politics. The U.S. position as weapons supplier to both Greece and Turkey, for example, when they were fighting over Cyprus in the 1960s and 1970s, led to a sustained period of difficult relations with Turkey, a country in which the United States has a critical strategic interest. (The United States embargoed arms deliveries to Turkey on several occasions in the 1960s.) Denial of military assistance at a time of crisis not only upsets the country directly involved, but also makes other arms recipients nervous.

In normal circumstances these "worst case" implications of arms sales are rarely considered by decision makers. Instead, the key word heard most often in justifications of arms exports is "influence," political influence. Sales of weapons are said to provide leverage to the United States in its dealings with other nations. Whether this leverage is derived from gratitude or from concern that future sales might otherwise be terminated, it is widely believed (in both the executive branch and the Congress) that the United States acquires political capital through arms sales and that this will at some point weigh positively in decisions that affect U.S. interests.

During a session of a working group of the National Security Council in 1977,* for example, cabinet-rank officials argued that arms sales to Saudi Arabia would cause that nation to: (1) modify its threatened hostility toward Egypt's participation in peace negotiations with Israel and (2) exercise a moderating influence on prospective increases in the price of oil. Such positions had not been promised nor even hinted at by Saudi leaders. Nor was there any discussion of offering the arms sale explicitly in exchange for such commitments. U.S. officials simply assumed, as is assumed widely throughout the foreign policy establishment, that arms sales lead to leverage with recipients.[7]

A former director of the Defense Security Assistance Agency, the unit of the U.S. Defense Department responsible for managing arms sales, described the presumed political benefits of arms sales succinctly:

> Arms sales give us a relationship with a country that we would not have otherwise, and a great deal of leverage. It survives the ups and downs of politics. It's often very low key, but when we need it we can use it. And it enables us to protect American interests without putting American lives at risk. . . . A few bucks go an awful long way with these countries . . . just a few bucks.[8]

* When serving as assistant director of the U.S. Arms Control and Disarmament Agency in 1977–1979 I took part in several of these meetings.

The most relevant political implication of arms sales may in fact be a more defensive one: the avoidance of loss of influence. Recipients consider it their right to buy whatever weapons they wish, a perception encouraged by manufacturers' representatives. When an arms request is turned down, the response is strong and negative, particularly as in most cases there are alternative Western suppliers. The executive branch fears that if a weapons request is turned down, it will be perceived by the purchasing nation as a hostile act, adversely affecting U.S. relations with that country and causing a decline in our influence. Thus, within the executive branch, the primary advocate of controversial weapon sales is most often the U.S. embassy in the purchasing country and the relevant regional bureau of the State Department—not lobbyists for the manufacturer, and certainly not the U.S. military.[9]

It seems clear that the further along in the arms sale decision process a turndown is made, the more severe is the adverse effect on U.S. interests. Ideally, if a prospective sale is to be declined it should happen at the earliest stage—for example, when the assistant chief of staff of the potential recipient's army first sidles up to the U.S. defense attaché at a cocktail party and says something like, ''I'm not asking, of course, but theoretically, as an intellectual exercise, how do you think that your country might respond if my country asked to purchase Conquistador guided missiles? . . . not that we would want them, you understand.'' At this point, there is no commitment to the request by officials of the recipient country, and thus no loss of face if the answer were negative. But once the request is made in any official conversation, there is a price to be paid for saying no. And once the request is known publicly, the political price of a turndown can become very high indeed.

It is perhaps for this reason more than any other that the executive branch finds the Arms Export Control Act so repugnant. The act not only puts the Congress into the decision process on arms sales, but it raises the possibility of public rejections of prospective sales when governments are fully committed to them. General Brent Scowcroft, national security adviser to both President Ford and President Bush, said:

> Congress ought to be involved in decisions of this sort. . . . The problem I have with the present procedure is that it is too late when Congress gets it. By that time, Congress cannot reject an administration proposal without doing grievous foreign policy harm.[10]

The act is thought to diminish the potential political influence of arms sales because it impairs the ability of the executive branch to utilize the promise of weapons as inducements for more cooperative behavior. Countries with reason to believe that they may run afoul of powerful forces in the Congress are said to seek alternative sources of weapons rather than risk being the subject of debate and possible rejection.

Congress's actual participation in arms sales since enactment of the 1974 legislation reflects the degree to which these executive branch complaints may be true, and illustrates how the political process operates on these sensitive transactions.

Congressional Limitations on Arms Sales

Congressional concern about sharp increases in U.S. weapon sales abroad heightened perceptibly in the summer of 1973 when rumors circulated that the Nixon administration was planning to sell F-4 Phantom jets, then the most modern aircraft in the U.S. inventory, to Saudi Arabia. Although this transaction was never consummated—the 1973 war in the Middle East intervened—the Nelson amendment, giving the Congress its first role in arms sale decisions, was passed the following year. The legislation, modified somewhat in 1976 as the Arms Export Control Act, required the president to notify Congress thirty days prior to completing all sales valued at $14 million or more for single weapons, and $50 million or more for sales of "defense articles and services." During the thirty-day period the Congress was authorized to veto the sale by passing a concurrent resolution of disapproval in both Houses. (Concurrent resolutions are not presented to the president for signature and are thus not subject to a veto.)

Following the Supreme Court's landmark *Chadha* decision (in *Immigration and Naturalization Service v. Chadha,* 1983) disallowing these so-called legislative vetoes, the act was amended in 1985 to require a joint resolution of both Houses to turn down a weapons sale. A joint resolution is subject to presidential veto, which can be overruled only by two-thirds majorities in both Houses; the executive branch, therefore, only has to persuade one-third plus one of the members of either House to permit a sale to go forward. Nonetheless, the Congress has intervened more frequently in arms sales decisions since 1985 and has made a greater impact than ever before.

The only case dealt with under the original Nelson amendment took place in 1974. The prospective sale of mobile Hawk missiles to Jordan generated opposition from members concerned about their potential use against Israel. In what has proved to be a repetitive pattern of behavior, the issue was never forced to a vote; instead, the Ford administration compromised by modifying the transaction to require that the missiles be made immobile.[11]

A second controversial arms transaction in the 1970s—the proposed sale of airborne warning and control system (AWACS) aircraft to Iran—illustrates some of the institutional aspects of the conflict between Congress and the president. The weapon system incorporated some of the most advanced technologies then available to U.S. forces; the aircraft were only beginning to enter U.S. inventories, and the European allies had only recently decided to acquire some for themselves. The sale of such an advanced system clearly ran counter to the Carter administration's just-announced arms sale restraint policy, an issue that had been prominent in Carter's presidential campaign. In addition, the administration demonstrated undue haste in pressing the Congress on the issue, notifying it of the sale on July 6, 1977, rather than waiting until after the summer recess, as congressional leaders had requested.

The key issue concerned the security of the advanced communications and control equipment on board the planes. Conservative members feared the compromise of this technology in the event an aircraft should fall into Soviet hands, perhaps through Soviet penetration of the Iranian air force. These concerns were fueled by public statements by Stansfield Turner, director of the Central Intelligence Agency, who echoed the fears of technological compromise. Combined with liberals who opposed the export of ever-more sophisticated military technologies in principle, and who were antipathetic toward the shah's regime in any event, an effective coalition was forged. The coalition gained the upper hand in the House Foreign Affairs Committee, which voted 19 to 17 to disallow the sale.

Although the administration dealt successfully with the technical factors in its testimony before the Senate Foreign Relations Committee, a majority wanted more time to consider the issue. Accordingly, Senator Robert Byrd, the new majority leader, requested the administration to withdraw the request and resubmit it in the fall. When President Carter refused, the substantive merits of the sale were forgotten, and the dispute turned into a power struggle between Carter and Byrd. The president regarded the Congress's demand as an unwarranted intrusion into the executive's prerogative to operate on its own schedule in conducting the nation's foreign affairs. The majority leader regarded the president's refusal as a challenge to his leadership and authority in the Senate.

Byrd did his work well as he prepared the Senate to vote on a resolution of disapproval. Disinterested observers were unanimous in predicting the measure's passage, when Senator Hubert Humphrey intervened and arranged negotiations between the White House and the majority leader. At literally the last minute, Carter backed down and withdrew the sale.

Once the dust settled, it turned out that the substantive issues had largely been resolved. The administration assured the Congress that the shah's AWACS would not be equipped with the most sensitive devices and that certain other measures would be taken to reduce the risks to national security. This assuaged conservative critics, some of whom were probably reflecting concerns emanating from the Pentagon and the CIA. Moreover, the administration had gotten the message and spent the summer intensively mending fences with Senator Byrd. When the sale was reintroduced in September, it sailed through without a hitch.[12]

The episode demonstrated the Congress's willingness and ability to stand up to an administration, even without the additional incentives provided by a powerful special interest lobby. It also illustrates the concern of leaders in both branches to protect the prerogatives (and power) of their respective offices, leading to a clash quite separate from the substantive merits of the case. These conflicts become more fierce when partisan politics enter the picture.

Just as the Ford administration had initiated the sale of the AWACS to Iran, and then left it for President Carter to conclude, the Carter administration began negotiations to sell AWACS to Saudi Arabia, and left it for President Reagan to complete. The issue was joined in 1981 when the Reagan administration notified the Congress of an $8.5 billion sale to Saudi Arabia, adding aerial tankers, air-to-air missiles, and improvements to the F-15 fighters acquired by the Saudis in 1978 to the prospective AWACS deal. In deciding to go ahead with the transaction, administration officials knew that a difficult struggle was in the offing. They wrote off the House from the beginning, concentrating instead on persuading a majority of senators to support the president.

As in the Iranian AWACS sale, security of the high-tech gear on board the aircraft was a special concern; Senator John Glenn took the lead on this issue. In the Saudi case, however, there were also the special concerns of the Israeli lobby. Not only the AWACS itself but other elements in the proposed package were said to give Saudi Arabia offensive capabilities that might be turned against Israel at some point in the future. The administration, largely through Secretary of State Alexander Haig, attempted to deal with both issues by giving a variety of assurances about special "safeguards" to be placed on the weapons. Not least of these was the fact that, because Saudi Arabia lacked the requisite trained personnel, Americans would partially man the aircraft well into the 1990s.

The leadership of the Democratic party saw this issue as an opportunity to reassert itself following the debacle of the 1980 election and the early triumphs of the Reagan administration in the Congress. The Democratic National Committee, under its new chairman Charles Mannatt, was active in organizing and supporting the opposition. Party leaders in both Houses worked hard to pass resolutions of disapproval, primarily to prove that the president was not invincible, as his triumph on the 1981 tax reform bill had seemed to suggest, and to show that the Congress could continue to play an effective independent role. Not unimportantly, some Democrats hoped that by accentuating this issue they could paint the administration as being anti-Israel, thus eroding the gains that the Republican party appeared to have been making among traditionally Democratic voters in the Jewish community.

As it turned out, the strategy backfired. Although a resolution of disapproval passed the House handily (301 to 111), and barely survived in the Senate Foreign Relations Committee (9 to 8), it failed on the Senate floor, 48 to 52. Two things seem to have swung the tide. First, there was some division within the Democratic ranks. High-ranking officials of the Carter administration testified in favor of the sale (which they had originated). President Carter himself, during his first visit to Washington since leaving office, spoke in favor of it. (In view of the great efforts of Democratic leaders to stand up to President Reagan, this first Carter foray was deeply resented.) More important, though, was the personal lobbying by President Reagan. Perhaps learning from Carter's AWACS experience in 1977, the new president worked hard; he is credited with turning around several of the key votes, including Senators Mark Andrews (R.-N.Dak.), William Cohen, Slade Gorton (R.-Wash.), Roger Jepson (R.-Iowa), Larry Pressler, and Edward Zorinsky.[13]

This AWACS example shows how difficult it is for the Congress to reject an arms sale when the administration has its act together and the president is in a general position of strength. With Ronald Reagan at the height of his popularity, members could not successfully stand up against him, even with the Democratic party and the Israeli lobby behind them, and even though the vote came when only a simple majority of both Houses would have been sufficient to veto an arms sale.

Now, with the *Chadha* decision, two-thirds majorities are required; nevertheless, the Congress has won several victories in the years since *Chadha*. A particular congressional concern has been the export of Stinger portable air defense missiles to the Middle East. Many members of Congress worry that these very advanced, relatively small, and very effective weapons could fall into the hands of terrorist groups and be used against civilian airliners. In early 1984 the administration notified Congress of its intention to sell Stingers to both Jordan and Saudi Arabia. Opposition mounted quickly, led by Senator Bob Packwood (R.-Oreg.) in the Senate and Congressman Larry Smith (D.-Fla.) in the House. This time the administration faced significant opposition not only from the Democrats and the Israeli lobby, but from within its own party; it was an election year, not a good time for Republicans to be seen to be opposing Israel's interests. The terrorist issue, moreover, was able to galvanize more powerful political emotions than virtually any other. Recognizing the inevitable, the administration withdrew the sale before any votes were taken. Later in the year, however, following Iranian attacks on shipping in the Persian Gulf, the administration exercised the emergency waiver clause of the Arms Export Control Act to transfer four hundred Stingers to Saudi Arabia.[14]

Over the next three years, informal soundings were taken on several occasions concerning the potential transfer of Stingers to Kuwait, Bahrain, and other small states on the Persian Gulf. In each case, congressional opposition mounted quickly and the sales never materialized. The revelation in late 1987 that Iran had obtained Stingers (apparently from Afghan guerrillas, but no one is really sure) made clear that congressional concerns about the difficulty of maintaining the security of these weapons had been well placed.

Stingers also figured prominently among a veritable potpourri of missiles in a proposed 1986 sale to Saudi Arabia. The issues were the same in this case—a threat to Israel, fear of terrorism—and again the critical test came in the Senate. This time the Senate overwhelmingly passed the joint resolution of disapproval, as did the House. The president vetoed the resolution, but removed the Stingers from the package. Even so, his veto was sustained in the Senate by only a single vote.[15]

There are two other recent instances of successful congressional interventions. One of these episodes stands as the sole explicit rejection of a complete arms package by the Congress. In September 1985 the administration made yet another attempt to sell previously denied weapons, including Stingers, mobile Hawks, and advanced aircraft, to Jordan. Congressional opposition centered this time on Jordan's refusal to reach a peace settlement with Israel. Despite a personal visit to Washington by King Hussein to persuade congressional leaders that the new weapons would not be used against Israel, the Congress remained unconvinced. Three days after formal notification of the intended sale, the Senate passed (97 to 1) a joint resolution to delay the sale until at least March 1986. The resolution was passed subsequently by the House, and was signed reluctantly by the president. The proposal has yet to be resubmitted.[16]

The second episode was in 1987 when the administration let it be known informally that it intended to sell another large arms package to Saudi Arabia, including a small number of F-15s to replace aircraft that had been lost, an improvement package for F-15s already there, some army equipment, and several sophisticated Maverick air-to-surface missiles. Despite the deepening military alliance between the United States and Saudi Arabia at the time (due to U.S. protection of Kuwaiti and other shipping in the Persian Gulf), overwhelming majorities in both Houses urged the president not to go ahead. After protracted negotiations, a compromise was struck: the most objectionable portion of the package, the Mavericks, was removed, and the sale went forward.[17]

Critics of the congressional role in arms sales maintain that the potential threat of intervention also prevents some arms transactions from ever being considered seriously by the recipient countries. The most prominent example of this is the Saudi decision in 1985 to acquire seventy-two British Tornado aircraft, instead of U.S. fighters, a deal valued at $6–8 billion plus another $20 billion in support contracts. According to a study by the Congressional Research Service, the Saudis returned to British suppliers—breaking what had been a long string of U.S. aircraft purchases—only after concluding that the Congress would not permit the sale of an additional large number of F-15s. In addition, the Saudis believed the British would not place restrictions on the armaments and basing of these aircraft, as the United States had done in response to congressional pressures at the time of the initial F-15 sale in 1978.[18]

In 1988 the Saudis expanded their military relationship with Great Britain sharply, concluding a deal valued at $29 billion (for combat aircraft, helicopters, mine-hunting vessels, and construction projects). A Saudi official made the reasons for the decision perfectly clear:

> We would prefer to buy weapons from the United States. American technology is generally superior. But we are not going to pay billions of dollars to be insulted. We are not masochists.[19]

The American League for Exports and Security Assistance, a lobby organized by the aerospace industry, estimates that sales worth $2–3 billion to U.S. defense companies are blocked each year by the deterrent effects of the Arms Export Control Act. According to a study prepared for General Dynamics, if U.S. aircraft sales to Jordan, Saudi Arabia, and the smaller Arab Gulf states were blocked for the remainder of the century, U.S. firms would lose an additional $28 billion in sales and 886,000 work-years in employment.[20] These figures, however, should be taken with a grain of salt. They assume, among other things, that U.S. firms would secure all the sales in the absence of the congressional role, a dubious assumption in today's world of cutthroat competition. Still, there is no doubt that the Congress's power has resulted in a cutback on U.S. weapons sales to Arab nations, at some cost to U.S. industry. Whether or not this sacrifice has served U.S. interests remains to be seen.

The Politics of Arms Sales

Surprisingly in this age of concern about the competitiveness of U.S. industry, the loss of U.S. weapon exports seems to be without political importance. The aerospace lobby has made hardly a ripple in Washington and apparently even had trouble persuading defense companies to support its efforts to loosen export controls. The Saudi decision to substitute British weapons for U.S. equipment and Jordan's decision to acquire French aircraft in place of denied U.S. F-16 fighters were hardly noticed in the Congress. As noted, the chief sponsor of legislation to give the Congress a greater role in arms sales decisions has one of the largest concentrations of aerospace companies in his own district. Idiosyncratically, and probably because of the special character of arms sales, congressional evaluations of these issues focus on their alleged international ramifications rather than on domestic economic effects. The confrontations are executive versus legislative power struggles more than dollars-and-cents issues.

Generally, the Congress is disposed to go along with weapon sales and is likely to support the executive branch's decisions. A prospective sale will gain attention only when some special characteristic triggers a political reaction; the 1977 AWACS sale to Iran, seeming to epitomize the trend toward the export of the United States's most advanced military technologies, put forward by an administration that had trumpeted its intention to halt such practices, galvanized such a reaction. Sales of equipment with a potential for use by terrorists have had a similar effect. Weapon transfers to Turkey at times of tension with Greece have elicited such a response. And any sale to Arab nations (other than Egypt since it made peace with Israel in 1979) has always had this potential. In the mid-1950s, for example, there was a minor storm of criticism in the Congress when an enterprising reporter discovered surplus U.S. tanks destined for Saudi Arabia on a dock in Brooklyn. With passage of the Nelson amendment in 1974, the Congress gained an instrument with which to do more than complain.

Once a prospective arms sale becomes a salient political issue, institutional factors play an independent role in fueling the controversy. The executive branch will fight hard to complete the transaction, fearing the effect of a turndown (or significant modification) on its credibility abroad—and on its future ability to dominate congressional decision making on related issues. Yet congressional effectiveness will also be judged to a degree by how well it does. Sometimes, as the contest is joined, personal qualities—or shortcomings—will become important. President Carter's refusal to take even small measures to placate Senator Byrd in the summer of 1977 greatly worsened the debate on the AWACS sale to Iran, just as President Reagan's effort to woo senators seemed to turn the tide in 1981.

Timing is also critical: arms sales that could probably pass congressional scrutiny with little problem during the first six months of an administration could face difficulties during the administration's final year, depending on what other events have transpired. In 1987, for example, badly weakened by the rejection of Judge Robert Bork to sit on the Supreme Court, the administration "compromised" on the proposed package to Saudi Arabia by removing the one truly objectionable element—Maverick missiles; it had no stomach for a pitched battle. The impact of prospective elections is also evident. For example, in the proposed sale of missiles to Saudi Arabia in 1986, five of seven senators who were retiring voted with the president to sustain the sale, but only four of twenty-eight up for reelection were on the president's side.[21]

What is the decisive factor in determining the outcome? The cases are too few and diverse, the variables too many, to reach any general judgment. The substantive merits of the prospective sale will be important in a few cases. It is rather difficult, after all, to argue convincingly that weapons particularly appropriate for use by terrorists should be exported to countries known to harbor terrorist organizations, a fact that goes a long way in explaining the administration's repeated difficulties in securing congressional approval of Stinger exports. But in most cases the substantive merits of a case will be far less clear, and rather too complicated, to play much of a role in political discourse.[22]

The international context plays some role, as suggested by the 1985 Jordanian case, when King Hussein refused to reach a peace settlement with Israel, but it does not appear to be an overriding factor either. U.S. relations with Saudi Arabia and other Arab countries on the Gulf have improved measurably over the 1980s, but selling arms to these countries has become far more difficult.

The political context of the transfer is clearly important, although also not necessarily dominant. The president's popularity, the administration's skill in deal making, the aspirations of key members, the timing of sales relative to elections, and the effectiveness of lobby groups all play a role. The success of the Congress in constraining arms sales to Arab nations during the second Reagan administration is probably explained best by the relative weakness of the White House after the Iran–Contra scandal, along with a coincident sharp increase in the Israeli lobby's willingness to intervene in the political process. One cannot forecast the reaction to a prospective sale simply by examining the current relative strength of the two branches.

The fundamental issue is that presidents and their subordinates simply resent having to deal with the Congress on these issues. They consider the congressional role in arms sales an unwarranted intrusion into the conduct of foreign policy and an unconstitutional and unwise breach of the separation of powers. Inevitably responsive to parochial interests, the executive argues, the Congress cannot evaluate these questions from the more lofty perspective of the national interest, a perspective that the president, they insist, has uppermost in his mind. As a result, they argue, congressional involvement leads inevitably—even when sales are ultimately approved—to disruptions in U.S. relations with purchasing nations that counteract the otherwise beneficial impact of weapon sales for U.S. influence abroad.

On Capitol Hill, there is no question of the Congress's right to be involved. The Constitution gives it the right "to regulate Commerce with foreign nations . . ." (Art. I, sec. 8[3]), but more importantly, insofar as arms sales can lead to tacit military alliances, the Congress's right to review prospective transfers stems also from its powers "to provide for the common defense," and "to declare war." Rather than reversing the congressional role, some members argue, congressional involvement in weapon sales decisions should be expanded—shifted from the current negative one of vetoing prospective sales to a requirement that the Congress positively affirm all sales to nations other than those with which the United States maintains formal alliances.

Assessing the Congressional Role

In the years since passage of the original Nelson amendment in 1974, the Congress has voted to deny (more precisely, "postpone") or has forced the withdrawal of two announced arms deals—the 1984 Stinger sale to Jordan and Saudi Arabia, and the 1985 sale of advanced aircraft to Jordan. It has caused the removal of specific types of weapons from four additional transactions of which it was notified formally—mobile Hawks to Jordan in 1974, Stingers to Saudi Arabia in 1984, and Mavericks to Saudi Arabia in 1987 and Kuwait in 1988. And it has persuaded the administration to place restrictions on the specific equipment or operations of certain weapon systems in at least four additional cases—Iranian AWACS in 1977, Saudi Arabian F-15s in 1978, Saudi AWACS in 1981, and replacement F-15s for Saudi Arabia in 1987. Moreover, in several cases the knowledge of the potential for congressional disapproval has deterred the conclusion of some prospective arms transactions.

Have these interventions harmed U.S. interests? Is the congressional role in arms transfers a problem for the conduct of foreign policy? The answers to these questions are subjective. The State Department's Saudi Arabia desk officer and the CIA's station chief in Riyadh have very clear points of view, as do most officials of U.S. aerospace and petroleum companies and the heads of the unions that work for them. The Defense Department's Office of Technology Transfers may see the question differently, however, as might the armed forces' long-range planning staffs, the officials concerned with the security of civilian air traffic, and certainly the members of the board of the U.S.–Israel Public Affairs Committee.

Is it possible to assess the consequences objectively? Not with any certitude. No doubt there are short-term problems in U.S. relations with nations denied weapons sales. To understand this, one need only imagine the first conversation between the U.S. ambassador in Amman and the Jordanian foreign minister following the Congress's rejection of King Hussein's request in 1985. But what of the mid-term impact? Events in the Middle East seem to have conspired to promote U.S. interests. Continued weakness in the oil market has dominated decisions on oil pricing; the economic laws of supply and demand are clearly of far greater import to the oil-producing nations than any political relationships. The war between Iran and Iraq drove the gulf Arab nations into closer relations with the United States. With sworn enemies like Iran in the neighborhood and the profound divisions between the values of these Arab governments and those of the Soviet system, conservative Arab governments have little choice but to turn to the United States for their security. Clearly, the internal economic and social objectives of these governments can be satisfied only in the West.

After years of dealing with the United States, sophisticated Arab officials seem to have developed a certain understanding of U.S. politics. After the 1987 Saudi deal was resolved by eliminating Mavericks from the package, for example, one diplomat was quoted as saying:

> [We are] happy that this issue has been settled for the moment, [and are] anxious to start the process of the transfer because [of a] pressing need

for this equipment . . . further discussions at a later time will certainly show that the Mavericks will not upset the balance of power in the region, and [they] will be part of some future purchase, hopefully [in] the near future.[23]

These are hardly the words of a deeply offended and permanently alienated representative of a foreign nation.

Yet, how close *might* U.S.–Saudi relations have been had the executive branch been able to carry out all the arms transfers it had contemplated? Might the Saudis have been willing to support U.S. naval operations in the Persian Gulf in 1987 and 1988 more visibly than they proved? Persuasive arguments can be made either way. And how about the Jordanians? It is certainly the case that the Jordanian–Israeli peace process is dead in the water. Might the United States have been able to persuade Hussein to enter direct negotiations with Israel had he not been repulsed so directly by the Congress in 1985? Again, there are no definitive answers.

The long-term consequences of congressional intervention in arms sales are even more murky. There can be no doubt that the decidedly pro-Israeli cast of U.S. policy, always emphasized when arms sales are considered by the Congress, has been exploited at times by Soviet spokesmen and by radical demagogues in the Arab world. But are these propaganda wars really significant in the broader context of international relations? And what of the long-term military consequences? To the degree that the congressional actions slow down the proliferation of advanced military technologies to the Middle East, aren't military threats to Israel, and thus to the United States, diminished?

And how can one assess the less visible deterrent effect of the congressional role? It seems clear that contracts have been lost for U.S. business, but the political effects are not so clear. To the degree that fear of congressional debate leads foreign governments to despair of U.S. assistance, it no doubt hurts U.S. interests. But executive branch protestations are often hollow. In fact, the ability to blame the Congress for turning off requests for certain types of arms is quite useful. It can permit U.S. diplomats and defense officials to deny arms sales prior to their reaching an official status—arms sales that they would prefer not to see consummated. It is sometimes handy for the executive branch to have the Congress as an excuse to do what it really would like to do anyway—and to do it without suffering damage in official relations as serious as might have occurred otherwise.

Reforming the Congressional Role

The ability of Congress to constrain arms sales, for better or worse, is here to stay. The legitimacy of the congressional role has been settled by over fifteen years of practice. While all presidents, Republican and Democratic, have been careful not to accept congressional demands for "war powers" formally, with regard to arms sales no administration, however unhappy, has officially denied the legitimacy of the Congress's actions.

This being the case, there are nonetheless several questions regarding congressional involvement:

Should the Congress act only on these prospective weapon sales for which some members seek a resolution of disapproval? Or should the Congress be required to evaluate all arms transfers affirmatively before they go forward?

Does the *Chadha* decision make it too difficult for Congress to block a prospective weapon sale? Shouldn't simple majorities of both Houses be sufficient to stop a transaction, rather than the two-thirds now required to overturn a presidential veto of a resolution of disapproval?

Is there any way to put the Congress into the decision loop earlier in the process? Do congressional debates and possible rejections have to occur only after governments are fully committed to a weapon sale, thus bringing public embarrassment to all parties?

The first two issues were addressed by the Biden–Levine Arms Export Reform Act, introduced in January 1987 but never acted on formally. The bill would have replaced the current system (in which the Congress has the option of disapproving any prospective arms sale meeting certain financial thresholds) with a requirement for both Houses to approve controversial transactions. In one sense, Biden–Levine would have narrowed the congressional role: it would have removed from congressional consideration weapon sales to nations with formal defense treaties with the United States (NATO members, Japan, Australia, and New Zealand), and also sales to signatories of the Camp David Accord (Egypt and Israel). By requiring positive congressional action before all other sales could go forward, however, the legislation would have induced congressional debate and possibly denial on a much larger number of transactions. Moreover, it would have made it possible for simple majorities to veto any controversial sale, thus further strengthening the potential for congressional action.

There were two fatal flaws in this legislation.

First, most members of Congress do not want to go on record on every controversial weapon sale, nor should they be required to do so. Yet Biden–Levine would have provided difficult-to-resist opportunities for members seeking publicity—or seeking to satisfy narrow interests—to compel on-the-record votes. In some situations, the political dynamics of arms transfers might have forced many members to vote against transactions they would have privately supported.

Consider, for example, U.S. weapon sales to Egypt in the mid-1970s. Following the 1973 war in the Middle East, President Anwar Sadat of Egypt began to move his nation from its previously close alliance with the Soviet Union toward a peace settlement with Israel. The U.S. government, mainly in the person of Secretary of State Henry Kissinger, understood and supported this process to the degree possible by mediating between the two belligerents and by gradually assuming a military relationship with Egypt. Arms sales played a growing role, reassuring the Egyptian military and providing concrete underpinnings to the United States's diplomatic assurances. Yet in the popular view Egypt remained both a Soviet client and the sworn enemy of Israel. Even those members of Congress who perceived the subtle changes taking place in U.S.–Egyptian–Israeli relations would have had a hard time voting for the arms sales; political realities would have made it extremely difficult.

One can easily imagine other scenarios—envisioning internal conflicts in Korea or the Philippines, for example—in which the United States might have good reason to continue making arms available but where most congressmen could not possibly go on the record favoring weapon transfers. One can even imagine situations involving Iran or Iraq for which the United States might wish to initiate a new arms sale relationship. The requirement of a positive vote would make such weapon transfers all but impossible.

The degree to which short-term election-oriented political interests dominate congressional decision making may be unfortunate, but it is inherent in our democracy and not to be ignored in designing an appropriate congressional role. This was recognized quite clearly by a congressman who had cosponsored the Biden–Levine legislation:

> I agree with the arguments against requiring a positive congressional vote on all controversial arms sales. For example, we are able to stop objectionable sales to Saudi Arabia without requiring affirmative votes. And if affirmative votes were required, no sales to Saudi Arabia would ever be approved, which would not be in the U.S. interest. *But I co-sponsored it anyway, because the politics were right.*

The second problem with Biden–Levine stemmed from its reversal of the *Chadha* decision's impact. Under its terms, the ability of a simple majority in either House to stop a prospective sale would give too great a sway to parochial political forces. A return to the early days of the Nelson amendment would also give short-term political considerations too great a role. Arms sales as an instrument of U.S. defense policy would truly be crippled; the worst fears of the executive branch would materialize, and the potential negative long-term consequences of congressional involvement might indeed be realized.

Apart from those powers derived from its budgetary authority, congressional involvements in defense policy (to declare war, to consent to treaties) typically require two-thirds majorities. Being derived from those same powers, congressional authority in arms transfer matters should require a comparable consensus.

The third aspect of the congressional role in arms sales decisions—the lateness of its involvement—could and should be corrected. Each year the executive branch makes up an arms sales plan—the so-called Javits list, named after the late Senator Jacob Javits (R.-N.Y.)—to be submitted to relevant congressional committees, as mandated by the Arms Export Control Act. No congressional action is currently required by the act, as the list simply outlines sales likely to reach a decision point during the coming year. Under President Carter the plan was taken relatively seriously, as his arms transfer policy placed a ceiling on the total value of weapons sold abroad each year (excepting sales to formally allied nations). The Javits list became something of a joke during the Reagan administration.

The Arms Export Control Act could be amended to require the Congress to approve the list, using a financial vehicle for this purpose; most sales require U.S. government loan guarantees, for example. Only simple majorities would be required for approval or disapproval. Approval of the list would not constitute final approval of each prospective sale, some of which may not actually come to fruition. However, the need to gain legislative approval would force the executive branch to take the list more seriously, and perhaps eliminate—early in the process—prospective purchases that might cause difficulties.

Legislative considerations of the Javits list, moreover, would provide the Congress an opportunity to make clear which sales it found objectionable prior to their culmination, and without going on record against the specific transaction. Hearings could provide the basis for serious consultations between the branches of government before controversial sales were put on the table. If the executive branch were sensitive to potential problems revealed during congressional review of the Javits list, it could use the congressional debate to help persuade potential recipients not to push for possibly difficult transactions, or to indicate necessary modifications in prospective purchases, while reaffirming the desirability of others.

Prior review of the year's prospective totality of arms sales would help avoid confrontations between the branches and avoid the embarrassment that foreign nations inevitably suffer from such conflicts. It would cause serious consultations to take place prior to any U.S. commitment to go forward with a weapon transfer. And it would permit the necessary play of domestic political forces to take place without jeopardizing the positive effects on U.S. security relations that arms sales are supposed to bring about.

5

Covert Operations

The withdrawal of Soviet troops from Afghanistan in 1989 concluded one of the largest and most successful covert operations ever mounted by the United States. Costing more than $2 billion over eight years, the program to arm and train Afghani *Mujaheddin* achieved an objective that Congressman Charles Wilson (D.-Tex.) characterized as being "completely beyond the realm of anyone's imagination" at its outset.[1]

The successful Afghan operation is a demonstration of cooperation between the executive and the legislature at their best. Not only was the Congress able to review and discuss the operation over a protracted period of time without any breach of security, but it was the Congress that took the initiative to expand the program's ambition and scope.

A resolution sponsored by Senators Paul Tsongas and Malcolm Wallop (R.-Wyo.), passed in October 1984, was the turning point. "It would be indefensible," the resolution stated, "to provide the freedom fighters with only enough aid to fight and die, but not enough to advance their cause of freedom." Six months later, President Reagan signed a classified order stating for the first time that the goal of the operation was to bring about the withdrawal of Soviet troops. The level of U.S. support was doubled in 1985 and doubled again in 1986. And the United States began to supply advanced technology weapons to the *Mujaheddin,* most importantly Stinger anti-aircraft missiles.[2]

The 1980s also witnessed one of the least successful covert paramilitary operations the United States has ever mounted—support of the Contra insurgents in Nicaragua. The operation was notably unsuccessful in the field. Moreover, it was extremely divisive for the United States, repeatedly the subject of recorded votes in the Congress and the source of heated disputes between the Reagan administration and the Democratic-controlled House of Representatives. A variety of incidents led members of Congress from Tip O'Neill to Barry Goldwater to charge executive branch officials with bad faith, if not outright deception; for its part, the administration accused the Congress of leaking classified information and compromising the Contras' security. Eventually, the administration's increasingly desperate attempts to continue the Nicaragua operation in the face of congressional opposition led to criminal actions by a number of officials (and charges of criminal activity against several others), allegations that the Federal Bureau of Investigation and other executive agencies had been misused for political objectives, and new legislation to strengthen the Congress's role in decisions on covert operations.

The contrast between U.S. involvement in Afghanistan and Nicaragua could not be more dramatic. Sponsorship of the key Afghan resolution by Senators Tsongas and Wallop, among the Senate's most liberal and most conservative members, showed that the operation had received the enthusiastic support of virtually all members. The cause was just, the U.S. interest obvious, the U.S. proxy in the field viable and determined. On Nicaragua, however, the Congress was deeply divided; "rights" and "wrongs" were far from clear, the U.S. interest was the subject of vitriolic debate, and the effectiveness of the United States's local client—even assuming full U.S. support—far from assured. Despite massive drives for congressional support on key votes, the administration could barely hold narrow majorities, and even these required extensive compromises on the size and character of U.S. aid and on the degree of involvement of U.S. agencies.

That the Congress had any role in these decisions is testament to the 1970s revolution in congressional participation in defense issues. Its involvement in covert operations was probably more traumatic than in any other aspect of U.S. defense policy, considering that for the first twenty-five postwar years, the U.S. intelligence community had every incentive not to tell the Congress anything about what it was doing, and the Congress had every incentive not to ask. The virtual absence of congressional oversight served the Congress's interests as much as it did the executive's.

After Vietnam, however, the legislature could hardly continue to turn a blind eye on covert operations. To many Americans, a central lesson of the Vietnam War was that large-scale, ostensibly covert, paramilitary operations lead inevitably to overt military involvement. If true, then to cede power over covert operations was to cede the

Congress's constitutional authority to declare war. Then-Representative (now Senator) Wyche Fowler, Jr. (D.-Ga.), put it clearly:

> You can't stop a covert war easily or painlessly or effectively once it has begun. If Congress can't approve them through its intelligence committees, before they begin, and can't effectively regulate the manner in which funds are obtained to initiate them, what else can we do? In such circumstances, how effective are the constitutionally-mandated congressional powers of declaring war and controlling the purse?[3]

Exactly in what way the Congress might carry out its mandated responsibilities, however—compromising neither the integrity of covert operations nor its own political interests—has been a source of continuing conflict between the branches. As in other areas of defense policy, congressional attitudes swung from overt hostility to executive branch initiatives in the early post–Vietnam War years to unquestioning, almost servile support in the very early 1980s. In more recent years, congressional attitudes have returned to the center, tending to judge each operation on its merits, and reflecting its new confidence in the Congress's rightful role in defense policy decisions. The Congress has concluded both that the executive has no monopoly of wisdom in this area, and that it can make an important contribution to sound judgments on these sensitive and risky operations.

Congressional "Undersight," 1947–1974

The National Security Act of 1947, which created the Central Intelligence Agency, provides a logical starting point for an analysis of the Congress's oversight role. The agency's creation was motivated in part by the intelligence failures of Pearl Harbor and the associated realization that good intelligence was essential in peacetime. Accordingly, the CIA was tasked primarily with intelligence-gathering and analytical duties. But the 1947 act also specified that the CIA could be called upon "to perform such other functions and duties related to intelligence affecting the national security as the National Security Council may from time to time direct." This provision served as the statutory basis for the agency's involvement in covert activities. The vagueness with which the act addressed the CIA's purpose became a source of consternation in the late 1970s when measures were proposed to draft a detailed legislative charter for the intelligence community.[4]

The act also created the director of central intelligence (DCI), an official who would not only run the CIA, but would coordinate the activities of all government agencies involved in intelligence. The DCI, furthermore, was to serve as the president's senior adviser on intelligence matters. In recent years, concern about the director's many, sometimes competing, responsibilities has prompted legislative proposals to divide his duties.[5]

A second early piece of legislation, drafted primarily to define the spending powers of the CIA and its officers, also affected the oversight process. In the Central Intelligence Agency Act of 1949 the agency was given the authority to "transfer to and receive from other Government agencies such sums as may be approved by the Bureau of the Budget . . . and any other Government agency is authorized to transfer to or to receive from the Agency such sums without regard to any provisions of law limiting or prohibiting transfers between appropriations."[6] The act exempted the agency from the normal procedures of public accounting for government expenditures and gave rise to the unique way in which CIA appropriations were, and essentially still are, handled: a select few legislators on the Defense Appropriations subcommittees were given the task of hiding the CIA's funds in other agencies' spending bills (primarily the Defense Department's), from which the money was transferred secretly to the CIA.

Attempts to hide the CIA's funds were not always successful. Former Senator Richard Schweiker (R.-Pa.), for example, recalled that he had once asked why a defense appropriations bill contained $1.7 billion for spare parts. "I was turned down and turned down," he said, "but finally someone called me aside and said, 'Hey, that's CIA money.' " In general, the fact that the CIA's budget was hidden in other accounts, as well as the existence since 1952 of a "reserve for contingencies" within the agency's budget, meant that all but a very few legislators—no more than two dozen at any one time—lacked access to the most powerful congressional instrument for controlling the activities of executive agencies: the power of the purse.[7]

Oversight of the CIA was formally vested initially in special intelligence subpanels of the Appropriations and Armed Services committees. The Senate Defense Appropriations Subcommittee established its own Subcommittee on Intelligence Operations; its House counterpart had a more informal arrangement, with CIA responsibilities reserved for the five senior members of the panel. Membership on the intelligence subcommittees often overlapped: in 1956, for example, of the five legislators on the Senate Armed Services Committee's Subcommittee on Intelligence, three also held seats on the Defense Appropriations Subcommittee's intelligence panel, meaning that ten slots were filled by seven senators. Indeed, for a period during the 1960s, the two Senate panels overlapped to such an extent that they began to operate jointly.

Restricted membership aside, the four intelligence subcommittees were never accorded high marks as watchdogs. As one former member of the House Armed Services panel said, "We met annually—one time a year, for a period of two hours in which we accomplished virtually nothing." In some years, apparently, the Intelligence Subcommittee of Senate Armed Services did not meet at all. Attendance at those hearings that did take place was low, and questioning tended to be less than vigorous. One source recounts a CIA official's story of an elderly committee chairman who, "when shown a diagram of covert actions, demanded to know 'what the hell are you doing in covert parliamentary operations?' When reassured that the chart read 'paramilitary operations,' he shot back: 'The more of these the better—just don't go fooling around with parliamentary stuff—you don't know enough about it.' "[8]

Critics of the oversight system contend that the CIA reduced the effectiveness of congressional scrutiny by co-opting the panel members, thus avoiding any antagonisms that might have led to rigorous inquiries, and by withholding details of operations except when questioned directly. One CIA official said, "[We] give them a peek under the rug and their eyes pop out. It doesn't take long before the congressional overseers acquire that old-school feeling." The 1949 act mandated that the director of central intelligence protect intelligence sources and methods from unauthorized disclosure, a provision that critics claim had been used to justify a lack of candor. But the agency needed little excuse. Its attitude was expressed clearly by former Director Allen Dulles when he reportedly told a colleague, "I'll fudge the truth to the oversight committee, but I'll tell the chairman the truth—that is, if he wants to know."[9]

The overseers denied any laxity on their part. Senate Armed Services Committee Chairman Richard Russell, for example, during floor debate on a 1956 measure to establish a separate intelligence committee, said that:

> The Central Intelligence Agency does report to the Armed Services Committee when it is supposed to do so. I have stated that they have answered frankly, forthrightly, and fully every question asked by the Armed Services Committee.[10]

Russell added that to his knowledge the CIA has behaved just as correctly in testimony before the appropriations panel. His statement, however, failed to address two key concerns: (1) Whether the committees knew enough about the CIA's operations to ask the right questions and (2) whether the members really wanted to find out much about them, because knowledge of covert operations would confer upon them some measure of responsibility for the consequences.

The intelligence panels' passivity meant that the only real oversight was exercised by a very few legislators, particularly Senator Russell, who for years chaired both the Senate Armed Services Committee and its intelligence subcommittee, and who from 1963 to 1968 chaired the Defense Appropriations Subcommittee (and, presumably, its intelligence panel) as well. Russell's enormous authority has been attested to by former Secretary of State Dean Rusk:

> I never saw a budget of the CIA, for example, although I was a statutory member of the National Security Council. The CIA's budget apparently went to two or three specially cleared people in the Bureau of the Budget, then ran briefly by the President, turned over to Senator Russell, and that was the end of it. He would lose the CIA budget in the defense budget and he wouldn't let anybody question it. There were no public hearings on it. So again his judgment, his word on that was the last word.[11]

Senator Russell was seen by many as sympathetic to the CIA, as were the two other prominent senators concerned with these issues, John Stennis and John McClellan (D.-Ark.). Less is known about how the House system operated, but it is likely that Congressmen George Mahon and Carl Vinson, longtime chairmen of the Defense Appropriations and Armed Services panels, respectively, as well as Vinson's successor, L. Mendel Rivers, played roles similar to, if not quite so powerful as, Senator Russell's.

Even more striking than most legislators' ignorance of CIA operations was the pronounced reluctance of the Congress to change the situation. By the early 1970s, between 150 and 200 legislative measures to alter the oversight system had been put forward, including at least a dozen proposals to create a joint intelligence committee. All were stymied, and only two got even as far as recorded floor votes. One was a 1956 proposal by Senator Mike Mansfield to establish a joint committee on the Central Intelligence Agency, modeled on the Joint Atomic Energy Committee, and drawing its twelve members equally from the two chambers. Although Mansfield indicated that the new panel would consist entirely of legislators already holding oversight positions, the members of the "inner circle" had no truck with the idea. Senator Russell's comment on the Mansfield measure well summarized prevailing congressional attitudes:

> It would be more desirable to abolish the CIA and close it up lock, stock, and barrel, than to adopt any such theory as that all the Members of the Congress of the United States are entitled to know the details of all the activities of this far-flung organization.[12]

Russell and many of his colleagues actually seemed insulted by the inference that they were not doing their jobs properly. Mansfield's proposal was defeated by a 59 to 27 margin.

Ten years later, Senator Eugene McCarthy (D.-Minn.) proposed the creation of a Senate Committee on Intelligence Oversight that would draw its nine members equally from the Armed Services, Defense Appropriations, and Foreign Relations panels. Senator William Fulbright supported the idea of giving the Foreign Relations Committee (which he chaired) an oversight role, and brought the McCarthy proposal to the floor. The plan was effectively defeated when the Senate voted to refer it to Russell's Armed Services Committee, from which, as was expected, it never emerged. Nevertheless, Russell offered to let Fulbright, Mansfield, and Bourke Hickenlooper (R.-Iowa), the ranking minority member of the Foreign Relations Committee, sit in on the briefings of his CIA panel. Fulbright apparently went a few times but gave up, saying, "They never tell you anything down there."[13]

The easy defeats of these legislative efforts suggest that the lack of rigorous congressional oversight cannot be blamed entirely on the CIA. As Senator Leverett Saltonstall (R.-Mass.) put it:

It is not a question of reluctance on the part of the CIA officials to speak to us. Instead it is a question of our reluctance, if you will, to seek information and knowledge on subjects which I personally, as a Member of Congress and as a citizen, would rather not have. . . .[14]

Many in Congress worried that they might disclose classified information inadvertently, or that, having been given access, they would be placed in a position in which they might be blamed for any leaks. For example, one source recounts a story about how Senate Foreign Relations Committee Chairman John Sparkman (D.-Ala.) treated a report he was given on CIA covert activities.

He is keeping that report on him at all times and he probably sleeps with it. He's scared that the agency will leak some of the information contained in the report and then discredit the committee by saying, "See, we told you you can't keep classified information."[15]

Legislators were content to distance themselves from CIA activities for political reasons as well. They wanted neither to appear to be hindering the CIA's fight against communism at a time when a powerful anticommunist consensus dominated U.S. foreign policy, nor to be seen as constraining the executive branch in what was considered its rightful monopoly in national security affairs. There were few political incentives to play an active role on intelligence matters because the public was not concerned, and the closed meetings and classified reports hindered grandstanding in any event. Moreover, there were political risks in the event an operation failed and embarrassed the United States. The legislators might share in the administration's culpability.

The Oversight Revolution

In the early 1970s a number of unseemly CIA activities came to light: among others, a secret war had been conducted in Laos; and the governments of Salvador Allende in Chile, Raphael Trujillo in the Dominican Republic, and Ngo Dinh Diem in South Vietnam had been destabilized and eventually overthrown (although the extent of CIA responsibility was disputed). Most troubling to members of Congress, assassinations of several foreign political leaders had been plotted by CIA officials and, in a few cases, efforts had been made to carry them out. Several attempts, for example, had apparently been made on Fidel Castro's life and, in the cases of Patrice Lumumba, a leftist political leader in the Congo (now Zaire), and Che Guevara, the famous Cuban revolutionary, the CIA's plans appear to have been implemented successfully.

Activism in the field of covert operations increasingly came to be regarded as a logical extension of the more assertive congressional role in foreign policy generally, a tendency spurred in large part by the Vietnam War. One lesson many lawmakers drew from that war was that clandestine operations could lead to deeper military commitments. Extensive CIA activity in the hills of Laos and Vietnam in the late 1950s and early 1960s, for example, was an important source of pressure for escalating overt U.S. military involvement when the South Vietnamese government's position deteriorated in the mid-1960s. A growing public impression that the intelligence community had run amok, particularly following subsequent revelations of CIA domestic activities, created additional pressures for congressional action. In the mid-1970s the Congress began to carve out a more visible role for itself.

Many of these legislative initiatives were unsuccessful. In 1973, for example, Senator Thomas F. Eagleton (D.-Mo.) was unable to include covert operations under the restrictions of the War Powers Act, an effort motivated by his concern that failure to close this loophole would encourage presidents to turn to covert operations more frequently. In 1974 Senators Howard Baker and Lowell Weicker proposed the creation of a Joint Committee on Intelligence Oversight. Said Baker, ''I do not think there is a man in the legislative part of the government who really knows what is going on in the intelligence community, and I am terribly upset about it.'' Their proposal never got very far. That same year, amendments offered by Senator James Abourezk (D.-S.Dak.) and Congresswomen Elizabeth Holtzman (D.-N.Y.) and Bella Abzug (D.-N.Y.), which sought in effect to bar CIA covert activities entirely, were soundly defeated; 1975 measures by Holtzman and Congressman Ron Dellums to prohibit the CIA from attempting to overthrow or to undermine any foreign government met similar fates.[16]

The Hughes–Ryan Amendment

The first successful effort to gain greater congressional oversight of covert operations was the Hughes–Ryan amendment to the 1974 Foreign Assistance bill. Named after Senator Harold Hughes (D.-Iowa) and Congressman Leo Ryan (D.-Calif.), the bill stated that the CIA could not conduct covert operations abroad in peacetime

> unless and until the President finds that each such operation is important to the national security of the United States and reports, in a timely fashion, a description and scope of such operation to the appropriate committees of the Congress, including the Committee on Foreign Relations of the United States Senate and the Committee on Foreign Affairs of the United State House of Representatives.[17]

The amendment stopped short of conferring veto power over covert operations to the Congress; it did not strictly require the Congress to be notified prior to their implementation, nor did it apply to CIA activities intended solely for obtaining "necessary intelligence." At the same time, the Hughes–Ryan amendment did establish a standard of "national security" against which each operation had to be measured. This may not seem like much, but it was an improvement over the 1947 National Security Act, the agency's original charter, which had no such criteria. Further, Hughes–Ryan required the president to be involved in approving all CIA covert operations—again, a step that by contemporary standards appears elementary, but that was revolutionary at the time. Perhaps most significantly, reports to the Congress on the CIA's covert activities, which previously had been given only sporadically, were now required each time an operation was carried out.

The revelations of CIA mischief lent support to the belief that the Armed Services and Appropriations committees, charged with monitoring the agency, had been co-opted. Growing congressional acceptance of this view, and a corresponding loss of confidence in the existing "appropriate committees," helps to explain why the Hughes–Ryan amendment added the foreign policy panels explicitly to the list of agency watchdogs. Indeed, proximal events may have reinforced this perception; the Senate Armed Services Committee failed even to hold hearings on any of the seven legislative initiatives referred to it during 1973–1974 that would have limited CIA activities or changed oversight procedures.

Similarly, although reports about the CIA's activities in Chile had begun to circulate in the Congress and were creating an uproar, Congressman Lucien Nezdi (D.-Mich.), chairman of the House Armed

Services Committee's Special Intelligence Subcommittee, ruled out any investigation of the matter because he considered it a question of foreign policy lying outside his panel's purview. The House Foreign Affairs Committee, however, did not have jurisdiction over the CIA, and thus was unable to summon key witnesses. These shortcomings associated with divided oversight soon became a persuasive argument for establishing separate intelligence committees.[18]

Creation of the Intelligence Committees

In late 1974 the *New York Times* published a shocking account of domestic intelligence-gathering activities during the Nixon administration. Through a special organization within the CIA, files had been amassed on at least 10,000 U.S. citizens. Subsequent revelations of massive programs to intercept mail and eavesdrop on Americans, in many cases in response to legitimate political activities, fueled the nation's outrage. The Congress quickly responded to the uproar over these disclosures; in January 1975 the Senate voted 82 to 4 to create the Select Committee to Study Government Operations with Respect to Intelligence, known more commonly as the Church committee after its chairman, Senator Frank Church. The committee's mandate was not only to investigate the propriety of the CIA's past activities, both domestic and foreign, but also to assess the system of congressional oversight.

After fifteen months of extensive investigations, including a series of hearings that confirmed and elaborated on many of the earlier press reports, the committee and its professional staff of sixty people finished their work. One of the principal recommendations of the committee's final report, which ran 641 pages, was to create a separate intelligence oversight panel that would have jurisdiction over the entire intelligence community and would have to be notified of covert operations in advance of their execution.[19]

The arguments for creating a separate intelligence committee proved compelling: (1) the committees then vested with oversight duties had other responsibilities and thus could not give intelligence matters close attention; (2) because authority was spread over a number of committees, none appeared to be getting the whole intelligence picture; (3) the division of authority complicated the Congress's efforts to speak with one voice on intelligence matters and thus blunted its influence.

Many arguments were made for establishing a single joint congressional committee, primarily as a way of reducing the risk of leaks. When consideration of intelligence oversight reform was delayed by the House, however, the Senate acted to create its own panel. Considerations of turf were not absent from the debate. Senators John Tower, Barry Goldwater, and John Stennis, all members of the Armed Services Committee, expressed the worry that by giving the Intelligence Committee jurisdiction over the budgets of the Defense Intelligence Agency, National Security Agency, and other military intelligence components, in addition to the CIA, the risk of security breaches would increase. Nonetheless, the Senate was determined to exert control over the entire intelligence community. A Tower–Stennis amendment that would have given the new committee oversight and investigative powers, but not legislative or budgetary authority, over military intelligence was defeated 63 to 31, though eleven of the sixteen Armed Services members favored it. Senator Walter Huddleston (D.-Ky.) expressed the majority opinion, saying, ''Oversight without legislative authority is toothless oversight.''[20]

The Senate Select Committee on Intelligence was established officially in May 1976. Authority over the CIA's legislation and budget was taken from the Armed Services Committee and given exclusively to the new panel. The Hughes–Ryan amendment was not repealed, however, meaning that the number of ''appropriate committees'' to which the administration was required to report covert activities was brought to seven (eight after the House intelligence panel was created). Under the new legislation, jurisdiction over the other elements of the intelligence community, such as the Defense Intelligence Agency and the National Security Agency, would be shared with the appropriate standing committees (Armed Services, in most cases). All intelligence agencies and departments were directed to keep the new committee fully informed of their activities in a timely manner, although this directive did not have the force of law.

In the spirit of bipartisanship, membership on the panel was split near evenly between the parties, consisting initially of eight senators from the majority party and seven from the minority, with the ranking minority member designated as the vice chairman. Two members each from Appropriations, Armed Services, and Foreign Relations, as well as two from the Judiciary Committee (because the Federal Bureau of Investigation was also covered by the bill), joined seven senators chosen at large by the majority and minority leaders. To prevent the members of the panel from being co-opted by the intelligence community, as many argued had happened to the Joint Atomic Energy Committee with respect to the nuclear weapons establishment, the law stated that no senator would be allowed to serve on the committee for more than eight years and that, to the extent practical, at least one-third of the panel would rotate with each new Congress.

The House also reacted to the revelations about the CIA's domestic spying. In February 1975 it set up a panel to investigate intelligence matters, but problems soon developed when liberal Democrats on the committee objected to the chairmanship of Lucien Nezdi. Unable to resolve their problems amicably, the panel was dissolved and reconstituted in July, with Otis Pike (D.-N.Y.), a widely respected liberal, as the new chairman.

The Pike committee set itself more prosaic tasks than the Senate's Church committee; it concentrated on assessing the costs and risks of intelligence operations, and the value of the intelligence that they produced. Even so, the committee quickly became involved in a controversy. In late January 1976 it voted to release its final report despite the administration's objections that it contained material that should remain classified. Three days later, a leaked summary of the report was printed in the *New York Times,* leading the House to embargo the complete report until the president certified that it contained no classified information. In February, however, the *Village Voice* published excerpts from a copy of the report leaked to it by CBS correspondent Daniel Schorr; Schorr refused to reveal his sources and was fired by the network. The House spent much of the rest of the year investigating the leaks and as a result did not establish its own intelligence panel until 1977. This turmoil led the Senate to change its own establishing measure from a bill to a resolution, thus obviating any need for House action and avoiding the possibility of a presidential veto.[21]

The House finally did vote (227 to 171) in July 1977 to create the Permanent Select Committee on Intelligence. Other than the slight difference in name, the House panel closely resembled its Senate counterpart. Committee members were drawn from the Armed Services, Appropriations, Foreign Affairs, and Judiciary committees, as well as at large, and were limited to a six-year term. Unlike the Senate panel's close split, however, the division of committee seats between Democrats and Republicans reflected the ratio in the full House, with an initial membership of nine Democrats and four Republicans; it was opposition to this partisan proviso that caused the relatively close vote on establishing the panel. A second important difference between the Senate and House committees is that the latter was given budget powers over the "intelligence and intelligence-related activities of the Department of Defense." In practice, this meant that the House panel gained budgetary authority over tactical military intelligence programs, an authority that has continued to elude its Senate counterpart.[22]

How did the revamped congressional oversight system actually operate in the late 1970s? As noted, with the creation of the separate intelligence panels, a total of eight committees received reports on the CIA's covert operations. Although the Hughes–Ryan amendment stipulated only that these reports be given in a timely fashion, as a rule they were filed less than forty-eight hours after the president had approved an operation in a "finding." Senator Daniel K. Inouye (D.-Hawaii), the first chairman of the Senate Intelligence Committee, ensured that committee members could always be reached on short notice, with the chairman having access to a "secure telephone" at home or abroad. Stansfield Turner, director of central intelligence under President Carter, recalled that during his tenure only three operations, all involving the hostages in Iran, were not reported within forty-eight hours.[23]

Having been designated to receive reports on CIA covert activities, the foreign policy committees had to establish procedures to accept them. According to one source, "In the Senate Foreign Relations Committee, it was agreed that the reports would be received orally from the director of the CIA by the chairman and ranking minority member, with the committee's chief of staff present and authorized to brief any other committee member who asked."

Apparently, not many asked; congressmen were still reluctant to learn too much about covert activities, even after Vietnam. While the Intelligence committees had requested to be kept fully and currently informed, the sheer volume of operations meant that not everything could be reported every minute. According to Stansfield Turner, the practice developed of having full briefings on all activities once a year, with more sensitive operations reported at more frequent intervals.[24]

The creation of the intelligence panels meant that separate authorization bills had to be prepared for them, giving all legislators access to the intelligence community's budget. The committees developed budget review processes that did not differ substantially from most other authorization procedures, but unlike most authorizations, the budget totals and component line items, as well as the committee's report containing its policy recommendations, were kept secret and made available only to members. The actual appropriations for the CIA, moreover, were still handled the old-fashioned way—hidden within other spending bills.

A recurring congressional debate in the late 1970s was whether to disclose the overall intelligence budget. Proponents of the idea argued that doing so would increase public confidence that the intelligence community was under control while permitting a useful debate about how to rank intelligence activities against other national priorities. Release of the aggregate figure, it was argued, would not compromise national security. Critics maintained that a lump-sum figure would be of greater benefit to the United States's adversaries than to the public. Additionally, they said, if any figures were made public, pressures would build to reveal greater details, a development that could end up compromising intelligence operations. As then-DCI William Colby put it, "I think it is inevitable that if you disclose a single figure, you will immediately get a debate as to what it includes, what it does not include, why did it go up, why did it go down, and you will very shortly get into a description of the details of our activities." [25]

In practice, the Congress has accepted Colby's argument; measures that would require disclosure of the intelligence budget total have been defeated consistently by wide margins. At the same time, the House Intelligence and Appropriations committees often disclosed the difference between the administration's request and the amount they approved, although without mentioning what either figure was. The Senate panels tended to be more tight-lipped.

How effective was the new oversight system? Turner, for one, gives it a favorable review:

> Most of all, the requirement to report to the Congress is valuable because it forces the DCI and his subordinates to exercise greater judiciousness in making decisions about which espionage operations are worth the risks. . . . There is a need for a responsible body outside the Executive Branch to make sure that the Executive is not over-enthusiastic in seeking to obtain information important to the national interest. Over-enthusiasm, as we have seen, may lead to excesses. [26]

This accolade leaves aside a number of obvious shortcomings in the oversight system of the late 1970s. The overarching problem was the number of legislators who had to be kept informed about covert operations. The system was generally unwieldy, conducive to leaks, and the number of times that intelligence officials had to testify before various committees was truly burdensome. These problems created an impetus for consolidating oversight procedures that, once the political environment shifted in 1980, occurred fairly rapidly.

The Intelligence Oversight Act of 1980

The Church committee had recommended that a legislative charter be drafted for the CIA and the other components of the intelligence community; in 1977 a subcommittee chaired by Senator Huddelston set about this task. In February 1978 Huddelston introduced the National Intelligence Reorganization and Reform Act, an ambitious 263-page document. It would have replaced the 1947 National Security Act (the fundamental statutory authority for the intelligence community) with a clearer framework stating the purposes of the CIA and the other agencies, and establishing guidelines for the use of covert operations.[27]

The charter proposal, however, was soon overtaken by events: the fall of the shah in Iran, the hostage crisis, and the Soviet invasion of Afghanistan. All of these increased the political risks of appearing to restrict the country's defense options. In the House, which tends to respond to changes in the public mood more quickly than the Senate, some urged a rollback of virtually all the constraints placed on covert operations in the 1970s. This mood made it probable that any Senate action on the charter would have been rejected in the lower chamber. Furthermore, apparently successful executive efforts at self-regulation, including a 1978 Carter administration executive order, undercut some of the impetus behind the charter. These various developments created an atmosphere too politically charged to build a consensus about the proper role of covert operations, a daunting task under any circumstances.

The issue was not fully joined again until 1980, when the Huddelston proposal was cut down to four pages in what became known as the Intelligence Oversight Act of 1980. Most importantly, the act mandated partial repeal of the Hughes–Ryan amendment, so that reports on CIA covert operations had to be filed with only the two Intelligence committees. Congressional conservatives had long considered the eight committees involved under Hughes–Ryan to be excessive, and the change persuaded many of them to back the new proposal. The widespread lack of support for the existing system was revealed when the House defeated 325 to 50 an amendment from Congressman Ted Weiss (D.-N.Y.) to keep the Hughes–Ryan amendment intact.

Liberals had many reasons to support the Oversight Act as well. Provisions that called on all the intelligence branches to keep the Intelligence committees "fully and currently informed" of all their activities were given the force of law. More importantly, the act stipulated that, except in rare circumstances, the committees should be notified prior to the execution of any "significant anticipated intelligence activities," which were defined in an accompanying report as follows:

> An anticipated intelligence activity should be considered significant if it has policy implications. This would include, for example, activities which are particularly costly financially, as well as those which are not necessarily costly, but which have . . . [significant] potential for affecting this country's diplomatic, political, or military relations with other countries or groups. . . . It excludes day-to-day implementation of previously adopted policies or programs.[28]

DCI Stansfield Turner had argued against putting prior notification provisions into law, stating that because of the risk of leaks, "Rigid statutory requirements regarding full and prior congressional access to intelligence information will have an inhibiting effect upon the willingness of individuals and organizations to cooperate with our country." He preferred the Hughes–Ryan language, which mandated notification "in a timely manner," but in fact the executive had in all but a few cases elected to report beforehand even under Hughes–Ryan.[29]

Many members of Congress agreed that prior notification of a covert operation might not always be advisable or even possible, and were willing to make allowances. Indeed, the main legislative battle over the Intelligence Act in the House took place over which members of Congress, if any, would have to be informed in the event the full committees were bypassed. The House Foreign Affairs Committee, and particularly its chairman, Clement Zablocki, fought the Intelligence Committee for a provision explicitly permitting a complete waiver of prior notification under certain circumstances. Zablocki's parliamentary maneuvers were defeated, in conference, and the House agreed with the Senate that prior notification should go to the chairmen and ranking minority members of both Intelligence committees, as well as the Speaker and minority leader of the House, and the majority and minority leaders of the Senate (a group sometimes referred to as the "gang of eight"). In such cases, the Oversight Act required the president to report to the full committees in a timely fashion, and to explain why notification was delayed. The conference report added that prior notification should be waived only in "rare, extraordinary, and compelling circumstances."[30]

The Senate debate on the oversight bill raised a point, obscure at the time, that became very relevant during the subsequent Iran–Contra affair, namely, that the 1980 act did *not* strictly require that at least some legislators be notified of covert operations in advance of their implementation. The Senate bill as reported to the floor (and as incorporated into the eventual law) prefaced its section on prior notification with the phrase, "To the extent consistent with all applicable authorities and duties, including those conferred by the Constitution upon the executive and legislative branches of Government. . . ." A colloquy between Senator Javits and Senator Huddleston made it clear that the bill deliberately left room for the president to cite constitutional authority as a basis for withholding prior notification even from the gang of eight.[31]

Nevertheless, a few senators maintained that, as Javits put it, "This language should not be interpreted as meaning that Congress is herein recognizing a constitutional basis for the President to withhold information from Congress." Huddleston offered his opinion that the only constitutional basis for withholding prior notice would be when time does not permit. At the same time, both senators qualified their remarks by noting that the White House held a differing view of the Constitution's dictates, and made it clear that the oversight statute had not settled the dispute. All that was strictly required by the act was that the committees be informed "in a timely manner"—as had been the case under Hughes–Ryan. The Congress cannot be held too blameworthy for leaving this loophole, however. As Stansfield Turner indicated, a strict prior notice requirement would likely have been vetoed by President Carter.[32]

The 1980 act did not, then, completely revamp the oversight system. It was careful to stipulate that congressional approval was not required for intelligence activities to be carried out—as with Hughes–Ryan, the Congress did not give itself veto power. Also retained was the requirement for a presidential "finding" for all CIA operations abroad, except for those intended solely to obtain necessary intelligence. During the debate, President Carter suggested reducing the number of operations that would require presidential approval, but this did not meet with congressional support. Senator William Proxmire (D.-Wis.) charged that removing the requirement of presidential approval of CIA covert actions would only give the executive "plausible deniability," what he called "that insidious doctrine which allows the Executive Branch to take secret actions and later deny the existence of such operations." This term became the focus of the greatest controversy between the Congress and the president on intelligence matters during the Reagan administration.[33]

Congressional Oversight in the 1980s

The 1980 act had left it to the president and the Intelligence committees to "establish such procedures as may be necessary to carry out" the law's provisions, and, for the most part, congressional attention to intelligence oversight was focused on working out these procedures. Particular efforts were made to clarify what should be reported to the Congress, and when. The most important development in the early and mid-1980s, however, was the gradual breakdown of trust between the committees and the intelligence community, as personified by its director, William J. Casey. This development contributed materially to the Iran–Contra affair, and demonstrated the limits of any legislated form of congressional oversight. It ultimately became clear that effective oversight requires an atmosphere of mutual respect between the executive and the legislature.

The doubts harbored by many legislators about whether Casey always told them the whole truth were a repeated source of friction. Some described Casey's behavior in terms evocative of the 1950s, when CIA officials seemed reluctant to provide any details about their activities unless a member happened to hit upon the right question to ask. In the words of Norman Y. Mineta (D.-Calif.), for example, a member of the House intelligence panel until 1984, "I've often said that if you were talking to Casey, and your coat caught fire, he wouldn't tell you about it unless you asked.''[34]

During hearings before the Senate Intelligence Committee on John N. McMahon's appointment as deputy director of the CIA, Senator Joseph Biden told McMahon that, ''With some of us at least, the utterances of Mr. Casey are not always as—well, we do not always leap at them to embrace them as being the whole story. . . .'' Many of the committee members, Biden included, had relied on Admiral Bobby Inman (McMahon's predecessor), rather than on Casey, to give them the ''unvarnished'' truth. Senator Goldwater took a moment to elaborate. ''[I]f the new deputy director [McMahon] will develop the habit of pulling up his socks when there was something being said [that was less than truthful] . . . you sit over here and the witness, if he is getting off a bit, just pull your socks up.''[35]

The clincher in the relationship between DCI Casey and the Intelligence committees was the CIA's action to help the Contras mine Nicaraguan harbors, an operation undertaken in the early months of 1984. When press reports about the operation appeared in early April, some members of the Senate Intelligence Committee complained vociferously that they had not been told about it. Committee Chairman Goldwater, normally supportive of covert activities, was particularly piqued because he had denied any CIA role during an early April floor debate on aid to the Contras and had subsequently been forced to apologize to his fellow senators for not having had the facts. He fired off an angry letter to Casey, telling the director, ''I am pissed off!''[36]

It was soon revealed that the House intelligence panel had learned of the CIA's role in the mining operations in late January, when the issue came up during routine questioning, and had received a full briefing about it in late March. Goldwater was furious that his committee had not also been notified. The CIA held that Casey had indeed informed the Senate panel on two occasions in mid-March but had received no indication of greater interest in the subject. Pointing to written transcripts of testimony in which he had mentioned the mining operation, Casey asserted that the CIA had met its obligations and had complied with both the letter and the spirit of the oversight law.

This was more than many members of the intelligence panel could stomach: Daniel Patrick Moynihan (D.-N.Y.), for one, tendered his resignation as committee vice chairman. Most of the senators, Jake Garn (R.-Utah) being the notable exception, did not consider a one-sentence remark in an eighty-four-page testimony—ten seconds of commentary in a two-hour-and-eighteen-minute briefing—to have constituted adequate notification. Indeed, the remark could easily have been lost in Casey's renowned mumbling. Finally, to head off a full-blown confrontation, Casey apologized to the committee in late April for having failed to notify it of the operation adequately and in a timely manner; Moynihan subsequently withdrew his resignation. Apparently the CIA had interpreted the 1980 act as requiring prior notification only of completely new covert operations, like aiding the Contras generally, not of specific activities within those operations, like mining harbors—a very convenient interpretation if one's purpose is to avoid anticipated congressional complaints.

In the aftermath of the mining affair, Senators Moynihan and Goldwater pressed for formal clarification of what activities the committee should be notified about, and when. A list of procedures was drafted by the committee and signed grudgingly by Casey in June. The essence of the understanding was well summarized in a later report on the committee's activities:

> while each new covert action operation is by definition a "significant anticipated intelligence activity," this is not the exclusive definition of that term. Thus, activities planned to be undertaken as part of on-going covert action programs should in and of themselves be considered "significant anticipated intelligence activities" requiring prior notification to the intelligence committees if they are inherently significant because of factors such as their political sensitivity, potential for adverse consequences, effect on the scope of an on-going program, involvement of U.S. personnel, or approval within the Executive Branch by higher authority than that required for routine program implementation. [The harbor-mining operation had been approved by the president in December 1983.]

The agreement was careful to specify that its provisions were subject to the possible exceptional circumstances contemplated in the 1980 Intelligence Oversight Act. Subsequent to the agreement, DCI Casey, "agreed to the establishment of specific time intervals for the notification process," a step that would set a precedent for current legislation.[37]

The agreement did little to strengthen Casey's relationship with the committees, however. Senator Patrick J. Leahy (D.-Vt.), for example, who succeeded Moynihan as Intelligence Committee vice chairman, was skeptical of its value, saying, "Casey, he could sign that as easily as he could birthday greetings." Senator Dave Durenberger, who succeeded Goldwater as committee chairman, also lashed out at the director: "There is no use in our meeting with Bill Casey. None of us believe him. The cavalier, almost arrogant fashion in which he has treated us as individuals has turned the whole committee against him." [38]

The Current Oversight System

Since its inception, the House Permanent Select Committee on Intelligence has grown to include seventeen members, while the Senate panel, which briefly expanded to seventeen members in the late 1970s, has returned to its original fifteen. The House committee currently has three subcommittees: Legislation, Program and Budget Authorization, and Oversight and Evaluation (which assesses the quality of the intelligence given to national policymakers); covert operations are addressed by the full committee. On the Senate side, similar subcommittees existed until 1985, but since then all intelligence matters have been handled by the full committee. The two committees have different staff arrangements: the House panel has a nonpartisan staff of thirteen professionals; the Senate committee has a staff of five (divided between majority and minority), but most of the committee's work is handled by designated members of senators' personal staffs, which brings the effective number to about twenty.

Limits on the number of years a legislator can serve on either committee have withstood the test of time, although there was a challenge made on the Senate side in 1984. Senator Malcolm Wallop, who stood to become chairman, sought to have the limit waived or repealed, while Senator Dave Durenberger, who stood to become chairman only if Wallop stepped down, defended it. Durenberger prevailed.

For reasons of secrecy, the activities of the committees are discussed only in vague terms. For example, the Senate panel's biennial reports on its activities have more than once contained language like the following:

> The Committee has received detailed reports and has heard testimony on covert action programs before implementation, and has actively monitored the progress of those programs once launched. Certain covert ac-

tion programs have been modified to take into account views expressed by the Committee.

According to a more recent Senate report, the Reagan administration gave either the Intelligence committees or the gang of eight prior notice of every covert operation, with the exception of arms sales to Iran (discussed later).[39]

The budgetary procedures of the Intelligence committees have changed little since the late 1970s. Each committee produces a classified "Schedule of Authorizations," as well as a secret annex to the report released to the public, which contains detailed discussions of the various intelligence programs. Prior to floor votes to authorize the intelligence budget, members of Congress (but not staff members) may read these classified documents after signing a statement promising not to reveal any of the information contained in them. Except when the intelligence authorization bills have been centerpieces of debate over controversial paramilitary assistance programs, the intelligence budgets have been passed by wide margins.

Since CIA appropriations are still hidden away in the spending bills of other agencies (most often the Defense Department), one of the few joys for outside budget analysts is to try to uncover where the pieces are buried. Once in a while it is easy. In the summer of 1984, for example, House Appropriations Committee member Charles Wilson added $40 million in aid for the Afghan rebels to an omnibus supplemental appropriations bill. When that amount, and no other, appeared in the air force's "other procurement" account, its true purpose was clear.

The Iran–Contra Affair and Current Oversight Issues

The Iran–Contra affair raised anew the most basic issues of congressional oversight. The Congress had been kept completely in the dark about the secret sale of arms to Iran. Notification was withheld not only from the intelligence panels, but from the gang of eight as well, for at least ten months–from the January 1986 presidential "finding" that authorized the sales to November of that year. It was revealed then only after a Lebanese newspaper broke the story. President Reagan had specified in the "finding" that the Congress was not to be informed until he had determined otherwise. To many legislators, this action represented a direct assault on the prerogatives that had only recently been clarified in the 1980 Oversight Act and the subsequent agreements with William Casey.

The Justice Department's ensuing investigation of the arms sales revealed a second concern: that profits from the sales had been diverted to assist the Nicaraguan Contras when the Congress explicitly had denied such funds, a move that seemed to challenge even the Congress's power over executive branch expenditures.

The House and the Senate reacted strongly to these revelations and moved quickly. In the course of testimony before joint hearings of special committees established to carry out an investigation, National Security Council official Lt. Col. Oliver North, the man operationally most responsible for both the arms sales and the diversion of funds to the Contras, mentioned a conversation with the late CIA director Casey about creating a permanent "off-the-shelf" capability to engage in clandestine operations. In North's words:

> Director Casey had in mind, as I understood it, an overseas entity that was capable of conducting operations or activities of assistance to U.S. foreign policy goals that was "stand-alone," it was self-financing, independent of appropriated monies and capable of conducting activities similar to the ones we had conducted here.[40]

Although North's testimony has not been independently corroborated, and there has been no indication that any such permanent clandestine organization or "enterprise," as it has been referred to, actually was constituted, the mere possibility that the Congress's power of the purse—and thus, in large measure, its vehicle for oversight—might be circumvented was particularly galling to many legislators.

The testimony of North and his superior, former national security adviser Admiral John M. Poindexter, as well as other executive branch officials, further revealed a deep distrust of the Congress and an extraordinary hostility toward the congressional role in covert operations. Resentment and contempt pervade the testimony, along with a sense that only the executive branch is in a position to understand and carry out the activities necessary to protect the nation's interests overseas. After the close cooperation between the legislative and executive branches during the Carter administration, and at least the appearance of a cooperative attitude during the first Reagan term, this hostility both surprised and chilled many legislators.

On what basis had President Reagan decided not to notify the Intelligence committees or the gang of eight of the arms sales to Iran? On the basis of the 1980 Oversight Act, which stipulated that notification had to be provided only "to the extent consistent" with constitutional authorities and duties. In contemplating the reaction to arms sales to the most virulent enemy of the United States, the White House determined indeed that prior notification could jeopardize the operation and thus the president's ability to conduct foreign relations. Further, the administration found the act's provision that Congress be notified "in a timely fashion" to be so vague as to allow the executive branch to delay notification for months, theoretically for years, until the risk of exposure no longer precluded sharing the information with the Congress.[41]

While obviously disturbed by the administration's circumvention of the requirement for notification, Senate Intelligence Committee Chairman David Boren and Vice Chairman William Cohen at first were reluctant to legislate any new requirements, preferring instead to work out a more informal arrangement with the White House. The committee thus sent a letter to President Reagan in July 1987 outlining a number of specific procedures that it believed should be adopted. The president responded in August, describing the contents of what would become a new National Security Decision Directive (NSDD). While most of the Intelligence Committee's recommendations were accepted, the Reagan letter and the NSDD still left open the possibility that, under certain circumstances, congressional notification of future covert operations could be delayed indefinitely.

This loophole left Boren and Cohen uneasy. In September 1987 Cohen introduced a bill (which Boren eventually cosponsored) to replace existing statutes, spelling out more clearly the oversight procedures for both covert operations and other intelligence activities. In its most significant aspect, no provision was made for withholding notification on constitutional grounds. The bill required at least a few legislators to be notified of *every* covert action within forty-eight hours of its approval in a presidential "finding," which itself would be required before the initiation of any operation. The Cohen–Boren position was expressed in the Intelligence Committee report accompanying the bill: "The Committee rejects the notion that the risk of disclosure justifies the Executive Branch's withholding such notice entirely from the Congress where sensitive cases are concerned." Indeed, according to the report, not being notified of covert operations precludes the Congress from discharging *its* constitutional duties.[42]

The administration strongly opposed the Cohen–Boren legislation, maintaining that a requirement for prompt notification under all circumstances constituted an infringement on the president's constitutional authority, and consequently threatened to veto the bill if it were passed. The Senate Intelligence Committee nonetheless reported the bill favorably by an overwhelming 13 to 2 margin. The stage was set for a confrontation between the White House and Capitol Hill when, in March 1988, the Senate passed the Cohen–Boren bill by a 71 to 19 margin, a majority more than large enough to override the threatened veto.

The overwhelming vote in favor of the Cohen–Boren initiative demonstrates once again how nothing unites the Senate like evidence of a violation of its prerogatives by the executive branch. During floor debate Senator Cohen revealed why he had changed his mind about legislating new notification requirements. He was particularly piqued that some rather shady characters had been used as middlemen in the arms sales, while senior members of Congress were kept in the dark. And he railed against the Justice Department's contention that notification of covert operations could be withheld from Congress indefinitely:

> When the executive branch ignores Congress or seeks to mislead it or circumvent it, the ship of state is going to be grounded; it is going to sink in political paralysis. This is the penalty which I think executives will pay, have paid in the past, and will pay in the future when they seek to do this.[43]

The House, meanwhile, had already reacted to the Iran–Contra revelations with a legislative proposal of its own. In April 1987, Congressmen Louis Stokes (D.-Ohio), chairman of the House Intelligence Committee, and Matthew McHugh, also a member of the panel, introduced a measure similar to Cohen–Boren—it would require congressional notification of all covert operations, beforehand in most circumstances, but always within forty-eight hours of the operation's approval or initiation. Hearings were held on the proposal, but when the more comprehensive Cohen–Boren bill was introduced, the House Intelligence Committee agreed to postpone action.

Time ran out on the Cohen–Boren bill in the 100th Congress, as the pressures of the presidential and congressional elections short-circuited the session. Action on the House side was made particularly difficult when Speaker Jim Wright revealed previously secret information about covert operations in Nicaragua, reopening the issue of the Congress's ability to keep secrets. These revelations were so damaging politically that, when the 101st Congress convened in January 1989, Cohen and Boren decided to drop the issue (see Chapter 7).

The Iran–Contra scandal also rekindled attention to a number of other oversight issues that have been raised over the years. The most frequently mentioned is the move to consolidate the two existing Intelligence committees into a single joint committee. A bill introduced in the House, for example, sponsored by the ranking minority member of the Intelligence Committee, Henry J. Hyde (R.-Ill.), would create an eighteen-member panel divided equally between the chambers. A comparable measure introduced in the Senate by then-Senator Dan Quayle would establish an equally divided ten-member joint committee.

Proposals for a joint committee are predicated on the assumption that the more legislators involved in oversight, the greater the threat of compromise. Those who favor the idea, Congressman Howard L. Berman, for example, or Senator Nancy Kassebaum, maintain that if fewer members were involved the executive branch would be more forthcoming in consulting with the Congress prior to carrying out covert operations. They argue that, no matter how detailed the legislated requirements for notification, the president will always find a way around informing the Congress of the most sensitive covert operations if he so chooses. The idea of a joint committee was endorsed by the Tower commission in its report on the Iran–Contra affair, which noted that the number of members and staff that currently are privy to the details of intelligence operations (about sixty-five) "provided a convenient excuse for presidents to avoid congressional consultation."[44]

A smaller committee would certainly reduce the statistical probability of leaks, but it is not clear that this logic should be applied one-sidedly to the legislature. Large numbers of executive branch officials are likewise privy to, and might leak, information. Indeed, the most spectacular leaks about covert operations during the Reagan administration originated within the executive. A decision to supply Stinger missiles to the Angolan rebel force the National Union for the Total Independence of Angola (UNITA), for example, originated with a

Pentagon official. And after his death it was revealed that CIA Director William Casey had divulged the details of dozens of covert operations to the *Washington Post* reporter Bob Woodward, subsequently embarrassing the United States and several of its allies when these incidents were revealed.

In a sense, it is rather naïve to believe that an administration that would withhold notification of a covert operation to a two-committee system would be more forthcoming with a joint committee. Certainly as concerns the Iranian arms sales, consolidation of the committees would have made no difference to the Reagan administration, which was unwilling even to notify the gang of eight months after the fact. And a joint committee would run a greater risk of co-option; it is just too cozy a setup, particularly with a topic as exciting as the derring-do of intelligence operatives. The existence of separate panels permits more members to learn how the intelligence community actually operates, leads to a more informed level of debate, and—as was demonstrated by the Nicaraguan mining operation, when the House's Intelligence Committee, but not the Senate's, uncovered the operation—provides a congressional double check on any administration's more harebrained schemes.

Congress seems well advised to protect its powers to oversee covert operations. The Cohen–Boren bill would have clarified many of the ambiguities in previous legislation about the executive branch's responsibilities for covert operations. More importantly, the proposed law would have closed the major loophole in the 1980 act, making clear that at least some members of the Congress must be informed of every covert operation.

This is not to say that some future president might not ignore, or rationalize an exception to, any new legislation. If a president so chooses, he can keep covert operations involving relatively few people secret from the Congress, just as he can keep them from the highest officials of his own administration. As Congressman Lee H. Hamilton (D.-Ind.), one of the most thoughtful members of Congress on these issues, noted, "There are limitations about what you can do with the language of legal requirements. Fundamentally, it remains an attitudinal problem." [45]

According to Bob Woodward, the Reagan administration's attitude toward the Congress was described by Director Casey in his usual earthy language: " 'These fuckers,' Casey called the senators. Their ideas and statements were 'bull shit.' '' The reasons for Casey's ire had little to do with risks of leaks and the possible compromise of operations, and it certainly was not prompted by perceptions of the Congress's institutional aversion to covert operations (throughout this period, it was the Congress that urged more extensive efforts in Afghanistan). Casey's rage stemmed from differences on substantive policy. Members of the Intelligence Committee disagreed with some of his plans; they found many operations too risky as compared to the potential gain, or simply not in the U.S. interest. The mining of Nicaraguan ports was only one such operation that drew opposition not only from Democrats on the committee, but from key Republicans as well. Briefed on one operation, Barry Goldwater is reported to have said, "That's the fucking dumbest idea I ever heard." And the operation in question was proposed before he learned of the Iran arms sale.[46]

One can only speculate that in contemplating the Iranian arms sales key administration officials recognized that the congressional response would be extremely hostile; negative views within the administration itself, including those of Secretary of State George Shultz and Secretary of Defense Caspar Weinberger, made this evident. Determined, nonetheless, to push on, the president decided to find a way around the 1980 act and found the "constitutional" loophole. A future administration would no doubt find a way around legislation tightening reporting requirements, such as that introduced by Senators Cohen and Boren, as well.

As shown by the failure of the Iran–Contra affair and its consequences, however, seeking paths around the requirement of congressional notification is a mistake for any president. Neither the Congress nor its Intelligence committees nor its "gangs of eight" and "four" actually vote approval or disapproval of covert operations, and no one is suggesting they should. All the Congress can do is to bring the weight of reason and political judgment to bear on ideas for covert operations. As Senator Leahy put it, "Notified of a covert operation, members of the Intelligence Committee can raise the key political question: Would the operation be worth the candle if it were discovered?" If such a discussion takes place early enough, and if questions are raised by members representing different political viewpoints, the notification requirement can prevent serious mistakes.[47]

The requirement for congressional notification might even have a useful deterrent effect. Executive branch officials might think of the need to notify the Congress as a sort of red-face test: if they can't describe a covert operation to a group of congressmen without becoming embarrassed, it probably should not be attempted. The Bay of Pigs invasion would have failed the red-face test had a notification requirement existed in 1961, so too the arms sales to Iran. The United States does not need any more political embarrassments stemming from ill-conceived covert operations. Even if it serves only to dissuade future administrations from doing foolish things, the Congress can play an important role in the secret side of the U.S. defense policy.

| 6 |

War Powers

The pattern, by now, should be clear. In each of the four dimensions of defense policy examined thus far—defense budget making, arms control, arms sales, and covert operations—the balance between the branches has shifted toward the Congress. The Reagan revolution (counterrevolution, really) failed; the procedures and institutions created by the Congress in the 1970s not only held but were reinforced. In the 1980s even more than the 1970s, the Congress has been a primary participant in the defense policymaking process, acting to curb and sometimes to reverse administration initiatives, and, on occasion, to initiate the general direction as well as the specific detail of U.S. policy.

The shift seems permanent, or at least enduring. The Congress shows no sign of relinquishing its greater involvement in defense policy as demonstrated by the strong reaction to the administration's sudden reinterpretation of the ABM Treaty in 1987, and even more pointedly by the rejection of President George Bush's first nominee to be secretary of defense, John Tower, in 1989. When challenged by the executive branch, the Congress has repeatedly shown the will and the means to carry out its prerogatives and, when necessary, to tighten existing legislative restrictions.

There is, however, a major exception to these trends. In one central element of defense policy, war powers, the Congress has drawn back from the power it claimed for itself in the 1970s. Faced with continued resistance from the executive branch, successive Congresses have been unwilling either to tighten obvious loopholes in the relevant legislation or even to enforce existing requirements. The executive branch has opposed congressional interventions in war powers with greater vigor and passion than any other aspect of defense policy. Faced with this opposition, there has been a distinct limit on the legislature's willingness to assume responsibility for the commitment of U.S. troops to combat.

The Congress's reluctance to enforce its legislated war powers is a very important exception to its general pattern of assertiveness, concerning, as it does, the very heart of defense policy. In a sense, all that we have been discussing so far is superstructure—proxies, or sometimes precursors, for the real issue. The vital center of defense policy lies neither in budgets nor in negotiations, but in the power to place American lives at risk. Power in defense policy, in the end, is the power to declare war, or what passes for such declarations in contemporary times—the power to commit U.S. troops to situations abroad in which they would face an actual or imminent risk of military conflict.

The political pressures that caused the Congress to become so centrally involved in defense policy in the 1970s had little to do with defense budgets, and even less to do with arms sales. They stemmed from one fact: that the United States had fought an undeclared war in Vietnam for more than seven years. Without direct authorization by the people's elected representatives, millions of U.S. troops had been sent to fight, more than 50,000 had been killed, and hundreds of thousands wounded, in a country halfway around the world that few Americans had ever heard of prior to 1964. The U.S. economy was wrecked by it; it took a decade to recover. U.S. society was divided more sharply over the U.S. involvement there, and with greater bitterness, than at any time since the Civil War. And all this occurred with only the congressional authorization that is implicit in its annual appropriation of funds for the Department of Defense.

By the end of 1968, regardless of their initial thoughts on the wisdom of the involvement, a majority of Americans wanted their government to find a way out. The political strength of the sentiment was strong enough to cause President Lyndon Johnson not to seek reelection. Both major parties' presidential candidates ran on promises to end the war, and still there was enough antiwar sentiment to create a third party dedicated to that one purpose that qualified for the ballot in nine states. Yet the U.S. combat involvement in Southeast Asia dragged on for four more increasingly bitter years.

During those four years, the antiwar movement was thwarted time and again in its efforts to persuade the Congress to act. The Senate had passed the Gulf of Tonkin Resolution in 1964 in the hot aftermath of an apparent attack on a U.S. destroyer on an apparently innocent mission on the high seas. The Johnson administration used this resolution on every conceivable occasion to argue against the need to seek a declaration of war or to submit to any other direct authorization of the conflict. The Congress also passed the Defense Department's budget each year, defeating in the process a variety of attempts to utilize the power of the purse to curtail the war effort. (Only in 1970 was such an effort successful, when the so-called Cooper–Church amendment to the fiscal 1971 Defense Authorization bill prohibited the use of funds to support U.S. troops in Cambodia. But it was passed only after U.S. troops had already been withdrawn, and proved ineffectual when the Nixon administration decided to resume air operations over Cambodia.)

Individual members of Congress adopted a variety of postures on the war. A very few from the beginning prophesied the futility of the effort and its divisive impact at home. As the war progressed, additional members took high-profile stances in favor of withdrawal, helping to orchestrate the grass-roots protests that eventually turned the executive branch around. But as an institution the Congress found itself without recourse. Despite its unchallenged constitutional authority and responsibility to declare war, the Congress was compelled time and again to acquiesce to unilateral executive branch decisions. The war was initiated, escalated, de-escalated, and eventually terminated by the executive. The Congress lacked effective means to influence those decisions, much less to dominate them. It was unable to transform the grass-roots political forces opposing the war into effective legislative action.

Between 1967 and 1973 the Congress considered several ways of applying its constitutional power to declare war to the situation in Southeast Asia. It sought to ensure timely participation in decisions affecting the deployment of U.S. military forces throughout the globe, at a point in world history when the margin between peace and war was ambiguous, and when technology was rapidly reducing the time available to reflect on decisions to enter combat. The result was a bold and controversial initiative, the War Powers Resolution, passed in 1973 over President Nixon's veto.[1]

In effect, the resolution specifies that three types of actions should take place whenever U.S. troops are introduced into situations of actual or imminent hostilities:[2]

1. The president should consult with the Congress prior to the event, and on a regular basis until U.S. forces have been withdrawn from the situation. This is a relatively weak provision for a number of reasons, not least of which is inclusion of the phrase, "in every possible instance," a loophole that both Presidents Carter and Reagan took advantage of.

2. The president should report to the Congress within forty-eight hours after the commitment of U.S. forces, describing the circumstances, legal basis, and expected scope and duration of the action. Such reports are to be submitted periodically as long as the combat involvement continues.

3. The report of a combat involvement initiates a sixty-day clock. If the Congress does not authorize the action during this period, the use of U.S. troops in combat is supposed to be terminated. This is the heart of the resolution and its most controversial element. In theory, it places the burden of legislative action on the administration and its supporters in the Congress because a positive act is required for the combat involvement to continue; if the Congress does not act, according to the legislation, the president is compelled to withdraw the U.S. forces.

Implementation of the resolution, born in controversy, has proven difficult. The debate over its practicality, wisdom, and legality has intensified tremendously in recent years. The participants in the debate—scholars and practitioners alike—can agree only on the fact that the resolution has not worked as intended and probably never could. It needs to be revised. From President Carter to President Reagan, the *New York Times* to the *Wall Street Journal*, Jesse Helms to Tip O'Neill, there is agreement on this point. As Senator Sam Nunn, a conservative Democrat, put it in 1988, "The War Powers Resolution is 'broke' and should be fixed."[3] Senator Alan Cranston, a liberal Democrat, expressed very similar views:

> the act has been a failure. It has not prevented Presidents from pursuing risky military adventures. . . . It has not facilitated unity between the legislative and Executive Branches. Instead, it has introduced new un-

certainties into U.S. diplomatic and military endeavors . . . the act needs
to be rewritten.[4]

Why has the resolution been such a failure? How might it be revised
to give the Congress an effective role in decisions on commitments of
U.S. forces abroad?

War Powers in Theory and Practice

The War Powers Resolution has been in effect for seventeen years,
covering the waning months of the Nixon administration, the complete
terms of Presidents Ford, Carter, and Reagan, and the first years of
the Bush administration. During this period, elements of the resolution
have been invoked for the fifteen separate incidents listed in Table
6-1. In each case, the executive branch addressed the requirements of
the resolution only with the greatest reluctance, complying only with
the minimum demanded by the political situation, and prompting questions by the Congress about whether or not the resolution's requirements had been adequately fulfilled. Moreover, charges were made
that the resolution should have been invoked, and was not, in at least
six additional incidents (also listed in the table). With only one exception, the executive branch appears to have carried out the absolute
minimum degree of compliance that it calculated was necessary to
avoid a confrontation with the Congress.

Executive branch hostility to the resolution runs deep—over its op-
erable provisions, but mainly over the very concept at the heart of the
resolution: that the Congress should participate in decisions to commit
U.S. forces to combat. From the perspective of the executive branch,
this power is the president's and the president's alone, deriving from
his constitutional authority as commander-in-chief of the armed forces.
In President Nixon's veto of the resolution, he stated it would be unconstitutional, as it would place restrictions on "authorities that the
President had properly exercised under the Constitution for almost two
hundred years." More practically, he argued, the resolution "would
seriously undermine the nation's ability to act decisively and convincingly in times of crisis."[5]

Judging by their actions, Presidents Ford, Carter, Reagan, and Bush

TABLE 6-1. Incidents Relevant to the War Powers Resolution

Resolution cited

President Ford

1. Evacuation of U.S. and Vietnamese personnel from Danang (1975)
2. Evacuation of U.S. personnel from Phnom Penh (1975)
3. Evacuation of U.S. and Vietnamese personnel from Saigon (1975)
4. Rescue of the crew of the freighter *Mayaguez* (1975)

President Carter

5. Attempted rescue of U.S. hostages from Iran (1980)

President Reagan

6. Deployment of U.S. troops in the Sinai Desert in support of the Israeli–Egyptian peace treaty (1982)
7. Deployment of U.S. Marines to Beirut as part of the Multi-National Force (MNF) to supervise the withdrawal of Palestinian forces (1982)
8. Deployment of U.S. Marines to Beirut as part of the second MNF to supervise the truce (1982)
9. Deployment of U.S. tactical air forces to the Sudan to assist the government of Chad against Libya.
10. First U.S. casualties in Beirut (1983)
11. U.S. intervention in Grenada (1983)
12. U.S. air strikes against Libya (1986)
13. U.S. naval actions against Iranian forces in the Persian Gulf (1987)
14. U.S. naval actions against Iranian forces in the Persian Gulf (1988)

President Bush

15. U.S. intervention in Panama (1989)

Resolution not cited

President Ford

1. Reconnaissance flights over Cambodia (1975)
2. Deployments of U.S. tactical air units to Korea in the aftermath of the "tree-cutting incident" (1976)

President Carter

3. Airlift of French and Belgian troops to Zaire (1978)

President Reagan

4. Military exercises, construction projects, and related activities in Honduras (1982–1988)
5. "Freedom of navigation" exercises in the Gulf of Sidra (1986)
6. Convoys of reflagged Kuwaiti tankers (1987)

each have agreed with their predecessor's assessment. As a result, questions have been raised about each of the three key requirements of the resolution—consultation, reporting, and congressional action.

Consultations

Section 3 of the resolution states that "the president *in every possible instance* shall consult with Congress before introducing United States Armed Forces into hostilities or into situations where imminent involvement in hostilities is clearly indicated by the circumstances. . . ."[6] [italics added] This requirement, of course, represents the minimal means through which the Congress could expect to participate in decisions to go to war. Even so, for most of the seventeen years the resolution has been in effect, presidents have generally been unwilling to consult in any serious way, justifying their use of the qualifying phrase "in every possible instance" on a variety of grounds. Jimmy Carter, for example, cited the need for secrecy to mean that the 1980 Iran hostage rescue operation was not an instance in which consultations were possible. Lack of time has been cited even more frequently. A number of mechanistic problems, beginning with the alleged difficulty of contacting key congressional leaders in a timely manner and including the Congress's unwillingness to designate a consultative body, also have been mentioned.

When consultations have taken place, there has been far more form than substance. In almost every instance, congressional leaders have been called in after the executive branch had already made a decision to commit U.S. forces. In the 1975 case of the *Mayaguez*, for example, combat operations were already under way when congressional leaders were first told of the incident; similarly, in 1983 forces were already being deployed when the Congress learned of the decision to invade Grenada.

Congressman Norm Dicks, in an interview, referred to the consultative requirement of war powers as "a joke." In the case of the 1986 air strikes against Libya, for example, he noted that the U.S. aircraft had already taken off from a base in Great Britain when the congressional leaders were consulted. "We will bring them back if you object," he reports the members were told. Yet there had been plenty of time for proper consultations. The administration had taken several days to decide whether or not to mount the raids, to prepare for it militarily, and to "consult" with European countries whose territories might have been involved in the operation.[7]

Indeed, the term *consult* has almost always been interpreted by the executive branch to mean "inform" rather than "seek the advice of." It was the latter, however, that was the intent of the authors of the resolution, as stated explicitly in the committee report accompanying the resolution to the floor of the House:

> A considerable amount of attention was given to the definition of "consultation." Rejected was the notion that consultation should be synonymous with merely being informed. Rather, consultations in this provision means that a decision is pending on a problem and that Members of Congress are being asked by the President for their advice and opinions. . . .[8]

Basically, as in the case of arms negotiations, executive branch resistance to true consultations stems from an unwillingness to share power. Officials do not seem to believe that the Constitution requires the Congress to share in decisions to commit U.S. forces to combat, nor do they wish to do so, fearing undue constraints on their freedom of action and untoward effects on the United States' position abroad. Moreover, the phrase "in every possible instance" ensures that the requirement need not be taken seriously, except when political considerations dictate a conciliatory approach.

The waning years of the Reagan administration may have witnessed a break in the executive's attitude on consultations, however. After a long and acrimonious debate between the branches (which had been aggravated by the administration's failure to consult in any serious way) concerning the growing U.S. military involvement in the Persian Gulf, the White House reversed course. First with an incident in October 1987, and then even more seriously before an incident in April 1988, the president and his subordinates went out of their way to give congressional leaders a feeling of real participation in the decision-making process. The Congress was both surprised and pleased with this first meaningful effort to elicit its views, and it helped to turn around congressional attitudes on U.S. military operations in the gulf, which previously had been distinctly hostile. These incidents demonstrate the feasibility and the benefits of a real consultative process and thus deserve elaboration.

When it first became known that the Reagan administration had decided to "reflag" eleven Kuwaiti oil tankers and to provide naval escorts to protect them from Iranian attacks during transits of the Persian Gulf, there was very little congressional reaction, even during several hearings and private meetings with executive branch officials. Following the attack on the U.S.S. *Stark* in May 1987, however—which occurred prior to the start of convoy operations and made clear the risks of the activity—legislators began to question the policy and to express concern about the administration's failure to consult with them. On May 21, for example, the Senate passed an amendment that would have blocked the planned "reflagging" until the Pentagon had answered a number of questions about its intentions in the gulf. The administration reluctantly briefed legislators to head off a confrontation, but the White House's erroneous attitude toward consultations was summarized succinctly by presidential spokesman Marlin Fitzwater, "We certainly intend to keep the Congress *informed* of every aspect of the reflagging."

Their desire to be consulted unfulfilled, the Congress continued threatening a variety of legislative devices to prevent the convoy operations. Finally, on June 30, a meeting was arranged between a bipartisan group of more than a dozen legislators and the administration's entire team of top national security officials, including the president. Many of the members hoped to use the meeting to convey their deep-seated misgivings about the escort policy, but the president strongly and immediately rejected the few proposals made to delay the reflagging. The congressmen emerged disgruntled, convinced the meeting had been an empty ritual. House Democratic leaders Thomas S. Foley (D.-Wash.) and Tony Coelho were particularly upset, complaining that a press release about the meeting had been given to some reporters even before the session had begun, clearly signaling the administration's insincerity.

While the House was ready, apparently, to take action to invoke the War Powers Resolution with respect to the convoy operations, the Senate proved unable to act, leaving the administration free to move ahead. Nonetheless, the atmosphere became increasingly bitter, and the debate tied up the Senate for months, delaying a number of administration initiatives. The threat of congressional intervention also remained a live possibility for months, making it more difficult to implement the convoy policy effectively. Some European nations, for example, may have delayed sending warships to the gulf, waiting to see how the debate within the U.S. government would come out. Administration officials claim also that Arab nations bordering the gulf were reluctant to make facilities available to support the U.S. forces there because they feared a sudden U.S. withdrawal.

Eventually, the administration seems to have recognized the costs of this standoff (even though the Congress had been unable to act officially) and initiated a less perfunctory consultative process. In October, following an attack on a reflagged tanker by an Iranian Silkworm missile, President Reagan briefed five congressional leaders the day before the United States retaliated against Iranian forces in the Persian Gulf. Although the decision had been made, it had not yet been implemented, a fact not unnoticed by the legislators.

Perhaps as a result of the congressional support that followed the October incident, consultations prior to the April 1988 incident came even closer to the model envisioned by the drafters of the War Powers Resolution. The president called in the five most senior congressional leaders prior to selecting the specific targets to be attacked (although a general decision to retaliate apparently already had been made). Speaker Jim Wright noted that he and other congressional leaders "expressed our thoughts freely" and had "a very frank and clear discussion. . . . We suggested some reservations," said Wright, although he declined to be more specific. Majority leader Robert Byrd said that "for the first time, we were consulted before the 'execute' order was sent out and before it was decided."

The Congress was satisfied with its role in the April 1988 incident, and, as a result, pressures to invoke the War Powers Resolution diminished sharply. Even after the Iranian counterresponse resulted in a much more extensive series of combat incidents than had been expected, the Congress was unanimous in its endorsement of the activities. It was probably the most visible demonstration of American unanimity with regard to a U.S. military operation since the Cuban missile crisis. The consultations helped elicit further support when the administration decided to broaden the scope of its protective umbrella in the gulf, again consulting with congressional leaders prior to the final decision. Congressman Coelho, previously in sharp disagreement with U.S. gulf policy, now promised to cooperate with the administration. "There will be no fight," he said, "as long as they keep consulting." For its part, the executive branch was equally pleased; an unnamed administration official commented, ''Maybe after eight years we've finally gotten it right.''[9]

Whether or not this experience foreshadows a turnaround in executive branch attitudes remains to be seen. Weakened by the Iran–Contra scandal during the months preceding the Persian Gulf controversy, the administration could ill afford the continuing conflict with the Congress and was in no position to ride roughshod over its opposition. A special circumstance was provided by the fact that the Persian Gulf issue arose shortly after Howard Baker, a three-term senator and former Senate majority leader, had taken over an embattled White House as chief of staff. Baker went so far as to suggest the relevance of the War Powers Resolution prior to the start of the ''reflagging'' operation, a view that was quickly overwhelmed by more conventional executive branch perspectives. Finally, the political popularity of ''Khomeini bashing'' practically guaranteed congressional support for military operations in the gulf. The administration could consult with impunity, knowing it was unlikely to be confronted with hostile views. Still, the consultations prior to the October 1987 and April 1988 incidents do represent a break from past practices; their positive results may encourage future administrations to follow suit.

Reporting Requirements

The War Powers Resolution requires the president to report to the Congress in three types of contingencies: (1) when the armed forces are introduced into situations of actual or imminent hostilities; (2) whenever combat-equipped forces are sent to foreign nations, except for certain specified routine purposes; and (3) when combat-equipped U.S. forces already in a foreign nation are ''substantially enlarged.'' The first contingency is by far the most important; it sets the sixty-day clock ticking. Unless the Congress acts within that period to authorize continuation of the operation, it must be terminated within sixty days, or ninety days if the president requests an extension.

Presidents Ford, Carter, and Reagan generally complied with the requirement to report to the Congress in a timely fashion. There were six incidents (listed in Table 6-1) for which many thought reports should have been submitted, but the disputes concerned ambiguities, not the central problems of War Powers.

The reports that have been submitted under the terms of the War

Powers Resolution have been phrased very carefully, both to underscore the presidents' continued opposition to the resolution's constitutionality and, importantly, to avoid any implication that they were setting the sixty-day clock in motion. Provision 4(a)(1)—the paragraph in question—has been cited only once, in President Ford's report on the *Mayaguez* incident. Insofar as the incident was completed well before the report reached the Congress, there were no implications for the sixty-day clock provisions.

With the exception of three additional incidents (Danang sea lift, Cambodian evacuation, and Sinai peacekeeping operation), when presidents reported deployments of combat-equipped forces in hostile situations, no other reports cited a specific provision of the resolution as their basis, nor have administration officials been willing to be specific in related testimony. In fact, the reports have generally been submitted "consistent with" the War Powers Resolution, not "in compliance with" or "pursuant to" its requirements. In this way presidents have hoped to avoid a confrontation with the Congress over the constitutional issue, yet have still not provided a precedent suggesting acceptance of the legitimacy of the resolution, should its constitutionality ever be tested in the courts. This ploy also put the presidents in a position to ignore the resolution's requirement that forces without congressional authorization be withdrawn, should a Congress ever refuse to sanction continuation of the military activity.

Gerald Ford initiated the practice of not citing a specific provision of the resolution (with the 1975 evacuation from Saigon), and it has been followed by each of his successors. Even when President Reagan reported the 1983 Grenada invasion, an incident clearly fitting the intent and letter of paragraph 4(a)(1), no mention of it was made. Admitting that "as a factual matter, there were hostilities there," Deputy Secretary of State Kenneth Dam refused to admit that the Grenada operation should therefore trigger the sixty-day clock.[10]

Congressional Action

The executive branch's refusal to comply directly with the resolution's reporting requirements has left it to the Congress to determine when a situation exists that should start the sixty-day clock. This has proven difficult for the legislature to do, as a few examples will make clear.

GRENADA

Given the clarity and relative brevity of the action, to say nothing of its popularity, the Grenada intervention posed only an indecisive test of the Congress's ability to act, even though the House of Representatives moved quickly to implement the resolution. After a brief hearing, the Foreign Affairs Committee reported out a joint resolution stating that "the requirements" of section 4(a)(1) had been met, and that the sixty-day clock had started on October 25, the day of the invasion. The resolution passed the full House of November 1, 1983, by a lopsided margin, 403 to 23.[11]

In the Republican-controlled Senate, action came more slowly and more circuitously. Senator Gary Hart introduced a resolution on October 26 very similar to the one passed by the House, but it was not acted upon by the Foreign Relations Committee, to which it had been referred. At the behest of the White House, Chairman William Percy (R.-Ill.) apparently found the need for expedited action unpersuasive. Two days later, however, Hart reintroduced the resolution, this time as an amendment to the debt limit bill then pending on the floor. Surprisingly, the motion passed overwhelmingly, 64 to 20. Given the vividness of the combat on Grenada and the size of the U.S. intervention, a rejection of the proposal would have constituted a clear and public rejection of the War Powers Resolution and of the congressional role in relevant decisions. Even a Senate dominated on defense issues by Republicans and moderate Democrats was unwilling to take this radical a step in 1983.

Because no comparable amendment was attached to the House version of the debt bill, the legislation came back from conference on November 17 with the Hart amendment dropped. What happened in the conference is unclear. The official story was that, because of the urgency of passing the bill (the government technically had already run out of authority to spend money), it was imperative to strip all nongermane amendments to avoid delays. More likely, the Republican leadership found this a handy excuse to drop the amendment, which the White House found onerous, and as the fighting on Grenada had already concluded, the Democrats had little political incentive to hold the leadership's feet to the fire. Somewhat lamely, Senator Robert Byrd, the minority leader, noted that although the Congress had not passed binding legislation the intent of the War Powers Resolution was sustained in that both bodies passed identically worded legislation. While perhaps constituting a symbolic victory, those separate actions would not have constrained the administration in any way.

Beginning before, and ending after, the Grenada intervention, the use of U.S. troops to enforce a truce in Beirut in 1982 and 1983 provided an infinitely more complicated test of congressional attitudes toward War Powers. In the end, the Congress was able to assert its will and force the administration to establish a time limit on the U.S. presence. Beirut proved a Pyrrhic victory, though, providing both the high point and the beginning of the decline in the Congress's assertiveness with respect to the resolution.

U.S. troops first entered Beirut in late August 1982, together with French and Italian units, to supervise the withdrawal of forces belonging to the Palestine Liberation Organization. The U.S. involvement was not popular, and the president wisely consulted with congressional leaders prior to reaching a decision to take part in the operation. The War Powers Resolution was cited in these discussions, and congressional leaders, including both chairmen of the Foreign Relations committees, Congressman Clement Zablocki and Senator Percy, made clear their view that the operation would qualify under paragraph 4(a)(1), requiring congressional authorization within sixty days, if it were to continue that long. Even so, the president's report did not cite any specific provision of the law. No effective congressional complaints were raised, however, and when the intervention ended successfully within a few weeks, the issue was forgotten.

When the internal Lebanese situation deteriorated sharply on the heels of the peacekeeping force's withdrawal, U.S. troops returned to Beirut. This time, consultations with the Congress were desultory. The president's report again did not cite a specific provision of the War Powers Resolution. Although Senators Percy and Claiborne Pell, the ranking minority member of Foreign Relations, jointly expressed their view in a letter to the president that the sixty-day clock would apply whether or not the administration sought congressional authorization for the deployment, no presidential action was initiated.

Instead, the administration argued that the U.S. troops, being on a peacekeeping mission, were not in imminent danger of hostilities. When calm prevailed during the early months of the deployment, this view appeared justified, and no effort was made to force their withdrawal. In June the Congress went on record in the Lebanon Emergency Assistance Act in support of the U.S. presence for an indefinite period of time, although language was added to the effect that the administration would have to seek congressional approval prior to expanding the size of the U.S. forces in Lebanon.

The situations both in Lebanon and in the Congress deteriorated during the summer of 1983, following conclusion of a U.S.-mediated peace agreement between Israel and Lebanon. In the Middle East, factions supported by Syria began to attack the U.S.-supported Lebanese Army, and even U.S. forces themselves. The first U.S. casualties were incurred on August 29. The next day, the administration submitted a new report on its activities in Lebanon consistent with the War Powers Resolution, but again refused to recognize the relevance of paragraph 4(a)(1) and the sixty-day clock.

As the fighting heated up, members of Congress increasingly called for withdrawal of the U.S. contingent, with the War Powers Resolution playing an important role in their efforts. Most importantly, on September 23, the House Appropriations Committee passed an amendment sponsored by Congressman Clarence Long (D.-Md.), which would have cut off all funds for U.S. forces in Lebanon as of December 1 unless the administration submitted a report to the Congress under the terms of paragraph 4(a)(1).

The Long amendment put the congressional leadership and the president in a difficult situation. Given the executive branch's hostility to War Powers, and given Republican control of the Senate, passage of the measure through the full Congress was unlikely. Democratic House leaders were not eager for such a demonstration of their institutional weakness, but at the same time, by forcing the issue, the Long initiative raised the prospect that responsibility for an increasingly unpopular and unsuccessful initiative in the Middle East would be nailed directly to the president and Senate Republicans, just as the country entered an election year.

Congressional leaders of both parties wanted an outcome that avoided making a final mockery of the War Powers Resolution. As Senator Lloyd Bentsen (D.-Tex.) put it, "If the War Powers Resolution is not invoked, it is worthless. It is a scrap of paper and we ought to throw it away." Even the Republican leadership believed this, although neither Senator Percy nor majority leader Howard Baker was prepared to defy the president. Nor were congressional leaders prepared to engage in the full-blown confrontation that might have occurred if the Congress had ordered the U.S. troops out of Beirut and the president had refused to comply.[12]

For their part, the Democratic leadership wished to be seen as acting constructively. Most importantly, Democrats were desperate to avoid a perception of having put American lives at risk or letting down the United States's allies by cutting funds for the operation. The fact that Israel strongly supported the U.S. presence (which was helping maintain Lebanese factions favorable to Israel) was no doubt vital in ensuring Democratic support. Speaker Tip O'Neill, to demonstrate his leadership and statesmanship, seemed to take a personal interest in working out a deal.

Negotiations among the House and Senate leadership and representatives of the administration resulted in the Multinational Force in Lebanon Resolution. The legislation stated that section 4(a)(1) of War Powers had gone into effect on August 29, the date of the first U.S. casualties. It then authorized the president to maintain U.S. forces in Lebanon for a period of eighteen months, with the possibility of an extended deployment if the Congress voted a new deadline.

The measure was passed by the Senate on a narrow vote along partisan lines. In the House, it was brought to the floor by Speaker O'Neill under a very restrictive rule that tightly circumscribed debate and limited amendments to a single proposal similar to Congressman Long's original initiative. According to a staff member who took part in these deliberations, Speaker O'Neill was convinced that the administration's support for the compromise was shaky and that any change would risk a presidential veto. He thus adopted these tactics to avoid changes in the agreement that were small enough to attract broad support on the Hill, but still disabling as far as the administration was concerned. Supported by the leadership and a broad coalition of moderate and conservative members, the resolution passed 270 to 161.[13]

The president signed the joint resolution into law on October 12, 1983. He was careful to assert that his signature in no way indicated acknowledgment of the legitimacy of the relevant portions of the War Powers Resolution, or of any modification of his presumed unlimited powers over military operations deriving from his constitutional authority as commander-in-chief. Even so, a practical precedent had been established. The War Powers Resolution had been utilized as a political instrument to force a true consultative process between the Congress and the president and, in fact, to give the Congress a voice in an important decision on the stationing of U.S. troops in a hostile situation. Senator Percy described the Congress's apparent victory well:

> We cannot legislatively prohibit the President from having reservations about the War Powers Resolution. But we can collectively reaffirm its validity and thereby assure that the next time around we will have a less difficult time reaffirming the clear intent of the Constitution.[14]

Two weeks after the president signed the Multinational Force in Lebanon bill into law, a truck crammed with explosives was driven into a marine barracks south of Beirut, killing 241 Americans. This tragic act transformed the political and military situation in Lebanon overnight, and the deal struck between the administration and the Congress unraveled just as quickly. In early January Speaker O'Neill declared that, unless there were rapid progress toward a diplomatic solution, he would join the many others reconsidering congressional authorization of the deployment. On February 1, a nonbinding resolution calling for "the prompt and orderly withdrawal of the Marines from Lebanon" was submitted to the House Foreign Affairs Committee. At the same time, the Senate Republican leadership was telling the White House privately that an election year was not the time to insist on persevering in a highly unpopular military operation, for which the responsibility seemed likely to be pinned solely on the Republicans. A few days later, the administration announced the "redeployment" of the marines to ships offshore.

The War Powers Resolution had the effect its authors hoped for. It gave the Congress a role in decisions on the commitment of U.S. forces to combat (apart from its appropriating function). In fact, the political dynamic it established in this case persuaded the administration to terminate the operation. But the impact of the War Powers Resolution in the Beirut case was far less direct than the mechanistic procedures provided for in the legislation. A House staff member deeply involved in this legislative history described it this way:

> War Powers is a law that simply doesn't work in conventional terms. If it works at all, it does so in mysterious ways. It can compel the President to act with restraint, and it definitely forces the Congress at least to talk

about the situation. It is a political instrument to force a political accommodation. It is not a legal instrument which can be self-executed.

A political instrument, however, is subject to the whims of politics, and in the subsequent debate on the applicability of the War Powers Resolution to U.S. military operations in the Persian Gulf, the political and institutional pressures bearing on most members of Congress typically caused them to wish to avoid any involvement in these decisions.

PERSIAN GULF

Senator Brock Adams, one of the leading proponents of the relevance of the resolution, put the case to invoke War Powers with respect to the situation in the Persian Gulf this way:

> The reflagging [of Kuwaiti tankers] committed U.S. forces on a sham. It got us started on a military commitment in the Persian Gulf, which can only get deeper. I support the Persian Gulf operation, but the Congress has to be a part of it. The Congress has *the* major role to play in long-term military commitments.[15]

Only a minority of the Senate agreed with Senator Adams, however, even after the United States began to experience casualties as a consequence of the operation.

As noted, the administration had ''consulted'' with congressional leaders for several months prior to the convoy operations, but these sessions had been intended to persuade the legislators to support a decision already taken rather than to seek their advice. The analog with the then-recent Beirut fiasco was clear; a military operation was beginning whose long-range outcome, or even objective, could not be foreseen. While congressional support for the Persian Gulf operations was limited, several legislative efforts to deny funds for the operations failed nonetheless. Both the House and the Senate passed a number of restrictive measures, but the Congress as a whole failed to take binding action. Particularly in the Senate, there was a clear reluctance to challenge the president's authority as commander-in-chief of the armed forces.

A resolution declaring hostilities to be under way and starting the sixty-day clock was introduced in the House after the Iraqi attack on the U. S. frigate *Stark* in May 1987 but was never brought to a vote. Following several incidents between U.S. and Iranian forces in July and September, comparable measures were introduced in the Senate. As described in Chapter 1, this eventually led to passage of the Byrd–Warner measure, requiring only a new report from the administration and some unspecified action by the Congress.

The House, meanwhile, had turned to the courts. In July 1987 Congressman Mike Lowry (D.-Wash.) and 109 other members of the Democratic Study Group filed suit in U.S. District Court seeking a judgment stating that President Reagan was required to file a report on the reflagging operation in the Persian Gulf pursuant to section 4(a)(1) of the War Powers Resolution, and requesting that the court order the president to submit such a report triggering the sixty-day clock. While this action was pending, the group urged the House leadership and Chairman Dante Fascell of the Foreign Affairs Committee to avoid any legislation, a request they were only too happy to honor given the political difficulties of the issue. As a result, a straightforward resolution introduced by Congressman Stephen J. Solarz (D.-N.Y.) that would have declared the resolution in force for the Persian Gulf, and would have authorized the U.S. naval actions "until the security situation no longer requires," did not even receive a hearing. Similarly, the Byrd–Warner measure passed by the Senate received no attention in the House.[16]

In December 1987 the district court dismissed the case, ruling that it would be "inappropriate and imprudent" for the courts to decide whether U.S. troops were involved in actual or imminent hostilities. The court reported its view that such a determination was intended to be made between the executive and legislative branches and, indeed, that the Congress itself had not achieved a consensus on the issue of hostilities. On these grounds, the court declined to accept jurisdiction. Lowry and his colleagues then brought the matter to the U.S. Court of Appeals, which permitted the issue to languish long enough to become irrelevant.[17]

The failure of the House to act on the Persian Gulf stemmed from factors far more basic than the complications of Lowry's legal action, however. Like the Senate, the House feared the political consequences. On the one hand, the actions against Iran were highly popular, fulfilling a desire to "get back" at the Ayatollah for humiliating the United States in 1979. And as long as U.S. forces were more than holding their own in the gulf, few legislators wanted to be seen as second-guessing the president. Yet at the same time, the actions in the gulf held the potential of escalating significantly, perhaps resulting in further losses of U.S. ships, aircraft, and servicemen. After the experience of Beirut, few members of Congress wished to share in the responsibility for future casualties.

More than one member interviewed for this study considered the Persian Gulf incidents to mark the death of the War Powers Resolution, at least with regard to the requirement of congressional authorization for the continuation of combat operations beyond sixty days. The efforts by the Congress to avoid the responsibilities assigned to it by the resolution highlighted the inherent strength of the position of the executive branch.

What's Really Wrong with the War Powers Resolution?

Resolving the impasse over War Powers will not be easy. The Congress is split sharply on the issue, as was made clear during the Persian Gulf debates. There is a substantial group of members who believe that it would be better not to have any legislation on this subject and who thus might welcome an initiative to amend the resolution as a step toward that objective. Senator Nancy Kassebaum, for example, stated that "Ideally [I] would abolish the legislation, as it ties the President's hands too much. There exist ample ways to influence policy without War Powers." She noted that "there was no stronger congressional power than the power of the purse." [18]

Senator John Warner expressed similar views. "War Powers was a mistake," he said. "It is unconstitutional. Congress should have a voice in long-term commitments of military forces, but only through the power of the purse." [19]

A few key individuals continue to support the legislation in its current form, however. Congressman Dante Fascell, chairman of the Foreign Affairs Committee and a drafter of the resolution, is one such supporter. His opposition to change makes any effort to reform the legislation difficult. Other members have no great love for the current resolution but recall the struggle to bring an end to the Vietnam War, and they are reluctant to yield any potential lever that might be used to pressure the executive branch in a comparable future situation. Another group of legislators believe that any change in the legislation would almost certainly reduce the Congress's authority and therefore argue that all revisions should be resisted as a matter of principle.[20]

If reform is to be achieved, the new legislation will have to build on the centrist group of members who believe that the current situation is intolerable. Senator Patrick Leahy expressed this view: "It would be better to have legitimate procedures which everybody supports, even if they are weaker than those in the current Resolution, than the ambiguity and embarrassment which results at present."[21]

By crafting the legislation to satisfy both those who would reduce the Congress's theoretical role and those who would like to see the Congress's real power expanded in practical terms, it may be possible to enlarge the group of potential supporters. Analysis of the history of the War Powers Resolution suggests four major groups of problems in its conception and implementation. An understanding of these may help in modifying the legislation.

CONSTITUTIONAL AUTHORITY

The fundamental problem concerns the relative constitutional authority of the two branches with respect to commitments of military forces. Four presidents have already denied the legitimacy of the War Powers Resolution, and it is almost certain that George Bush will do the same, should his position ever be tested. No president can voluntarily accept public restraints on his authority to direct the armed forces, most importantly on his power to commit them as he believes necessary to support the nation's interests abroad. The struggle between the president's authority as commander-in-chief of the armed forces and the Congress's powers to declare war and to raise and support the army and navy is implicit in the Constitution. The *Washington Post* addressed the problem in an editorial during the impasse over the Byrd–Warner amendment:

> In fact, 200 years of history under the Constitution shows that conflict over "war powers" has been continuous and unending. Far from being a temporary and unfortunate accident of the day, conflict is built into the basic checks and balances of the Constitution and into its very language, which necessarily is sufficiently broad to prevent any settled and final resolution. This is the basis of the assertion that the Congress is an invitation to struggle for the privilege of directing American foreign policy.[22]

Irreconcilable in itself, the constitutional issue has been aggravated by the burden of action required by the resolution. Insofar as a positive joint authorization is required for U.S. forces to remain in combat once the sixty-day clock has been started, a simple majority in only one House can stop any initiative to support the involvement. Even a forty-percent-plus-one minority in the Senate, in principle, might be able to prevent action through filibusters and other delaying tactics. This is equivalent to a legislative veto, an action ruled unconstitutional in the *Chadha* case, as noted in Chapter 4.

The ease with which authorizing legislation could be defeated has hardened the executive branch's antagonism. In fact, in most cases the executive branch has simply refused to play by the rules specified in the resolution. It has issued the requisite reports to avoid forcing the Congress to take action, but it has also carefully avoided making any statement in those reports that would trigger an automatic start of the sixty-day limitation on combat involvement without congressional authorization. It has thus been left to the Congress to declare that those provisions of the legislation are in play. This expanded degree of responsibility has proven to exceed the boundaries of congressional tolerance.

At an absolute minimum, therefore, and as a first step, it seems clear that the burden of action required by the legislation needs to be revised. The Congress should be given the option of either authorizing or terminating any combat involvement. The fate of the operation should not be prejudged; neither its automatic termination nor its continuance should be assumed. Toward this end, the "default setting" should be reversed. In those cases when the Congress chooses not to act, resolution of the situation should be left up to the president in the exercise of his powers as commander-in-chief.

CONSULTATIONS

Problems concerning consultations are both mechanistic and fundamental. The mechanical concerns involve questions of whom to consult, and how to contact them expeditiously in the event of a fast-breaking crisis; these are easy problems to fix. In fact, one suspects that these questions are more artificial than real, being used as excuses by administration officials who are unwilling to consult for other reasons. Situations that require action in less than a matter of days are rare events. An administration sincerely seeking to elicit congressional views prior to reaching its own decision can generally find a way around the absence of a formal consultative mechanism, as was shown during the April 1988 incident in the Persian Gulf.

Still, if the Congress is serious about being consulted prior to commitments of U.S. forces abroad, it is hard to understand why it would not designate a formal consultative body and make arrangements to ensure that all or most of these key legislators could be contacted quickly. The failure to take steps has to do with turf and personal prerogatives. If the group is going to be kept to manageable size, and executive branch concerns about maintaining secrecy assuaged, a number of individuals with some claim to participate will have to be disappointed. In fact, of course, when consultations are carried out, such exclusions are made de facto—but by the administration. The congressional leadership is not accountable, and because the exclusion is done on an ad hoc basis, no member is confronted with formal recognition of his "second-class" status. In the world of politics, being seen to be involved is half the game. This rule of political survival will have to be violated if the War Powers Resolution is to be put into working order.

The more basic problem concerns the executive branch's fundamental antipathy to real "consultations." The word is anathema to most officials, who consider themselves not only far more knowledgeable about international problems than members of Congress, but also far more able to take a national perspective, unburdened by the parochial demands placed on elected representatives.

Yet the benefits of congressional involvement in the actual decision to commit forces are clear—both for tranquility at home and for the effectiveness of any protracted action abroad. It was the unavoidable recognition of this fact with respect to Vietnam that prompted conservative members of the Congress to support the War Powers Resolution in 1973, and it continues to be recognized by some very conservative figures. At his confirmation hearings, for example, Secretary of State-designate Alexander Haig stated, "Heaven help us as a nation if we, once again, indulge in the expenditure of precious American blood, without a clear demonstration of popular support for it. I think the legislature is the best manifestation of popular support."[23] Two years later, then-Secretary of Defense Caspar Weinberger made an equally clear statement, "Before the U.S. commits combat forces abroad, there must be some reasonable assurance that we will have the support of the American people and their elected representatives in Congress. We cannot fight a battle with Congress at home while asking our troops to win a war overseas.''[24]

While honored in principle, the benefits of consultations tend to be ignored in the heat of practice, particularly when legislative requirements are worded as loosely as those in the current resolution. A tightening of consultative requirements is thus highly desirable and might help to persuade a majority of the Congress to relinquish some of the other powers theoretically conferred on it by the existing legislation.

IMPACT ON THE EFFECTIVENESS OF AMERICAN MILITARY POWER

Like so much of the debate on war powers, the resolution's alleged impact on U.S. military power contains a large number of red herrings. By providing the possibility of a deadline on U.S. involvement, the legislation is said to encourage the United States's enemies to persevere in hostile actions. One former executive branch official opined, for example, that ''the Shi'a gunmen in Lebanon carried out their attacks with one eye on the war powers' clock,'' making the Congress, in his view, responsible for the deaths of the marines in 1983. (Obviously, this is nonsense. The terrorists involved in these incidents almost certainly never heard of the legislation, much less were familiar with its provisions, nor founded tactical decisions on the eighteen-month authorization—with the explicit possibility of renewal—provided prior to the bombing of the marines' barracks.)

There is a more serious argument, however; namely, that by potentially reducing the flexibility with which U.S. military forces can be deployed abroad, the legislation automatically limits the potential effectiveness of U.S. military power. A strange little incident during the Carter administration has been cited as giving credence to this view, but in fact it suggests that any deterrent effect of the legislation on the commander-in-chief's willingness to utilize the armed forces is self-imposed.

In 1978 and 1979 the nation of South Yemen, then allied fairly closely with the Soviet Union, carried out a campaign of border incidents and internal subversion against the neighboring state of North Yemen. The events in Yemen apparently greatly worried the Saudis, already concerned about a deteriorating situation in the Horn of Africa, the turmoil in Iran, and the weak response of the United States to visible increases in the Soviet Union's military and political role in the region. While it understood neither the ancient tribal rivalries that underlay the conflict between North and South Yemen, nor the cynical way in which the situation was being manipulated by the Saudis for their own reasons, the Carter administration sought a means of demonstrating its resolve to Saudi Arabia. During a Saturday morning meeting in the White House "Situation Room" called to discuss the "crisis," one administration official stated, "We must show the world and the American people that we understand the permanence of U.S./ Soviet struggle, and that we can take effective action to uphold the interests of those who choose to stand with us in that struggle."

In January 1979, therefore, the administration sent a squadron of F-15 fighters to Saudi Arabia to demonstrate the United States's ability to move military forces to the region quickly. The novel use of U.S. air power was also intended to warn Soviet officials and their friends in the region that the United States was not indifferent to the situation and might act militarily if the hostile forays continued.

Under paragraph 4(a)(2) of the War Powers Resolution, the introduction of U.S. armed forces "equipped for combat" into foreign territory requires a report to the Congress. Not wishing to file such a report, the administration in announcing the deployment made a point of noting that the squadron's weapons had not accompanied the aircraft to Saudi Arabia. Not only were the aircraft's missiles left at home, the administration stated, but even the ammunition for their 20 mm cannons was omitted. This of course ensured precisely the opposite effect as had been intended. It confirmed the then-growing view that the United States was so hampered by the legacy of Vietnam that it could no longer employ military power effectively. The announcement highlighted the political weakness of the president, rather than demonstrating his ability to act.

Why the administration felt it so important to make this statement in order to avoid filing a War Powers report is hard to say. This type of report would not have triggered the sixty-day clock. One can only speculate that the president and his political advisers believed it would dramatize the incident out of proportion to its importance, casting an aggressive light on an administration that had entered the White House committed to pursuing peaceful and cooperative policies in the Third World. Filing a War Powers report might also have been seen as giving credence to conservatives, who were already calling for a more aggressive stance toward the Soviet Union, thus further weakening political support for the administration and its more typically peaceful policies. It might even have been the case that those making the decision simply did not understand the details of the legislation, and feared that if the forces were equipped for combat they would need to obtain congressional authorization of the action.[25]

In fact, of course, the War Powers Resolution confers no special authority to the Congress with respect to this type of gunboat diplomacy; it in no way ties the president's hand. This was demonstrated clearly in 1983 when the Reagan administration deployed tactical and AWACS aircraft to demonstrate support for the government of Chad. A report was filed, and that was that. In the previous case, the Carter administration deterred itself, probably because it did not understand the resolution.

There are more serious implications of the resolution for the utility of U.S. military power, however. They all stem from the fact that, as currently crafted, the powers conferred on the Congress can be implemented only after a military operation has already begun. In principle, by not acting to authorize a military action *already initiated by the president,* the Congress can compel the withdrawal of U.S. forces. In this sense, the resolution accentuates what—in political/military terms—must be considered an intrinsic weakness of democratic societies:.they find it difficult to persevere in protracted military struggles.

The resolution provides an official channel to expedite popular actions to end an unpopular war; it does not create the problem of sustaining long-term democratic support for military involvements. Even so, the resolution's emphasis on termination of a military involvement after the fact, as opposed to before it begins, is troubling. Like any law, the resolution is a blunt instrument; its provision must apply to any situation of actual or imminent combat and cannot be implemented selectively in only those situations in which there is a significant chance of protracted involvement. Thus the War Powers Resolution epitomizes the difficulty that democracies have in persevering in conflicts, by reminding friends and foes of the possibility of a unilateral U.S. withdrawal. This is reason enough for the executive branch to have gone out of its way to avoid invoking the resolution, or at least those of its provisions that would initiate the sixty-day clock.

In practice, the resolution has proven a very weak restraint on executive action. Any Shi'a terrorist counting on the law would do well to study the history of its application as well as its theoretical constructs. As a practical matter, efforts to implement the resolution have led to procedural compromises between the branches in which the president received the authority to continue a military operation, but only in return for accepting a deadline for completing it. (While these deadlines can be extensive, as in the Beirut case, and always subject to renewal, even the suggestion that a point exists at which the United States might withdraw might weaken the U.S. negotiating position.)

The emphasis in the legislation on ex post facto congressional involvement not only complicates the use of U.S. military power, but counteracts the intent of the legislation as well. No politician wants to be seen to be second-guessing the president, particularly with regard to actions in which American lives have been put at risk. According to Congressman Dicks, "The Congress simply does not want to be seen to be weakening the President. It's a political problem."[26] This is the heart of the dilemma.

The desirable direction of reform is thus clear; to the degree that any new legislation mandates a need for congressional approval of combat involvements, the emphasis should be placed on approval prior to the fact. No special legislative authority is necessary for the Congress to terminate a protracted military involvement that, like Vietnam, has gotten out of hand. The Congress's power of the purse will always remain the weapon of last resort. If the country has become so disturbed by a military operation that it is willing to accept the consequences of a unilateral withdrawal, the Congress will always have the option to deny the president the funds he needs to continue to carry it out.

POLITICAL RESPONSIBILITY

The real weakness in the Congress's war powers, in 1990 as in 1970, is the legislature's reluctance to accept political responsibility for actions with the potential to lead either to the deaths of U.S. servicemen or to damage to U.S. interests abroad. Although most members would be reluctant to admit it publicly, the prevailing view is that the executive branch is not only in a better position to reach informed judgments, having the necessary information, expertise, and experience, but also that congressmen have nothing to gain by becoming involved. There are few political rewards for second-guessing the commander-in-chief.

Whenever commitments of U.S. forces are involved, the presumption is that the president knows what he is doing. The War Powers Resolution, as it is now written, puts the Congress in the awkward position of either questioning the president (and thus becoming responsible for the consequences of a unilateral U.S. withdrawal abroad) or standing with the president (and thus sharing the blame in the event of a military disaster or extensive loss of American lives). Most members prefer to do neither. By forcing the issue, the War Powers Resolution makes the Congress's understandable political timidity highly visible. Little wonder that the resolution may be the Congress's least favorite law.

Nonetheless, some members believe that the Congress should share in decisions on U.S. combat actions. Senator Brock Adams, for example, said "Congress has *the* major role to play in long-term military commitments. The Congress cannot run the war, but it should decide whether we're in it." He dismissed the question of political responsibility:

> To me, that is what being a congressman is all about. You have got to share the heat. Those who want to fight the war, or at least want to pose as standing with the President, have to be willing to go on the record in support of the conflict, and an American role in it.[27]

There is no legislative solution to this problem. Most members prefer to defer to the executive branch, letting the administration make decisions on the involvement of U.S. military forces abroad and take the consequences that result from the decision. At best, they would prefer the appearance of involvement at the outset—through consultations—but no requirement to go on the record when it comes to the commitment of U.S. troops abroad.

Resolving the War Powers Impasse

During the debate on war powers with respect to the Persian Gulf, the balance between the political difficulty of revising the legislation and the political cost of continuing to operate with seriously flawed legislation finally led the senators most closely involved in the debate to press for reform. The most comprehensive proposal was drawn up by Senators Byrd, Nunn, George J. Mitchell (D.-Maine), and Warner.

Tabled on May 19, 1988, and referred to the Foreign Relations Committee for "quick" action, the proposal nonetheless died in the 100th Congress, and did not resurface in the 101st. Its provisions, however, merit attention.[28]

Consultations

The Byrd–Nunn–Mitchell–Warner proposal would facilitate the current requirement that the president consult the Congress "in every possible instance" before introducing U.S. forces into situations of actual or imminent hostilities by establishing two consultative groups and specifying requisite procedures:

1. The president would be required to consult "in all possible instances" with a small (six-member) group, consisting of the Speaker of the House, the president pro tempore of the Senate, and the majority and minority leaders of each chamber.

2. A majority of the leadership group could request the president to consult also with a larger (eighteen-member) "permanent consultative group," consisting of the members of the smaller groups plus the chairman and ranking minority members of the Foreign Relations, Armed Services, and Intelligence committees. The president would be authorized, however, to deny a request for consultations with the larger group if he determined that the more limited consultation "is essential to meet extraordinary circumstances affecting the most vital security interests of the United States."

Reports

The proposal would not change the requirement to submit reports to the Congress following the introduction of U.S. forces into situations of actual or imminent hostilities and other circumstances as specified in the resolution.

Congressional Actions

Most importantly, the Byrd–Nunn–Mitchell–Warner proposal would remove the sixty-day limitation on military involvements that had not received specific authorization by the Congress. In the absence of congressional action following the decision to send U.S. forces into a hostile situation, the president would be free in law, as in practice, to continue the conflict for as long as he wished.

The revised War Powers Resolution would create expedited procedures to consider a joint resolution proposed by a majority of the permanent consultative groups to either: (1) require the president to disengage from a situation of actual or imminent hostilities or (2) provide a specific authorization for the action to continue. Such resolutions would be introduced following receipt of a report from the administration of involvement in actual or imminent hostilities, or simply following a conclusion by the consultative group that such a situation existed, regardless of what the administration might or might not have reported. The proposal notes explicitly that any individual member of Congress could submit similar resolutions at any time, but individual actions would not be considered through expedited procedures.

Evaluation

If adopted by the full Congress, changes like those in the Byrd–Nunn–Mitchell–Warner proposal would represent a step back from the war powers asserted by the Congress in 1973. Few would argue against removing the sixty-day clock or deleting the presumption of troop withdrawal in the absence of specific congressional approval. These provisions have few remaining supporters, and their replacement with expedited procedures to either support or require termination of the president's action would move toward a more appropriate neutral evaluation of future military activities. It would permit the Congress to act expeditiously without prejudging the direction of its action.

The Byrd–Nunn–Mitchell–Warner proposal fails, however, by not shifting the focus of congressional action to the consultative process. By preserving the emphasis on congressional options following a presidential decision to commit U.S. troops to combat, the revised resolution would still put the Congress in the position of second-guessing the president. The only real advantage here is that, by removing the presumption that the Congress should act in these situations, it would make it easier for the Congress to avoid taking a position, thereby eliminating what has proven to be a great source of political embarrassment.

The establishment of designated consultative bodies and special procedures as set forth in the Byrd–Nunn–Mitchell–Warner proposal is an improvement over the current resolution in that it provides for greater congressional involvement prior to decisions to commit U.S. forces to combat. However, these measures fail to go far enough. Three additional steps would be desirable.

First, the requirement for consultations "in every possible instance" should be strengthened and tightened. The phrase should be removed and replaced with a phrase that defines the grounds for exclusions in precise terms. Specifically, consultations could be required in every instance, with the sole exclusions of those cases in which the United States itself, or U.S. military forces, or U.S. citizens abroad were facing actual or imminent attack. While a phrase like this could conceivably be abused by a president determined to circumvent the Congress, at least the legal basis for such exclusions would exist, and thus the president's political rationale would have to be drawn more narrowly.

Second, the consultative body and procedures should be defined more broadly. The Byrd–Nunn–Mitchell–Warner proposal would require the president, when he chooses to consult, to consult only with the six-member leadership group. Even if they request a meeting with the eighteen-member group, the president is authorized to refuse on the undefinable grounds of "vital national security interests." This gives the president too much leeway. He should be required to consult with the larger group, and be permitted to ask to meet with the smaller group only on grounds that would be defined extremely narrowly. The language of the amended resolution should make clear that consultation with the smaller group should only take place in exceptional circumstances.

Most situations involving the possible involvement of U.S. forces in combat develop over a sufficiently long period to permit the larger group to be convened. Special procedures could be instituted by the Congress—for example, staggering of trips abroad—to ensure the availability of a quorum within easy range of Washington at any one time; as already noted, the Senate Intelligence Committee's procedures could be used as a model. As for the argument that such a group cannot maintain secrecy, those charges are demonstrably untrue. There have been leaks of classified information from the Congress; there have been many, many more leaks from the executive branch. To maintain that the senior congressional leaders who would comprise the consultative groups would be unable to restrain themselves from compromising information that could jeopardize the success of a U.S. military operation and, with it, American lives, is absurd and insulting.

Moreover, the larger consultative group should be expanded to include four additional members elected by each party's caucus in each chamber. One reason why the War Powers Resolution was introduced and passed in the early 1970s is because the views of the congressional leadership and the views of the broad membership of the Congress diverged increasingly through most of the Vietnam period. As antiwar sentiments played larger roles in elections, support for the war lingered far longer among the more senior members of the two Houses than among the Congress's rank and file. (As described earlier, members seeking a more active role for the Congress in defense policy had to reform the Congress first, and through those reforms gain control of the leadership, before they could even begin to challenge the executive branch.) Election of consultative group members representing the rank and file could facilitate the expression of such changing political views should a comparable situation ever develop in the future. It would also ease the appearance of elitism associated with the current proposal and thus help build support for it in a future Congress.

Third, provision should be made for congressional action prior to the commitment of U.S. forces. This is tricky business in view of the intrinsic conflict between the president's constitutional powers as commander-in-chief and the Congress's constitutional power to declare war. Still, an amended War Powers Resolution could express a preference for U.S. forces to be committed to combat as a result of a joint decision by the president and the Congress, and describe procedures through which such a decision could be acted upon. The consultative groups might be empowered to determine when prior congressional deliberations were desirable and feasible. In such cases, the larger consultative body could replace the usual committee system, reporting out a resolution of approval or disapproval that would be considered simultaneously by both Houses. Limits could be placed on the amount of time each chamber was permitted to consider the measure to facilitate expeditious action.

Obviously, some military actions would not be appropriate for such congressional deliberations. Isolated retaliatory actions, for example, such as the air strikes against Libya in 1986, require secrecy to protect American lives and do not result in a continuing commitment to military action. Similarly, congressional deliberation about responses to hostile initiatives taken by foreign powers, such as the *Mayaguez* incident, would be inappropriate, due to time constraints if nothing else. And in cases of attacks against U.S. territory or military forces or citizens abroad, not even consultations should be required.

Congressional deliberations about military involvements implying a long-term commitment of U.S. power, however, such as the Beirut peacekeeping mission or the decision to convoy Kuwaiti tankers, are not only appropriate, but would strengthen American effectiveness. Because these initiatives have become the functional equivalent of declarations of war, a congressional role is constitutionally appropriate. Political support, moreover, is essential if the country is to persevere successfully in these situations.

Determining which military involvements may or may not be appropriate for congressional deliberation will sometimes be difficult. The Persian Gulf case, for example, would have evoked sharp debate under any circumstances. As a practical matter, and in view of his powers as commander-in-chief, the president must have the ultimate authority. The revised War Powers Resolution, while making clear a preference for joint commitments, should permit the president to forgo congressional deliberations beyond the consultative group, to use the words of the current proposal, ''in those extraordinary situations affecting the most vital security interests of the United States.''

In effect, then, Congress should deliberate commitments of U.S. troops in combat situations only when the executive branch chooses to engage in such deliberations. Nonetheless, formalized procedures for joint actions should exist, and the administration should view recourse to them as politically desirable and practically feasible in most situations. The law should endorse this view and facilitate its implementation.

In the words of Senator Cranston, the adoption of a clause expressing the importance of a joint legislative–executive decision ''would go a long way toward reaffirming the Framers' original intent and lending greater credibility to our military and diplomatic endeavors throughout the globe.''[29]

No legislation, no matter how cleverly worded, can compel either executive branch officials or members of Congress to take a consultative process seriously. While it may be clearly in the nation's interest, as suggested by former Secretary of Defense Weinberger, for U.S. troops to be involved in combat only when there is clear evidence of political support for the operation, the ambiguities of international events, the difficulties of expressing motives and objectives publicly and clearly, and the reluctance of any president to accept curbs on his freedom of action as commander-in-chief suggest that congressional debate and decision prior to U.S. military actions always will be the exception rather than the rule. In most situations, moreover, most legislators will not be unhappy with this, because participation in decisions on war and peace is highly desirable in principle, but raises all sorts of practical political difficulties.

The strengthening of the consultative process proposed here is "user-friendly." It does provide for more extensive and serious private discussions between representatives of the two branches prior to executive branch decisions. And it provides a means for joint decisions prior to a U.S. combat involvement when circumstances warrant such an unusual procedure. By permitting either branch to avoid formal consideration by the full Congress, however, it permits both to avoid public debate without embarrassment in the more usual cases when such discussions are not desirable—for reasons of either policy or politics.

|7|

Reappraising the
Congressional Role
in Defense Policy

The typical executive branch view of the congressional role in defense policy is epitomized by a story told about the 1968 *Pueblo* crisis by John P. Roche, who served in the LBJ White House as special consultant to President Johnson. The *Pueblo* was a U.S. Navy "environmental research" ship that was attacked by gunboats and aircraft while carrying out an electronic espionage mission in international waters off the coast of North Korea. Virtually unarmed, the ship surrendered after a very brief exchange and was taken to a North Korean port, where its crew was held for nearly a year. International humiliation compounded the other serious negative effects for the United States, specifically that highly sensitive, secret cryptographic equipment and procedures had been compromised. The *Pueblo* incident, coming just before the Tet Offensive—the turning point in the Vietnam War—contributed significantly to the nation's increasing malaise and subsequently to President Johnson's decision not to seek reelection.

Roche reports that soon after the outbreak of the crisis the president and his key aides gathered in the White House Situation Room to determine the facts of the seizure. It was unclear at the time, Roche says, whether or not the ship had already been seized and, if so, whether it might still be at a location where a rescue mission could be attempted. Officials conversed frantically on the telephone with military commanders in the field, attempting to determine which U.S. forces were in the vicinity and what options might be available. Aides dashed in and out with maps, photos, and messages. The information in the White House was fragmentary, at best. In the midst of this chaos, a message was passed to President Johnson from Senator John Stennis, chairman of the Armed Services Committee. The senator had called, the message said, to be sure that the president understood that, coming in an election year and on top of the war, the *Pueblo* incident would be a political disaster. If the ship were not rescued, or something else done to seize the high ground, Johnson and the rest of the Democratic party would be made to look like weak and incompetent fools. The message concluded, ''For God's sake, do *something!*'' Looking up from the map board, Johnson is said to have muttered sarcastically, ''Please thank the Senator for his helpful advice.''[1]

This anecdote illustrates the executive branch belief that members of Congress are irrelevant at best, and distinctly bothersome on more frequent occasions. Congressional concerns are said to focus narrowly on elections and politics and hardly at all on the national interest. The Congress is seen as being unrealistic and naive about international affairs; ''Do something,'' they say, without having a clue about either the options or the consequences of action or inaction.

Is this perception of the Congress valid? If anything, it is a rather quaint view, more appropriate, perhaps, for the period when Washington was a sleepy little southern town than for the 1990s (although, thinking back to such greats as Senator Arthur Vandenberg, one wonders whether the caricature was ever valid). Clearly, the picture is too simplistic, but it persists, poisoning the atmosphere for a reconciliation between the branches on defense policy and thus prolonging the struggle between them—a struggle that serves the interests of neither the legislature nor the executive, and certainly not the interests of the nation as a whole.

It may be the case, as suggested by one House aide, that most legislators simply do not have strong feelings on most substantive defense policy issues. The majority may be motivated primarily by personal agendas, legislative relationships, and national constituency politics. A particularly candid congressman reiterated the view: ''When I look at these issues I ask, first, what's good for the Democrats? Unless the Russians are at the gates, and that hasn't happened yet, the substance of the issue has to take second place.''

This attitude is not universal, however. At least those members who sit on relevant committees, where the real action on defense questions takes place, are extremely concerned about policy aspects.

Fifteen years ago, a study by Richard Fenno found that the members of the House Foreign Affairs Committee tended to be motivated by policy considerations to a far greater extent than members of other House committees.[2] Based on my interviews, the assessment appears to be valid for other defense-related committees as well. Congressman Howard Berman, for example, said that he received very little constituent pressure on defense policy questions, leaving him a relatively free hand. What motivated him, then? "I have views on these issues, and I pursue them. I came here for a reason . . . an ability to influence government policy is one of the few advantages of being a congressman.[3]

Stephen Solarz, a senior member of the House Foreign Affairs Committee, echoed the view:

> I came to Washington in order to have an impact on policy and how we [as a nation] conduct ourselves. . . . I have no interest in being a glorified councilman. . . . The Congress has a role to play in determining the nation's defense posture, and I do what I can to implement my beliefs about what that role should be.[4]

Members of relevant committees differ substantially from their colleagues with respect to their knowledge of the issues as well. Many Foreign Affairs Committee members can more than hold their own with senior executive branch officials. Indeed, someone like Lee Hamilton, for example, who has chaired the House Subcommittee on Europe and the Middle East for more than ten years, is likely to be at least as knowledgeable as his senior counterparts in the executive branch and working-level "experts." The former are often political appointees with only limited relevant experience, and the latter (military officers, foreign service officers, civilian bureaucrats) have typically been in the job only a few years, having rotated frequently through a series of assignments intended "to broaden" their expertise.

Senior members of the Armed Services committees can similarly claim greater longevity in dealing with their issues than most executive branch officials with whom they interact. Chairmen Sam Nunn and Les Aspin are among the top experts in Washington on defense questions, while ranking minority members John Warner and William Dickinson have a depth of experience that few executive branch officials can match. By most accounts, members serving on the Intelligence committees have similarly tended to take their responsibilities especially seriously, working hard to come up to speed on relevant issues.

Nonetheless, one should not draw too clear a distinction between members and nonmembers of the relevant committees. Committee members are not motivated solely by policy preferences, nor do nonmembers focus exclusively on political considerations. Committee members are not always well informed, nor are the rank and file always ignorant. In the Congress, as in the executive branch, the resolution of any issue depends on a mixture of institutional, personal, and substantive considerations, and the individuals involved in making decisions on defense policy questions vary widely in the depth of their substantive knowledge. Individuals develop special interests in particular topics for a variety of reasons, often pertaining to their committee assignments, but sometimes based on previous employment, family members' or friends' or constituents' suggestions, or even whim.

Often, what is regarded by the executive branch as congressional ignorance or malfeasance is, in fact, simple disagreement over facts, or differences in judgment. Neither branch has a monopoly on knowledge or on virtue. Individuals in the executive branch, as well as in the Congress, sometimes pursue personal and institutional agendas, just as they both believe that they are seeking to advance the nation's interests. What they are doing, of course, is seeking to advance their perception of the national interest (which itself is shaped by personal and institutional factors as much, or more, as by the facts of the situation). Even if the concept of national interest were an objective phenomenon, the most sincere and well-informed individuals could disagree upon its definition in any specific situation. But because it is subjective, considerations of politics are certainly never far from mind when defense policy issues are evaluated, not only in the Speaker's office, but also in the White House. Officials in the Pentagon have been known to act on the basis of parochial interests, as have members of the Defense Appropriations subcommittees. If the Armed Services committees have been known to take a short-sighted view of an issue, so too has the State Department.

One certainly should not be Pollyannaish about the Congress's role.

There are lazy congressmen, and indifferent ones, and members whose priorities simply will not allow time for defense questions. These are not the ones who invest the energy necessary to learn the facts of defense policy issues. There are also venal members determined to advance their own interests and those of certain constituents or financial backers, regardless of the effect on the national interest. The Congress as a whole, moreover, can sometimes act in a wholly irrational way. At times, when a specific issue seizes the public consciousness, these "feeding frenzies" can bring hordes of members to their feet in a fierce competition to out-demagogue one another. Although flamboyant rhetoric usually suffices as a substitute for tangible action at such times, there is always a risk that totally irresponsible decisions will be taken.

Still, these are exceptions. Most of the time, most members are serious and responsible, hard-working, reasonably well informed on most issues, and extremely knowledgeable about their specialties. The majority, moreover, seek within the confines of their personal and institutional positions to do the "right" thing—"right" for themselves, for their party, and for their country. The differences between the motives of members of Congress and officials of the executive branch are differences of degree and style; they are neither fundamental nor irreconcilable.

The Congress, moreover, brings certain special perspectives to the resolution of defense issues, which permit it to make a unique contribution. The Congress, particularly the House with its two-year election cycle, is clearly in closer touch with the national mood than the executive branch, an important factor in determining which policies can, and cannot, be sustained. The Congress can take more explicit account of competing U.S. interests as well. For many defense issues, there is no single position that serves the national interest. Rather, different outcomes can serve different elements in American society. From the special interests of ethnic groups to decisions about the allocation of the defense budget, the Congress's ability to resolve diverse interests in a democratic fashion is an essential feature of our representative government.

As I. M. Destler, a noted scholar of executive–congressional relations, has pointed out, national security issues are rarely simple struggles between the two branches. More often, advocates of a certain policy in one branch conspire with like-minded allies in the other branch against similar cross-branch coalitions favoring alternative policies. The military services, for example, are notorious for seeking to sidestep decisions by the secretary of defense by appealing to friends on the Armed Services or Appropriations committees. But the services are not alone among executive agencies in finding common cause with like-minded congressmen against the preferences of senior officials, or even the president. Anyone who has served successfully in the executive branch quickly learns these tricks, if only in self-defense. Deliberate leaks of information, forewarnings to congressional allies about forthcoming decisions, carefully rehearsed lines of questioning during congressional testimony intended to draw certain information from a "reluctant" official, wired-up congressional requests for studies or other specific actions, these and many other techniques reside happily in the successful bureaucrat's bag of tricks.[5]

But in a more fundamental sense, debates about the appropriateness of the congressional role in defense policy and about the Congress's ability to play that role are irrelevant. The Congress has been asserting a more intrusive role in the determination of U.S. defense policy for twenty years now—nearly a generation. Many of the members who fought those battles have left the legislature, while others are in senior positions. Every two years, new members enter each chamber who presume an influence in defense policy to be their due. For these younger members, the notion that they should defer to the executive branch on defense issues is totally foreign. For better or worse, the congressional role in defense policy is a reality.

The incentives provided by politics and personal ambitions reinforce the continuance of the new congressional roles. As described earlier, there is now political resonance in many defense issues. They command media time; they inspire campaign workers; they can be used to please important constituent groups and other potential supporters; they can help create fund-raising networks. Even within the Congress, positions on defense policy can be essential—with respect to ambitions for committee assignments, for moving up the leadership ladder in each party caucus, and for relationships with other members.

But political motives are not the primary reason for the Congress's new assertiveness on defense. The "culture" on the Hill has changed to the point where members simply expect to be involved in these issues. It is considered their due, part of the job, and part of the reason for running for office. Congress has consequently developed a far greater confidence in its ability to deal with defense issues, and far less reluctance to challenge the executive branch; indeed, the feeling increasingly on Capitol Hill is that—after the Bay of Pigs, after Vietnam, after Iran, after the aborted 1980s defense buildup, after the Iran–Contra scandal, after so many other lesser incidents of executive branch malfeasance—the Congress cannot possibly do as much damage to U.S. interests as the executive branch already has done.

John Tower, former chairman of the Senate Armed Services Committee and chairman of the commission established by President Reagan in 1987 to investigate the Iran–Contra scandal, laments this greater congressional activism, an attitude that perhaps contributed to the Congress's failure to confirm its former colleague as secretary of defense in 1989. Even Tower believes, however, that the attitude on the Hill has been transformed fundamentally and will not be reversed: "The Iran/Contra incident reinforced the belief that the Executive cannot be trusted. The Congress now believes that oversight is no longer sufficient; the Congress must be active and engaged."[6]

A Compact Between the Legislature and the Executive

The continuing conflict between the branches about responsibilities for defense policy is lamentable. They each have strengths to bring to bear on the nation's problems. They each have a contribution to make. By working together, the executive and the legislature can reconcile the basic dilemma in the American approach to international affairs, namely the conflict between the desire for democratic government, on the one hand, and the need for effective policy, on the other. The former requires a process to resolve competing interests and perspectives. The latter needs coherence and constancy. By sharing power, the branches can narrow the gap to the extent possible. I. M. Destler has described this eloquently:

> In general, the genius of Congress is democracy, diversity, debate. Often Congress nurtures creativity. Nelson Polsby describes the Senate as, "a great incubator of policy innovation in the American system." . . . The executive, by contrast, offers the hierarchy and concentrated formal authority that make coherent policy execution at least possible; . . . there is a need for "decision, activity, secrecy, and despatch" which only the president and his senior advisors can supply.[7]

When the two work cooperatively, the results can be impressive. The positive results of a true consultative process concerning war powers, for example, were evident in the genuine exchanges that occurred prior to decisions (in April 1988) to retaliate against Iranian facilities in the Persian Gulf and to expand the scope of protection offered to neutral foreign shipping by the U.S. Navy. The process resulted in wide-ranging support for the retaliation, which conveyed a far stronger political signal than the action itself. U.S. allies took comfort in the fact that, for once, the Americans were united in support of a military operation and thus the threat of a sudden withdrawal could be put to rest. For their part, the Iranians could hardly have been comforted by the outpouring of congressional support.

Two other recent examples of executive–congressional collaboration are worth mentioning, one pertaining to the defense budget, the second to arms control.

As noted in Chapter 2, the administration repeatedly proposed defense budgets from fiscal 1984 to 1988 far exceeding the totals that a bipartisan consensus on the Hill was willing to support. As the debate on the allocation of government spending became more and more acrimonious, the Congress became more and more assertive in its annual mark-up of the defense budget, departing widely from the administration's spending priorities. The conflict peaked in the fall of 1988, with the Congress moving inexorably toward a budget that the president convincingly vowed to veto. After a lengthy period of exquisitely delicate maneuvers intended largely to avoid responsibility for any tax increases that might be forthcoming, a "budget summit" was held toward the end of the year.

The outcome of the domestic summit was agreement on a fiscal package for both fiscal 1988 and 1989 envisioning a modest increase in revenues, some cuts in domestic programs, and substantial reductions in the planned defense budget. Neither branch achieved all its objectives, and the deficit reduction that resulted fell short of the total that many economists and financiers had hoped for. But the agreement was a true compromise reached on the basis of competing perspectives on the nation's economic needs. As a result of the agreement, the Defense Department had to cut $33 billion (twelve percent) from its planned fiscal 1989 request, a sum that most observers thought regrettable but also necessary in view of the overall fiscal situation.

The effect on congressional consideration of the fiscal 1989 defense budget was electrifying. The process went far more smoothly than had been the case for many years, and the adjustments imposed by the Congress were far fewer. The fiscal 1988 Defense Authorization bill, for example, had not been passed by the Congress until November, well into the new fiscal year. The fiscal 1989 bill was completed in July, in plenty of time for the authorization to serve as the basis for the work of the appropriating committees. In fiscal 1988, the Congress adjusted more than one-half the line items in the defense budget; roughly one-third the line items were adjusted in fiscal 1989.

The Congress certainly did not abdicate its review and oversight functions in fiscal 1989. However, by bringing the overall budget request into line with the consensus on the total amount that could be spent in view of the nation's fiscal situation, the executive provided far less leeway for congressional changes. When the Congress had to cut as much as ten percent of the budget, as it did in fiscal 1987 and 1988, all items were up for grabs. In fiscal 1989, however, when changes had to be kept in balance due to the summit agreement and when every increase in a weapon program had to be offset by decreases in other programs, the room for initiative was constrained. If this practice had been continued, not only would the Pentagon have been more likely to see its programs ratified during the appropriating process, but U.S. defense planning would have become more stable and the management of U.S. defense resources would have become far more efficient.[8]

One other little-noted positive example of collaboration occurred in 1988, this time concerning arms control. The Committee on Foreign Relations reported favorably on the U.S.–Soviet Treaty on Intermediate-Range Nuclear Missiles in March. In late April, prior to the treaty being considered on the floor, the Congress learned of differences in U.S.–Soviet technical discussions over the details of the treaty's inspection provisions. Despite weeks of intense, secret discussions, nine specific issues remained unresolved, four of which were considered extremely important. Yet the administration had assured interested members of Congress that the talks were going well, largely out of concern that the impasse would give weight to opponents' claims that the original negotiations had been rushed so the treaty would be ready for the 1987 Washington summit.

On April 29 Senate Majority Leader Robert Byrd and Minority Leader Robert J. Dole (R.-Kans.), with the chairmen of the Foreign Relations, Armed Services, and Intelligence committees, announced that the start of floor debate on ratification would be delayed at least two days, until May 11, to permit resolution of the inspection issues, and to gain a commitment from the administration to fund new intelligence systems. The Soviet response to the U.S. demands on the inspection system was made in a May 8 letter to Secretary of State George Shultz, conveyed by Ambassador Yuri Dubinin. The response was far from satisfactory, however; indeed, the Soviets linked resolution of the inspection to a wholly new demand on their part. The Intelligence Committee was briefed the next day, after which administration officials and Senate leaders showed a united front when Senator Byrd announced that floor debate on ratification would be delayed indefinitely.

The new delay was announced two days before a previously scheduled meeting between Secretary Shultz and Soviet Foreign Minister Edouard Shevardnadze in Geneva, the last meeting prior to the planned 1988 Moscow summit. The inspection issues immediately rose to the top of the agenda. As a result of the Senate action, Shultz left for the meeting in a greatly strengthened bargaining position; he took with him the implicit threat that if the issues were not resolved to the Americans' satisfaction the treaty would not be ratified prior to the summit and Mikhail Gorbachev would be denied the political fruits of this major accomplishment in foreign policy. Facing a critical Party Conference the following month, Gorbachev could hardly have contemplated the prospect with equanimity.

Indeed, Shultz proved triumphant at Geneva. The Soviet negotiators relented on virtually every point raised by the American side. National Security Advisor Colin Powell flew back to Washington with the agreement; the Senate leaders agreed to bring the treaty to the floor, where it passed overwhelmingly; Senators Byrd and Dole flew to Moscow to deliver the document to a beaming Gorbachev and Reagan.

The incident represents a clear case of the Congress conspiring with the executive branch to put pressure on the Soviet negotiators. Both Republican and Democratic senators were pleased to take credit for the result. Given Gorbachev's desire to celebrate the agreement at the summit, the Senate's refusal to consider the treaty until the implementation issues were resolved was an effective way to strengthen the U.S. position. Collaboration between the branches not only improved the outcome but also led to a smoother ratification process once the treaty reached the floor. Given the last-minute concessions on the Soviets' part, the few possibly effective arguments against ratification had been pointedly undermined.

In this case, the Senate carried out its advisory role extremely effectively, just as the executive branch carried out the actual conduct of the negotiations with great competence. Cooperation permitted each branch to fulfill its responsibilities, bringing its unique perspectives and talents to the problem, with a result that greatly enhanced the U.S. interest. In the words of Senator David Boren, chairman of the Intelligence Committee:

> The Senate's firmness in this regard was crucial, I am certain, in convincing the Soviet Union to meet all U.S. concerns on these issues. The success in Geneva on this matter is an example of what can be achieved when the executive and legislative branches work together and speak with a single voice.[9]

There is a lesson in these three incidents. U.S. interests are best advanced when the branches exercise a degree of comity. They will continue to have differences to be sure—differences of interest, of perspective, of substance. But most disagreements can be worked out in the branches' mutual interest, and in the interest of the nation as a whole. What is required is a degree of tolerance and understanding, and a recognition of the legitimacy of the other's perspective (not necessarily its correctness).

Such collaboration is what was intended by the Framers of the Constitution. As stated by Lloyd Cutler, counsel to President Carter and a noted constitutional expert, "Contrary to popular belief, the powers are not separated in the foreign policy–national security area; they are shared for the most part, and neither Congress nor the President can do much without the other."[10]

As the examples suggest, we may be witnessing a reaffirmation of the Framers' intent. If so, it will have been a reaffirmation born of necessity, the result of the Congress's seizure of greater power over a period of years, and the political circumstances that caused the Reagan administration to cease its efforts to roll back the congressional role and withdraw recognition of the legitimacy of the legislature's undertakings. Reluctantly, in 1987 and 1988 the administration came to the conclusion that it could not defeat the trend toward greater congressional assertiveness, and thus a more cooperative attitude would be the path best calculated to confine its effects. Executive branch officials seem to have concluded, at least in the three instances cited, that by cooperating with the Congress they stood the best chance of ensuring that the outcomes of the defense policy process did not deviate too radically from the policies they preferred.

Assuming that the reality of the Congress's new authority causes the executive branch to again adopt a more cooperative posture, the next step should be to modify the congressional role. In the flush of asserting its prerogatives, it is natural that the Congress may have overstepped reasonable boundaries. Examples of such excesses have been given in previous chapters. Pragmatic means can be devised to ensure that the Congress minimizes its tendency to promote parochial and short-term interests that hinder its effective oversight of the broad outlines of U.S. defense policy. Steps also should be taken to allow the Congress to carry out the specific functions assigned to it by the Constitution without interfering needlessly in the day-to-day management of the nation's defense affairs.

Such reforms, many of which have been noted here, are more likely to be forthcoming in the context of a positive executive branch affirmation of the legitimacy of the congressional role in defense policy. Only then is the legislature likely to make a serious reappraisal of the way it approaches defense policy issues. Confidence is necessary for any institution to reform itself—confidence borne of an acceptance that has yet to be forthcoming in the case of the Congress and defense policy.

What may be necessary, therefore, is an informal compact of understanding between the branches that they share responsibility for the formulation and conduct of U.S. defense policy, and a recognition that it is in the nation's best interest to define their roles cooperatively. On this basis, over time, the two branches might review the various aspects of defense policy with an eye toward improving the effectiveness of current laws and procedures.

A Collaborative Process

The key to effective relations between the branches on defense issues is "collaboration." Existing institutions and procedures must be modified to take account of the reality of the distribution of power mandated by the Constitution: when it comes to national security affairs, power is not separated; the executive and the legislature share it. Neither can function effectively without a degree of collaboration with the other. Emerging arrangements for discussions and consultations might be strengthened to ensure continuity through changes of administration and congressional leadership.

Specific guidelines for improving cooperation might include the four steps described below:

1. When required, congressional decisions should be sought prior to executive actions. As often as possible, executive branch consultations with the Congress should take place prior to even generalized decisions on defense policy and certainly prior to the determination of a specific course of action that would require congressional collaboration. Ideally, procedures should encourage legislative action prior to, or in conjunction with, the executive decision. Nothing is more disruptive for the effective conduct of the nation's defense policy than the reversal of an executive initiative after it has been launched. Even if the Congress chooses not to act, the prospect of such action can have adverse effects on U.S. policy by encouraging the perception of a lack of resoluteness and constancy of purpose.

The tightening of the requirement for prior congressional notification of covert operations, as suggested by Senators Cohen and Boren in 1988, described in Chapter 5, would be a good step in the direction of this guideline. The changes to the War Powers Resolution proposed in Chapter 6 would similarly shift congressional participation in decisions on war and peace from evaluations following a presidential decision to participation in the decision itself. Obviously, this is not always possible, as when U.S. forces or the United States itself were under attack; but in most situations there is plenty of time for a collaborative approach.

2. The Congress should avoid revisiting decisions as much as possible. Procedures for congressional action on defense policy issues should seek to reduce the frequency of congressional interventions while preserving the possibility of action if conditions change or if the original action is demonstrated to have been a mistake. The revisiting of decisions is one of the least desirable characteristics of congressional behavior. To the degree that they impinge on defense policy, they make it more difficult for the executive to impart coherence and constancy to U.S. policy. The practice undermines the effectiveness of U.S. policy by encouraging those who seek alternative outcomes to think that, if they can only persevere, the decision might be reversed.

There are other negative effects of the tendency to revisit decisions. It gives more leeway for parochial interests to come to the fore and encourages the practice of micromanagement through excessive congressional involvement in details. Defenders of current practices note correctly that decisions must frequently be revisited because conditions change or new information becomes available. Such contingencies can be accommodated by preserving the possibility, although not the expectation, of congressional adjustments to established policies.

The proposal in Chapter 4 to have the Congress legislate the comprehensive Javits list of prospective arms transfers each year rather than rule routinely on individual transactions illustrates how this guideline for avoiding revisiting decisions might be implemented. Moreover, it would help shift congressional involvement in arms transfer decisions from its current reactive mode to active participation with the executive branch in original decisions.

The recommendations in Chapter 2 concerning the defense budget process are even more important with respect to revisiting decisions. By shifting to a biennial defense budget and distinguishing more clearly between the authorizing and the appropriating process, most defense programs would be subject to far fewer congressional votes. While specific provision would still be made for the Congress to adjust its decisions as circumstances change, the presumption would change from "all programs must be reviewed several times a year," to "programs should be reviewed only when there are compelling reasons to do so." The net effect should be far greater stability and efficiency in the defense program.

3. The Congress should be encouraged to take a longer-term view. Most significant initiatives in defense policy take a long time to implement. Weapons programs now require an average of twelve to fifteen years from developing a concept in the laboratory to engineering it into an operational capability on a potential battlefield. The SALT I agreements required three years to negotiate, SALT II took seven, and talks in Vienna on conventional military forces in Europe have been going on for fifteen years. The U.S. involvement in Vietnam continued for seven years; the Soviets stayed nine years in Afghanistan; the Iran–Iraq war lasted seven years.

The Congress, particularly the House of Representatives, operates on a relatively short time horizon, however. (So, too, for that matter, does the executive branch in many cases.) Short-term results influence electoral prospects: if a defense initiative cannot be completed in a year or two, politicians at least want constituents to be able to see movement in the desired direction. This short-term focus skews decisions on the types of initiatives that receive the highest-level attention. It also causes an unwise search for "shortcuts," risky options that often backfire. And it leads to frequent changes in U.S. policies that bewilder friends and enemies alike. To the degree that the Congress can be encouraged to take a longer-term view of defense policies, it would add constancy and deliberateness to U.S. policy. The effect could be dramatic if it encouraged the executive branch to take long-term planning more seriously as well.

Fulfilling this guideline, for the most part, is a matter of altering individual outlooks. But a few specific procedural changes could facilitate such an alteration in attitudes. With respect to the defense budget, for example, the adoption of a biennial budget would be a step in the right direction. So, too, would be the proposal (in Chapter 2) to refocus deliberations in the Armed Services committees from the budget itself to the Five Year Defense Program.

4. Greater responsibility should be given to specialized groups. Finally, experience has shown that members of Congress tend to be much better informed and tend to behave more responsibly with regard to subjects within the jurisdictions of their committee assignments. This alone is good reason to depend (to the degree possible) on committees to carry out much of the work of the Congress in defense policy. There are other reasons, as well, including the need for secrecy in many defense initiatives, and the need for rapid decisions in many others.

To a large extent, this is already the case. The Intelligence committees, of course, exercise the Congress's sole influence on covert operations, and most congressional actions on the defense budget take place in committee settings as well. The proposal to legislate the Javits list of prospective arms sales would similarly give the Foreign Relations committees a greater role in this area.

War powers and arms control, on the other hand, span the jurisdictions of several standing committees, requiring innovative organizational schemes. Various legislative initiatives have proposed the creation of standing consultative groups for war powers (proposals with

which I concur; see Chapter 6). These proposals call for a large consultative body consisting of the majority and minority leaders of each
chamber, and the chairmen and ranking members of the Foreign Relations, Armed Services, and Intelligence committees, as well as a
smaller group consisting solely of each chamber's leadership.

If the Congress is to accept and trust such elite units, however, care
must be taken on two accounts: First, emphasis should be placed on
consulting with the larger body; the smaller group should be used only
in situations in which the need for rapid action or some other exceptional circumstance rules out convening the larger body. Second, the
larger body should be expanded to include the Congress's less senior
members. One representative to the larger consultative body should be
elected by each party's caucus in each chamber. There have been situations in the past, notably Vietnam, when the Congress's leadership
was as much out of touch with the popular will, and with the will of
the Congress, as was the executive branch. A voice for hoi polloi, as
it were, could be an effective safety valve should a similar situation
develop in the future.

Although it would be created in the context of the War Powers
Resolution, the consultative body could be used for a wider variety of
tasks. Some proposals suggest that the group receive regular briefings
on world trouble spots so that, should a war powers contingency arise,
they could consider the matter from an informed vantage point.

The executive branch might also utilize the larger group for consultations on arms control, although it might want to initiate such discussions in the smaller leadership body at first. As noted in Chapter 3,
the original intent of the Framers of the Constitution was that the Senate's advice on treaties should be given prior to their negotiation. If
the president accepted that advice and negotiated an agreement in ac-
cordance with it, the presumption would be that the Senate would
ratify the agreement without modification. Serious consultations with
the larger group, in the sense of genuinely seeking congressional views
with a real possibility that the executive branch would seek to accommodate them, could help to restore such a collaborative process.

Former senator John Tower suggests the creation of a "Cabinet
Council" consisting of the individuals proposed for the War Powers
consultative group. This would expand the consultative process to include not only war powers contingencies, but also arms control and
other international negotiations. The council could even be used as the
instrument for regular budget summits, although in that event it would

have to be expanded to include the chairmen and ranking members of the Appropriations, Budget, and Finance committees.

Others have proposed creating a Joint Committee on National Security, patterned after the Joint Economic Committee, to serve as the focus for all consultations on defense issues. As I. M. Destler and others have pointed out, however, excessive centralization can be as harmful as excessive proliferation of contact points. Not least of the dangers would be a rising danger of co-option by the executive branch. A more differentiated approach, building on the functional specialties of the different standing committees, is probably the wiser course.

The Congress's Role

The Constitution has given great powers to the Congress in the area of national security affairs. The powers, among others, to declare war, to issue letters of marque and reprisal, to raise an army, to provide and maintain a navy, to regulate land and naval forces, to tax and spend for the common defense, to regulate commerce with other nations, to advise and consent on appointments, and to ratify treaties, confer great potential for tremendous influence in all aspects of defense policy. These powers cannot be implemented independently, however. The Congress requires the executive branch to execute its decisions faithfully.

Similarly, the president, as commander-in-chief of the armed forces, as the nation's chief diplomat, as the initiator of most policies, and as the operator of all the instruments of the nation's defense, has tremendous powers. Yet the president cannot spend money for any of these activities unless the Congress has appropriated it. He cannot make treaties or appoint officials without the Senate's consent. And, in principle, at least, he cannot make war without congressional authorization.

Clearly, for the nation's interests and security to be protected, the two branches must work together, preferably in harmony. The two branches represent complementary approaches to national security affairs. Louis Henken put it this way:

In foreign affairs, the president represents the United States, and the people of the United States, to the world. Congress represents the people at home, the sum of different groups, constituencies, interests (general and specific). The president leads; Congress legislates. The president represents needs for expertise, secrecy, speed, efficiency. Congress provides wider, soberer, more deliberate, more cautious, longer-term values and judgments.[11]

As the branch of government most directly attuned and necessarily most responsive to currents in public opinion, the Congress has a very special role to play in all aspects of defense policy. It is in the best position to ensure that there is some conformity between the public's expectations and the government's actions. It is clear that the government most often errs when the executive exceeds the boundaries of public tolerance. Jimmy Carter's misjudgment about the public's acceptance of Soviet inroads in the Third World, and Ronald Reagan's misunderstanding of the public's concern about nuclear war, are two recent examples. In cases like these, executive policies have largely been based on ideological viewpoints, or on abstract conceptions of international politics, rather than on the realities of contemporary circumstances. In such cases, the Congress has an absolutely crucial role to play in articulating the public's concerns and, if necessary, in compelling the executive to modify its course. And when the Congress speaks, presidents would be well advised to listen. Both they, and the nation, can benefit from the Congress's contribution to the formulation of U.S. defense policy.

Notes

Chapter 1

1. Public Law 93-148, 87 Stat. 555, 50 U.S.C. 1541–48.
2. After a six-month hiatus another round of assaults and reprisals took place in April 1988. See Chapter 6.
3. *Washington Post,* May 21, 1987.
4. *New York Times,* October 6, 1987.
5. Ibid. Efforts to invoke War Powers in the House fared no better during this period, leading a group of 110 House members to seek judicial remedy by filing suit in federal court to direct the president to fulfill the law's requirements. The suit is discussed in Chapter 6.
6. *Washington Post,* October 22, 1987.
7. Nor did the "War Powers" debate in the Senate end with the passage of the Byrd–Warner bill in October. In November, Brock Adams (D.-Wash.), one of the Senate's most active supporters of the War Powers Resolution, introduced a bill to invoke its sixty-day clock, retroactive to the October 19 attack on Iranian platforms. In order to avoid a confrontation, Senate leaders worked out a deal with Adams under which his resolution was not brought to a vote. In return a new procedure was adopted, making it more difficult to filibuster any subsequent efforts to invoke War Powers during the 100th Congress. In April 1988 Adams introduced a new resolution, this one linked to more recent incidents in the gulf. But the new procedure did not prevent a now-familiar outcome—the Adams measure was shelved on a procedural vote, 54 to 31. See "Clock Set for Senate Vote on Gulf, War Powers," *Congressional Quarterly,* April 30, 1988, p. 1148; and the *New York Times,* June 7, 1988.
8. In the 1950s and early to mid-1960s Congress passed a number of resolutions giving the president broad authority to take military action in various places. Resolutions were passed in the late 1950s covering Formosa (Taiwan) and the Middle East. In the 1960s a number of resolutions were adopted on Cuba, one on Berlin, and, of course, the Gulf of Tonkin

Resolution. For a discussion of most of them, see Marc Smyrl, *Conflict or Codetermination: Congress, the President, and the Power to Make War* (Cambridge, Mass.: Ballinger, 1988), pp. 8–13.

9. *New York Times,* April 19, 1976.
10. *New York Times,* January 19, 1976.
11. Thomas M. Franck and Edward Weisband, *Foreign Policy by Congress* (New York: Oxford University Press, 1979), pp. 155–56.
12. Interview with Senator Nancy Kassebaum, December 15, 1987.
13. Public opinion data taken from Roper polls, in "Opinion Roundup," *Public Opinion* (June/July 1985), pp. 34–35.
14. "1980 Republican National Convention Platform," *Congressional Record,* July 31, 1980, pp. 20630–31, 20633.
15. John Tower, "Congress versus the President: The Formulation and Implementation of American Foreign Policy," *Foreign Affairs* (Winter 1981/82): 234, 242.

Chapter 2

1. There were two military legislative committees in each House, Military Affairs and Naval Affairs, until 1946, when they were combined in each House into Armed Services by the Legislative Reorganization Act. A good description of the Congress's treatment of the defense budget in the early postwar years can be seen in Bernard K. Gordon, "The Military Budget: Congressional Phase," *Journal of Politics* 23 (November 1961): 689–710.
2. Raymond H. Dawson, "Innovation and Intervention in Defense Policy," in *New Perspectives on the House of Representatives,* ed. Robert Peabody and Nelson W. Polsby (Chicago: Rand McNally, 1963), p. 277.
3. Samuel P. Huntington, "Strategic Planning and the Political Process," *Foreign Affairs* 38 (January 1960): 286–88.
4. Until 1990, under congressional rules, members could accept for personal use up to $2,000 honoraria for individual speeches and other appearances before private groups. Congressmen were permitted to retain up to $25,000 in honoraria each year, senators up to $35,000. See "Bombs Away," *Common Cause News,* June 30, 1988.
5. "Congressional Oversight of National Defense," floor speech by Senator Sam Nunn, *Congressional Record,* October 1, 1985, p. 25351 (S12341).
6. Stanley J. Heginbotham, "Congress and Defense Policy Making: Toward Realistic Expectations in a System of Countervailing Parochialisms," in *National Security Policy: The Decision Making Process,* ed. Robert Pfaltzgraff, Jr., and Uri Ra'anan (Hamden, Conn.: Archon Books, 1984), pp. 251–61.

7. In addition to Dawson, Gordon, and Huntington, cited above, analyses of the Congress's early involvement in defense decision making can be seen in Samuel Huntington, *The Common Defense* (New York: Columbia University Press, 1961); Elias Huzar, *The Purse and the Sword* (Ithaca, N.Y.: Cornell University Press, 1950); Edward A. Kolodziej, *The Uncommon Defense and Congress, 1945–63* (Columbus: Ohio State University Press, 1966); and Herbert W. Stephens, "The Role of the Legislative Committees in the Appropriations Process: A Study Focused on the Armed Services Committees," *Western Political Quarterly* 24 (March 1971): 146–62.

8. Michael Glennon, "Committee Has History of Controversial Chairmen," *Congressional Quarterly,* March 31, 1984, p. 732.

9. Ibid.

10. James M. Lindsay, "Congress and Defense Policy: 1961–86," *Armed Forces and Society* 13 (Spring 1978): 378.

11. Interview with Senator Carl M. Levin, November 30, 1987.

12. Alton Frye, *A Responsible Congress: The Politics of National Security* (New York: McGraw-Hill, 1975), pp. 101–4.

13. In the first few years of the budget committees there was some experimentation with reviewing details of the defense program in order to achieve budgetary objectives. In 1975, for example, Senators Edmund S. Muskie (D.-Maine), then-chairman of the committee, and Henry Bellmon (R.-Okla.), the ranking minority member, persuaded the Senate to reject the Armed Services Committee's attempt to add an additional nuclear-powered cruiser to the Defense Authorization bill on the grounds that it would "break the budget." These incidents were few and far between, however, and by the 1980s the committees were setting the defense budget total in consultation with the chairmen of Armed Services and Defense Appropriations. See Nancy J. Berg and Edwin J. Deagle, Jr., "Congress and the Defense Budget," in *American Defense Policy,* ed. John E. Endicott and Roy W. Stafford, Jr. (Baltimore: Johns Hopkins University Press, 1977), pp. 335–36.

14. "Armed Services Panels Counterattack on Veto," *Congressional Quarterly,* September 2, 1978, pp. 2401–7; "House Easily Sustains Carter Weapons Veto," *Congressional Quarterly,* September 9, 1978, pp. 2415–17; and "House, Senate Committees Approve New Defense Bill Without Major Revisions," *Congressional Quarterly,* September 16, 1987, pp. 2491–92.

15. An excellent summary of these trends in public views on defense spending is presented in "Opinion Roundup," *Public Opinion* (June/July 1985): 34–35.

16. Speech by Senator Charles Grassley at Central College, Pella, Iowa, November 13, 1985; copy obtained from the senator's office.

17. Aspin quote from *Washington Post,* February 6, 1986; Hatfield quote from *Washington Post,* February 3, 1985.

18. Quayle quote from *Washington Post,* April 20, 1983.

19. Interview with Congressman Norman D. Dicks, December 9, 1987.

20. "Aspin Ousted as Armed Services Chairman," *Congressional Quarterly,* January 10, 1987, pp. 83–85; "Aspin Makes a Comeback at Armed Services," *Congressional Quarterly,* January 24, 1987, pp. 139–42.

21. For 1986–1988, the number of amendments ranged from 83 in 1986, to 114 in 1987, and back down to 83 in 1988. Data through 1986 taken from Lindsay, "Congress and Defense Policy," p. 374; data for 1987 from *Congressional Record,* relevant dates (May–October 1987); data for 1988 from *Congressional Record,* relevant dates (May 1988).

22. Data on size of staffs of congressional institutions provided by each organization.

23. Employment data from David K. Henry and Richard P. Oliver, "The Defense Buildup, 1977–85: Effects on Production and Employment," *Monthly Labor Review* (August 1987): 8.

24. This account of the fiscal 1988 Defense Authorization bill is based on interviews with both committee members and staff, and also the personal staff of several committee members. Staff members shall remain nameless so that their children may continue to have roofs over their heads.

25. The appropriating process is not very much different. The staff prepares the initial mark-up based on broad fiscal guidance and a very loose budgetary macrostrategy. In 1987, for example, they decided as the highest priority to protect personnel and operational accounts. Considerations of efficient program management are the most important influence on decisions; sometimes, individuals in the armed services or the office of the secretary of defense will aid the staff in identifying those programs that could be cut most expeditiously. In recommending cuts, staffers are well aware of members' special interests and act to protect them, seeking "to avoid problems in mark-up." This consideration pertains to a degree to the special interests of members outside the subcommittee, as well, if they make their needs known to subcommittee members or staff. Staff also takes account of the "traditional balance" among the armed services and among the different types of appropriations in making recommendations for reductions. Policy issues play a lesser role in the appropriating process, but are not absent altogether.

26. These generalizations about the committees' staffs were drawn from biographies found in Charles B. Brownson, ed., *Congressional Staff Directory* (Washington, D.C., 1987).

27. Interview with Senator Carl M. Levin, November 30, 1987.

28. Interview with Representative John Spratt, December 13, 1987.

29. See the Project on Monitoring Defense Reorganization, *Making Defense Reform Work* (Foreign Policy Institute of the Johns Hopkins University and the Center for Strategic and International Studies, 1988).

30. Interview with Senator John Warner, December 22, 1987. Demonstrating the value of old adages, Congressman Bill Chapell (D.-Fla.), chairman of House Defense Appropriations Subcommittee, was defeated in 1988.

31. Interview with Congressman Norman D. Dicks, December 9, 1987.

Chapter 3

1. Ellen Collier, *U.S. Senate Rejection of Treaties: A Brief Survey of Past Instances* (Congressional Research Service, Report no. 87-305 F, Washington, D.C., March 30, 1987).

2. Paraphrased from a speech by Senator Alan Cranston at Stanford University, December 6, 1987.

3. *New York Times,* December 12, 1988.

4. *Congressional Record,* May 25, 1988, p. S6614.

5. Glenn T. Seaborg, *Kennedy, Khrushchev, and the Test Ban* (Berkeley: University of California Press, 1981), pp. 269–70, 277–79. The standby atmospheric test capability still exists.

6. Rowland Evans and Robert Novak, "The Indigo-Lacrosse Satellite Gets the Nod," *Washington Post,* April 6, 1988; *New York Times,* April 29, 1988; *Congressional Record,* May 20, 1988, pp. S6300–6301.

7. Melvin Laird, secretary of defense at the time of the 1972 arms control agreements, devised perhaps the most memorable compensatory package. Testifying in support of the agreements, Laird urged the Senate to vote "a triple play for peace," to include the ABM treaty, the SALT agreement, and a package of accelerated weapons programs, including the first significant appropriations for developing cruise missiles.

8. Anonymous interview; George Moffett, *The Limits of Victory: The Ratification of the Panama Canal Treaties* (Ithaca, N.Y.: Cornell University Press, 1985), p. 95. Zorinsky eventually voted against the treaties anyway. Presumably, he was one of Carter's pocket votes.

9. Alan Platt, *The U.S. Senate and Strategic Arms Policy, 1969–1977* (Boulder, Colo.: Westview Press, 1978), pp. 9, 12–13.

10. Ibid., p. 17.

11. Aaron and Gelb deny that Perle had any influence on the formulation of the administration's position; Strobe Talbott, *End Game* (New York: Harper & Row, 1979), p. 54.

12. Platt, *The U.S. Senate and Strategic Arms Policy,* p. 116.

13. Senate Document 99-7, "Report of the Senate Arms Control Observer Group Delegation," June 10, 1985.
14. Only the unkind would suggest that the senator's enthusiasm for the fray had anything to do with the fact that Carter had defeated him for the Democratic nomination less than a year before, or that Jackson's primary advisers and experts, notably Paul Nitze, were conspicuously absent from Carter's appointments in the executive branch.
15. *New York Times,* January 28 and February 27, 1983; "Confirmation Struggle Looms over Adelman Nomination," *Congressional Quarterly,* February 26, 1983, p. 423. Adelman's confirmation experience shows vividly the dangers of relying on political "spin-controllers" for guidance in dealing with the Congress, a lesson apparently not taken to heart by the Bush administration when contemplating the nomination of John G. Tower to be secretary of defense.
16. *New York Times,* April 14, 1983.
17. *Congressional Record,* June 20, 1984, p. S7715.
18. The General Advisory Committee was created at the same time as the Arms Control and Disarmament Agency to assure conservative members of Congress concerned that the new agency would become a hotbed of Communist subversion within the government. For most of its history, however, the GAC has served mainly to encourage very cautious ACDA directors to take more forthright positions in favor of arms control. Only in the 1980s has it returned to the role originally intended for it.
19. In a testament to the realities that constrain all administrations, the compliance reports submitted by President Reagan have been cautious and nuanced in their charges of Soviet cheating.
20. *Congressional Record,* September 22, 1983, p. S12688.
21. Jodie Scheiber, ed., *Congressional Yellow Book: A Directory of Members of Congress, Including Their Committees and Key Staff Aides* (New York: Monitor Publishing Company, various editions).
22. Alan Cranston, "How Congress Can Shape Arms Control," in *Congress and Arms Control,* ed. Alan Platt and Lawrence Weiler (Boulder, Colo.: Westview Press, 1978), p. 218.
23. The following sources are useful for the political history of the nuclear freeze movement: Fox Butterfield, "Anatomy of the Nuclear Protest," *New York Times Magazine,* July 11, 1982, pp. 14–17 ff; Adam M. Garfinkle, *The Politics of the Nuclear Freeze* (Philadelphia: Foreign Policy Research Institute, 1984); Steven E. Miller, ed., *The Nuclear Weapons Freeze and Arms Control* (Cambridge, Mass.: Ballinger, 1984); Douglas C. Waller, *Congress and the Nuclear Freeze* (Amherst: University of Massachusetts Press, 1987). Much of this section is based particularly on the Waller book.

24. Waller, *Congress and the Nuclear Freeze,* p. 165.

25. Interview with Senator Nancy L. Kassebaum, December 15, 1987.

26. This perspective is elaborated brilliantly in Janne E. Nolan, *Guardians of the Arsenal* (New York: Basic Books, 1989), chapter 1.

27. Platt, *The U.S. Senate and Strategic Arms Policy,* p. 14.

28. Ibid., p. 15.

29. Ibid., p. 18. Also, in the early 1970s there were repeated efforts to deny funding for certain research programs intended to improve the accuracy of U.S. ballistic missiles, thus increasing the nation's ability to carry out a first strike against Soviet strategic forces. Among other negative consequences, the sponsors of this legislation, particularly Senators Edward Brooke (R.-Mass.) and Tom McIntyre (D.-N.H.), believed the achievement of such capabilities would make it more difficult to negotiate meaningful reductions in strategic arms. A very excellent account of this early effort by the Congress to utilize the power of the purse to promote arms control negotiations is contained in Alton Frye, *A Responsible Congress* (New York: McGraw-Hill, 1975).

30. The build-down proposal would have permitted each side to modernize its strategic arsenal, but only as long as a number of older warheads were retired for every new warhead deployed. The number required to be dismantled varied according to the type of weapon being introduced, with the idea of penalizing either side for deploying those types of weapons considered most dangerous. Unlike the freeze, the build-down thus would have permitted the modernization of nuclear weapons to continue. Also unlike the freeze, however, the build-down would have brought about substantial reductions of nuclear arsenals as both sides continued their long-standing quest for more modern and capable weapons.

31. The ASAT, SALT II, and nuclear-testing case studies are based largely on interviews with roughly two dozen congressional staff aides who were involved directly in the events in question. I am grateful to Margaret Sullivan for carrying out many of these interviews.

32. Glenn's intention to run for the presidency in the 1984 election made him particularly sensitive to the demands of the antinuclear movement, while his generally conservative outlook (and base in the conservative wing of the Democratic party) ruled out an endorsement of the nuclear freeze. Visible action in the Senate to promote SALT II seemed a logical way out of the dilemma.

33. "Strategic Arms Top List of Defense Cuts," *Congressional Quarterly,* August 21, 1982, pp. 2059–65.

34. "House Could Win Big Victory on Partial Nuclear Test Ban," *Congressional Quarterly,* August 30, 1986, pp. 2037–39.

35. The two partial test limitations were the 1974 Threshold Test Ban Treaty,

which limited nuclear explosions at test sites to explosive yields of 150 kilotons or less, and the 1976 Treaty on Peaceful Nuclear Explosions, which imposed the same yield limit on nuclear explosions outside of test sites—those presumably being used for peaceful purposes. The Carter administration had decided not to press for the ratification of either treaty, seeking instead to negotiate a comprehensive ban on all nuclear explosions. The Reagan administration, while strongly opposing a comprehensive test ban even in principle, considered the partial treaties unverifiable and demanded additional means of ensuring Soviet compliance. The administration lobbied hard against congressional test ban initiatives throughout its first term. The only measure to pass either House was a nonbinding resolution that was passed by the Senate in 1984.

36. According to House procedures, members are not permitted to use appropriation bills to legislate new laws or to change old laws. The Rules Committee, however, which specifies the "rule" that will govern debate for every piece of legislation that reaches the floor of the House, is empowered to grant waivers to this procedure. Members intending to amend an appropriation bill, therefore, must first obtain a waiver from the Rules Committee. Such waivers typically also state that no point of order can be raised against the legislative initiative. In this case, the Rules Committee denied such a waiver.

37. The idea of limiting nuclear tests is repugnant to many conservative and moderate senators and congressmen. Senator Hart's compromise was probably accepted by the more conservative senior Senate conferees solely because of their determination to conclude the conference successfully. In previous years, the appropriating committees had been paying less and less attention to defense authorizations, and there was increasing worry that the entire authorizing process, and thus the Armed Services committees, were becoming less relevant. A failure to complete the authorization bill would have seemed to ratify this viewpoint, encouraging the appropriators to pay even less attention in the future. Given the House's adamancy on the arms control issues, compromise was essential.

   Even so, Hart's proposal received less than an enthusiastic welcome from many House conferees. In the conference, for example, Congressman Ron Dellums accused Senator Hart of "playing numbers games with the survival of the human race," thus demonstrating the incredible chasm between the pragmatic center of the Democratic party and the more doctrinaire liberal wing.

38. Interview with Congressman Norman D. Dicks, December 9, 1987.
39. Interview with Congressman Les Aspin, January 21, 1988.
40. *Wall Street Journal,* January 25, 1988.
41. "The Nunn Letter: A Text," *Congressional Quarterly,* February 14, 1987,

p. 274. Demonstrating the total eclipse of the Senate Foreign Relations Committee in arms control matters, the entire burden of the battle over the interpretation of the ABM treaty was carried by the Armed Services Committee, even though, initially at least, the issue was strictly one of treaty powers. Foreign Relations made an abortive effort to gain access to the negotiating record soon after the new interpretation was announced, but backed down when the administration objected. The Senate acted only after Senator Nunn first insisted that the Congress had a right to examine the negotiating record and then, after studying that record, issued a report stating that, in his view, the new interpretation was inappropriate in light of the negotiating record and the Senate's understanding at the time the treaty was initially debated.

Chapter 4

1. Interview with Senator John Culver, October 5, 1987.
2. Data on weapon deliveries from U.S. Department of Defense, Defense Security Assistance Agency, *Foreign Military Sales, Foreign Military Construction Sales, and Military Assistance Facts* (annual reports, 1984–1987); data on total exports and exports of manufactured goods from *U.S. Trade Performance in 1985 and Outlook* (Government Printing Office, 1986), p. 119; U.S. Department of Commerce and U.S. Census Bureau, *Highlights of U.S. Imports and Exports* (annual reports, 1975–87); and U.S. International Trade Commission, *Composition of the U.S. Merchandise Trade Deficit, 1983–87* (annual report, 1988), p. 22.
3. Quoted in David C. Morrison, "In Person: Joel J. Johnson," *National Journal,* September 26, 1987, p. 2438.
4. As quoted in the *Washington Post,* May 1, 1978.
5. Data on U.S. personnel in Iran and Saudi Arabia provided by the U.S. Department of State. The dividing line between official U.S. government representatives and Americans working for private companies is rather vague in these situations. The Vinnell Corporation, for example, has been training the Saudi National Guard—under contract—since the mid-1970s. The Vinnell team in Riyadh is headed by a recently retired three-star U.S. general; he directs roughly three hundred former U.S. military personnel, from senior officers to noncommissioned officers. All the senior personnel, a Vinnell Corporation official confided to me, are cleared with the U.S. Army before being offered a position.
6. The first direct sale of a U.S. weapon system to Israel took place during the Kennedy administration. Previously, Israel had depended primarily on French weapons, although it also had obtained U.S. tanks and other army

equipment from the West Germans. The first direct sale of a highly visible, state-of-the-art U.S. weapons system, F-4 Phantom fighters, took place in 1968, over the objections of both the Department of State and the Department of Defense.

7. In the instance cited, the arms sales were approved, but the Saudis reacted even more strongly to the Camp David peace agreement than had been feared—acting not only to sever official support for Egypt but to terminate such unofficial subsidies as aid for the Sudan and remittances from Egyptian workers in Saudia Arabia. What efforts may or may not have been made to curb increases in oil prices are harder to discern, but in any case, the price of oil seems to have responded primarily to market forces, not to politics.

8. Backgrounder, October 8, 1987.

9. There have been a few instances, particularly in Central America, in which U.S. decisions not to supply certain weapons were welcomed by foreign officials. In these cases, the U.S. turndown enabled political leaders to resist the demands of military officers for expenditures on weapons that the civilian leadership had preferred to avoid but felt unable to resist in the absence of U.S. support. Prospective sales of jet aircraft to Mexico and Guatemala in the late 1970s are cases in point.

10. Quoted in "Congressional Role in Arms Sales," *Congressional Quarterly*, April 10, 1982, p. 798.

11. An excellent account of this incident can be found in Thomas M. Franck and Edward Weisbank, *Foreign Policy by Congress* (New York: Oxford University Press, 1979), pp. 100–3. Some critics of the congressional action argue that the changes made in the Hawks could have been easily reversed by Jordan at any time, making the action ineffective militarily, as well as damaging politically.

12. "Case Study: Carter and Congress on AWACS," *Congressional Quarterly*, September 7, 1977, pp. 1857–63; *New York Times*, September 6 and 20, and October 8, 1977. Lucky for the United States, given the subsequent situation in the Persian Gulf, Iran never actually obtained the AWACS, as the shah was overthrown before the aircraft were ready for delivery.

13. "Test of Administration's Clout in Congress Established by AWACS Announcement," *Congressional Quarterly*, September 5, 1981, p. 1665; "Panel Rejects AWACS Deal but Reagan Gains Support among Senate Republicans," *Congressional Quarterly*, October 10, 1981, p. 1942; "House Rejects Sale: Reagan Loses AWACS Votes but Picks Up Some Support among Senate Republicans," *Congressional Quarterly*, October 17, 1981, pp. 2006–8; "Senate Supports Reagan on AWACS Sale," *Congressional Quarterly*, October 31, 1981, pp. 2095–2100.

14. "Administration Seeks to Give More Help to Jordan," *Congressional*

Quarterly, February 18, 1984, p. 304; "Arms to Jordan, *Congressional Quarterly,* March 3, 1984, p. 528; "Israel's Friends on Hill Take Aim at Missile Sales to Jordan," *Congressional Quarterly,* March 17, 1984, p. 612; "Reagan Yields to Congress on Jordan Missiles," *Congressional Quarterly,* March 24, 1984, pp. 667–68; "Administration to Revive Sale of Stinger Missiles to Saudis," *Congressional Quarterly,* May 26, 1984, p. 1278; "As Gulf War Escalates, Reagan Sends Stinger," *Congressional Quarterly,* June 2, 1984, pp. 1304–6; "Republicans Sound Alarm on U.S. Role in Gulf," *Congressional Quarterly,* June 9, 1984, pp. 1351–53. The Arms Export Control Act permits the requirement of prior congressional notification to be waived when the president declares that "an emergency exists which requires such sale in the national security interests of the United States."

15. *New York Times,* March 11, April 2, 7, 8, 21, 22, and June 6, 1986.
16. "Middle East," *Congressional Quarterly,* August 3, 1985, p. 1542; "Administration to Press for Mideast Arms Sales," *Congressional Quarterly,* September 14, 1985, p. 1805; "Hussein Courts Wary Congress, but Arms Sale Is Uphill Struggle," *Congressional Quarterly,* October 5, 1985, pp. 2018–20; "Shultz Pleads with Skeptical Hill for Jordan Arms," *Congressional Quarterly,* October 12, 1985, pp. 2077–78; "Senate Deals Blow to Reagan, Hussein on Arms," *Congressional Quarterly,* October 26, 1985, p. 2135; "Middle East Arms Bazaar: Weighing the Costs," *Congressional Quarterly,* November 2, 1985, pp. 2241–46.
17. "Saudi Sale Required Dropping Mavericks, Sets F-15 Ceiling," *Aerospace Daily,* October 13, 1987, p. 60. Mavericks were dropped from a proposed sale to Kuwait in 1988, as well, following the emergence of congressional opposition.
18. "Memorandum from Richard Grimmet, Congressional Research Service, to Senator Daniel J. Evans on 'Sale of Advanced Fighter Aircraft to Saudi Arabia,' " August 25, 1987, published in the *Congressional Record,* October 8, 1987, pp. S13868–69
19. *New York Times,* July 11, 1988.
20. American League for Export and Security Assistance, "Talking Points on Biden-Levine Arms Export Control Act Amendments" (unpublished report, Washington, D.C., n.d.); William D. Bajusz and David J. Louscher, "The Domestic Economic Impact of Restricted Military Sales to the Middle East" (unpublished report, Washington, D.C., April 15, 1987).
21. American League for Export and Security Assistance, "Talking Points on Biden–Levine."
22. In 1988 the House of Representatives passed a bill, introduced by Howard L. Berman (D.-Calif.), that would prohibit sales of all weapons to nations found by the secretary of state to support international terrorism; such a list is compiled annually. If passed by the Senate, the Berman bill would

have prohibited covert transactions, as well as public ones, and—in an unusual provision—provide for criminal penalties for government officials found in violation. See *Congressional Record*, May 24, 1988, pp. H3561-69; *Washington Post*, May 25, 1988.

23. "Saudi Sale Required Dropping Mavericks, Sets F–15 Ceiling," *Aerospace Daily*, October 13, 1987, p. 60.

Chapter 5

1. *New York Times*, April 18, 1988.
2. For the text of the Tsongas–Wallop resolution (S.Con.Res. 74), see *Congressional Record*, October 4, 1984, pp. H11474–75.
3. Congressman Wyche Fowler, Jr., "Legislative Controls," *First Principles* (March/April 1984): 5.
4. Section 102(d)(5) of the National Security Act of 1947, 50 U.S.C. 403(d)(5).
5. Besides the Central Intelligence Agency, the intelligence community consists primarily of Defense Department agencies—the Defense Intelligence Agency, each of the armed services' intelligence arms, the National Security Agency, the National Reconnaissance Office, and others—but also includes elements of the Federal Bureau of Investigation, the State Department's Bureau of Intelligence and Research, and many others. The ability of the director of central intelligence to coordinate the operations of these diverse organizations has never been good. Indeed, competition between the CIA and the defense agencies, particularly, has been an important source of policy incoherence virtually throughout the postwar period.
6. Section 5(a) of the Central Intelligence Agency Act of 1949, 50 U.S.C. 403f(a). For the text of this act, as well as most of the other legislation discussed in this chapter, see, U.S. Senate, House, Permanent Select Committee on Intelligence, "Compilation of Intelligence Laws and Related Laws and Executive Orders of Interest to the National Intelligence Community" (Washington, D.C., March 1987).
7. *Congressional Quarterly Almanac*, 31 (1975): 389.
8. Statement of Congressman Walter Norblad (R.-Ore.), *Congressional Record*, August 14, 1963, p. 15086, quoted in David Wise and Thomas B. Ross, *The Invisible Government* (New York: Random House, 1964), p. 265n; CIA official's story from Thomas G. Paterson, "Oversight or Afterview? Congress, the CIA, and Covert Actions Since 1947," in Michael Barnhart, ed., *Congress and United States Foreign Policy: Controlling the Use of Force in the Nuclear Age* (Albany, N.Y.: SUNY Press, 1987), p. 158.

9. "The CIA's New Bay of Bucks," *Newsweek*, September 23, 1974, p. 51; Dulles quote from Paterson, "Oversight or Afterview?" p. 159.

10. *Congressional Record*, April 11, 1956, p. 6052.

11. Loch Johnson, "Paramilitary Operations," *First Principles* (March/April 1984): 2.

12. *Congressional Record*, April 11, 1956, p. 6048.

13. Thomas Powers, *The Man Who Kept Secrets: Richard Helms and the CIA* (New York: Knopf, 1979), p. 277. The period between the Mansfield and the McCarthy–Fulbright proposals witnessed two notable exceptions to the Congress's prevailing lack of interest in covert operations. The Senate Foreign Relations Committee held hearings on both the U-2 incident and the Bay of Pigs fiasco. The former led some senators to question whether the intelligence agencies were taking into account the possible foreign consequences of their actions, while the latter both generated doubts about executive judgment and established a precedent for the utility of congressional consultation. It seems that President Kennedy invited his friend William Fulbright to a White House meeting on the Bay of Pigs plan, at which the senator raised the only dissenting voice. This episode may help explain Fulbright's support for the McCarthy proposal. For a discussion of the Foreign Relations Committee's investigations, see Cecil V. Crabb, Jr., and Pat M. Holt, *Invitation to Struggle: Congress, the President, and Foreign Policy*, 2d ed. (Washington, D.C.: Congressional Quarterly Press, 1984), pp. 166–68.

14. *Congressional Record*, April 9, 1956, p. 5924.

15. Norman D. Sandler, "Twenty-eight Years of Looking the Other Way: Congressional Oversight of the Central Intelligence Agency, 1947–75" (Ph.D. diss., Massachusetts Institute of Technology, 1975), p. 157. A similar anecdote comes from the 1974 floor debate over an amendment from William Proxmire, which would have disclosed the total cost of U.S. intelligence activities. Senator Harold Hughes alluded to a floor statement made by Senator John McClellan, chairman of both the Appropriations Committee and its Subcommittee on Intelligence Operations, in which McClellan said he did not want to know the total intelligence budget, for fear that he would talk in his sleep and reveal it. See *Congressional Record*, June 4, 1974, p. 17492.

16. "The C.I.A." Congress Seeks Better Oversight," *Congressional Quarterly*, December 7, 1974, p. 3279.

17. Section 662 of the Foreign Assistance Act of 1961, as amended, 22 U.S.C. 2422. Note that the Hughes–Ryan amendment was itself subsequently amended, as discussed later in the chapter.

18. The apparent jurisdictional problem between the House Armed Services and Foreign Affairs committees seems exaggerated in view of the fact

that the Senate Foreign Relations Committee was able to investigate the Chilean affair, as well as certain other incidents mentioned previously; see *Congressional Quarterly,* December 7, 1974, p. 3278.

19. The Church committee's final report, which was accompanied by five supplementary volumes, also recommended changes in the executive branch's internal organization for overseeing covert operations, and suggested that some types of operations, including assassinations, be prohibited by law. See Senate Report 94-755, "Foreign and Military Intelligence, Book I," April 26, 1975.

20. *Congressional Quarterly Almanac* 32 (1976): 299; for the resolution establishing the Senate Select Committee on Intelligence, see S. Res. 400, 94th Congress, 2d sess. (1976). Members of the Armed Services Committee were worried even more about jurisdiction over tactical military intelligence, which is designed to serve combat commanders, but conceivably could also be of interest to political leaders, and thus could become fair game for the intelligence panel. The members were more successful on this point: the final bill excluded "tactical foreign military intelligence serving no national policy-making function" from the Senate Intelligence Committee's province.

21. Like its Senate counterpart, the Pike committee recommended the creation of a permanent intelligence committee. Interestingly, the Pike committee also counseled two steps that are the subject of more recent legislative initiatives: (1) that the Intelligence committees should be told of all covert operations, in writing and in detail, within forty-eight hours of the president's approval, and (2) that the director of central intelligence should be separated from the CIA.

22. For the resolution establishing the House Permanent Select Committee on Intelligence, see H. Res. 658, 95th Congress, 1st sess. (1977).

23. For Turner's revelation, see U.S. Congress, House, Permanent Select Committee on Intelligence, "H.R. 10013, H.R. 13171, and Other Proposals Which Address the Issue of Affording Prior Notice of Covert Actions to the Congress," 100th Congress, 1st sess. (April 1, 8, and June 10, 1987), pp. 45–46, 48–49 (hereafter, House Intelligence Committee hearings); for Inouye's statement, see, Thomas M. Franck and Edward Weisband, *Foreign Policy by Congress* (New York: Oxford University Press, 1979), p. 126. It is not clear whether these procedures for contacting committee members survived past Senator Inouye's chairmanship.

24. Crabb and Holt, *Invitation to Struggle,* p. 170; see also, Stansfield Turner, *Secrecy and Democracy: The CIA in Transition* (Boston: Houghton Mifflin, 1985), pp. 146–47.

25. "Congress Weighs Proposals to Control the CIA," *Congressional Quarterly,* July 19, 1975, p. 1549.

26. Turner, *Secrecy and Democracy,* pp. 150–51.

27. For a more detailed discussion of Huddleston's 1978 proposal, see John M. Oseth, *Regulating U.S. Intelligence Operations: A Study in the Definition of the National Interest* (Lexington: University Press of Kentucky, 1985), pp. 122–29, 142–48.

28. Senate Report 96-730, "Intelligence Oversight Act of 1980" (May 15, 1980), p. 8.

29. "Intelligence Charter Disputes Emerge Again on Key Issues," *Congressional Quarterly,* February 23, 1980, p. 538.

30. House Report 96-1350, "Intelligence Authorization Act for Fiscal Year 1981" (September 19, 1980), p. 16.

31. For the Javits–Huddleston colloquy, see *Congressional Record,* June 3, 1980, p. 13125; June 28, 1980, p. 17693. A similar colloquy took place on the House floor between Congressmen Edward P. Boland (D.-Mass.), then the chairman of the House Intelligence Committee, and Lee H. Hamilton (D.-Ind.): *Congressional Record,* September 30, 1980, p. 28392.

32. *Congressional Record,* June 3, 1980, p. 13124. The Reagan administration's case that it could cite constitutional authority as a basis for withholding prior notification entirely was made in a Justice Department memo. The memo was printed in House Intelligence Committee Hearings, pp. 247–73.

33. *Congressional Quarterly,* February 23, 1980, p. 538.

34. "Intelligence Panels: Fresh Faces, Familiar Issues," *Congressional Quarterly,* January 19, 1985, p. 120.

35. U.S. Congress, Senate, Select Committee on Intelligence, "Nomination of John N. McMahon to Be Deputy Director of Central Intelligence," 97th Congress, 2d sess. (May 26 and 27, 1982), pp. 56–57.

36. "Goldwater to Casey: 'This Is No Way To Run a Railroad,' " *Congressional Quarterly,* April 14, 1984, p. 833.

37. Senate Report 98-665, "Report of the Select Committee on Intelligence, United States Senate, January 1, 1983 to December 31, 1984," October 10, 1984, pp. 14, 15n. The text of the June 1984 agreement between Casey and the committee, "Procedures Governing Reporting to the Senate Select Committee on Intelligence (SSCI) on Covert Action," as well as the text of a June 1986 addendum, can be found in the House Intelligence Committee Hearings, pp. 38–43.

38. Senator Durenburger is quoted in Bob Woodward, *Veil: The Secret Wars of the CIA, 1981–87* (New York: Simon & Schuster, 1987), p. 333; Senator Leahy is quoted in *Congressional Quarterly,* January 19, 1985, p. 120.

39. Senate Report 98-10, "Report of the Select Committee on Intelligence, United States Senate, January 1, 1981 to December 31, 1982," February

28, 1983, p. 2. The Reagan administration's compliance record is noted in Senate Report 100-276, "Intelligence Oversight Act of 1988," January 27, 1988, p. 23.

40. *New York Times,* July 13, 1987.

41. The Reagan administration's case was made in the Justice Department memorandum cited in note 32.

42. Senate Report 100-276, p. 24.

43. *Congressional Record,* March 3, 1988, p. S1859.

44. "Report of the President's Special Review Board," February 26, 1987, p. V-6.

45. *Congressional Quarterly,* January 19, 1985, p. 120.

46. Woodward, *Veil: The Secret Wars of the CIA,* p. 281. If there is one thing demonstrated by these various exchanges, it is that both members of the Congress and officials of the executive branch share a propensity to use profane language when discussing covert operations; greater public scrutiny of covert operations might have the side benefit of cleaning up their acts.

47. Interview with Senator Patrick J. Leahy, December 9, 1987.

Chapter 6

1. There have been extensive writings on the War Powers Resolution. The better sources include Thomas Franck and Edward Weisband, *Foreign Policy by Congress* (New York: Oxford University Press, 1979), an overview of the Congress's actions during the 1970s with special emphasis on war powers; Jacob Javits, *Who Makes War?* (New York: William Morrow, 1973), historical analysis of war powers from George Washington through Vietnam, by one of the bill's chief authors; Marc Smyrl, *Conflict or Codetermination: Congress, the President, and the Power to Make War* (New York: Ballinger, 1988), examines war powers in the broader context of executive-legislative struggle over foreign policy during the 1970s and 1980s; John Sullivan, *The War Powers Resolution* (Washington, D.C.: House Foreign Affairs Committee, 1988), legislative history and overview of the record of executive branch compliance.

2. The resolution also requires certain actions when (1) U.S. forces, "equipped for combat," are introduced into foreign territory, except for certain routine operations, and (2) when the U.S. presence in a foreign nation is significantly increased in size. These requirements are far less controversial, however, as they do not start the sixty-day limitation on the operation in the absence of a congressional authorization. Formal reference for the Resolution is Public Law 93-148 (H.J. Res. 542), 87 Stat. 555, 50 U.S.C. 1541-1548, passed over the president's veto, November 7, 1973.

The text of the War Powers Resolution, together with related congressional documents and reports, and the reports submitted by presidents either in compliance with or consistent with its requirements can be seen in U.S. Congress, House, Committee on Foreign Affairs, "The War Powers Resolution" (committee print; May 1988).

3. Senator Sam Nunn, "Summary Statement: War Powers Act," press release, May 19, 1988.
4. Alan Cranston, "Revise the War Powers Act," *Washington Post,* October 22, 1987.
5. House Document 93-171, "Vetoing House Joint Resolution 542, Message from the President," October 25, 1973.
6. Public Law 93-148.
7. Interview with Congressman Norm Dicks, December 9, 1987.
8. House Report 93-287, "War Powers Resolution of 1973," June 15, 1973, pp. 6–7.
9. "Republicans Hold Off Critics of 'Reflagging,' " *Congressional Quarterly,* July 4, 1987, pp. 1425–26; "House Votes to Delay Oil-Tanker 'Reflagging,' " *Congressional Quarterly,* July 11, 1987, pp. 1508–10; "New Gulf Incident Rekindles Old Debate," *Congressional Quarterly,* April 23, 1988, pp. 1051–58; *New York Times,* May 23, September 23, October 19–21, 23, 1987, and April 19, 1988; *Washington Post,* April 19, 1988.
10. U.S. Congress, House, Committee on Foreign Affairs, "U.S. Military Actions in Grenada: Implications for U.S. Policy in the Eastern Caribbean," 98th Congress, 1st sess., November 2, 1983, p. 15.
11. H.J. Res. 402, 98th Congress, 1st sess., 1983.
12. "Congress Wants Greater Role on U.S. Presence in Lebanon," *Congressional Quarterly,* September 3, 1983, p. 1876.
13. A number of people involved in the negotiations expressed the view that the Speaker "was taken to the cleaners." There was considerable give in the administration's position, they thought, which had not been tested at all.
14. *Congressional Record,* September 29, 1983, p. S13164.
15. Interview with Senator Brock Adams, January 21, 1988.
16. The Solarz resolution (H.J. Res. 387) was introduced on October 22, 1987, and committed to the House Foreign Affairs and House Rules committees, neither of which acted on it. See *Congressional Record,* October 22, 1987, p. H8963.
17. U.S. District Court for the District of Columbia, *Michael E. Lowry, et al. v. Ronald W. Reagan,* "Memorandum Opinion and Order," December 18, 1987. Presidential actions overseas have been challenged in the courts on several previous occasions; the courts have refused consistently to take jurisdiction.

18. Interview with Senator Nancy L. Kassebaum, December 15, 1987.
19. Interview with Senator John W. Warner, December 22, 1987.
20. For Fascell's position, see his testimony before the Committee on Foreign Relations, Special Subcommittee on War Powers, July 13, 1988.
21. Interview, Senator Patrick J. Leahy, December 9, 1987.
22. "War Powers: More Than Tinkering," *Washington Post,* October 7, 1987.
23. U.S. Congress, Senate, Committee on Foreign Relations, "Nomination of Alexander M. Haig, Jr., to be Secretary of State (Part 2)," 97th Congress, 1st sess., January 14, 1981, p. 40.
24. *New York Times,* November 29, 1984.
25. *New York Times,* January 11 and March 5, 1979; *Washington Post,* March 7, and 9, 1979; Frank and Weisband, *Foreign Policy by Congress,* p. 157; personal notes. The consequences of the incident were revealed quickly. In March, following an outright attack by South Yemen on the North, the Carter administration offered to send an armed squadron of F-15s to Saudi Arabia, but the Saudis declined.
26. Interview with Congressman Norm Dicks, December 9, 1987.
27. Interview with Senator Brock Adams, January 21, 1988.
28. For the full text of the Byrd–Nunn–Mitchell–Warner proposal, see S.J. Res. 323, 100th Congress, 2d sess., May 19, 1988. On the House side, Congressmen Howard Berman, Lee Hamilton, and Stephen Solarz have introduced major revisions of the War Powers Resolution for consideration by the Foreign Affairs Committee, but have been stymied by Chairman Fascell's support for the existing law.
29. Cranston, "Revise the War Powers Act."

Chapter 7

1. Letter from John P. Roche, June 27, 1988.
2. Richard F. Fenno, Jr., *Congressmen in Committees* (Boston: Little, Brown, 1973), pp. 9–13.
3. Interview with Congressman Howard J. Berman, October 9, 1987.
4. Interview with Congressman Stephen Solarz, November 17, 1987.
5. I. M. Destler, "Executive-Congressional Conflict in Foreign Policy: Explaining It, Coping with It," in *Congress Reconsidered,* 3d ed., ed. Lawrence C. Dodd and Bruce I. Oppenheimer (New York: Praeger, 1977), p. 345.
6. Presentation by Senator John Tower at Georgetown University, April 14, 1988.
7. Destler, "Executive–Congressional Conflict in Foreign Policy," p. 345.
8. The cooperation in defense budgeting proved to be short-lived. President

Reagan vetoed the Defense Authorization bill in August 1988, claiming it contained too little funds for the Strategic Defense Initiative and other onerous conditions. Taken *against* the advice of Secretary of Defense Frank Carlucci, National Security Adviser Colin Powell, and Senator John Warner, the ranking Republican on the Armed Services Committee, the veto was widely understood to have been intended solely to help Vice President George Bush make defense a key issue in the presidential campaign, proving conclusively that it is not only the Congress that plays politics with defense policy.

9. *Congressional Record,* May 26, 1988, p. S6710.
10. *Washington Post,* May 17, 1988.
11. Louis Henken, "Foreign Affairs and the Constitution," *Foreign Affairs* (Winter 1987/88): 307.

Index